Managing the
Information Center

Managing the Information Center

Kurt A. Christoff

The Scott, Foresman Series in
Computers and Information Systems
Thomas H. Athey, Consulting Editor

SCOTT, FORESMAN/LITTLE, BROWN HIGHER EDUCATION
A Division of Scott, Foresman and Company
Glenview, Illinois   London, England

Library of Congress Cataloging-in-Publication Data

Christoff, Kurt A.
    Managing the information center / Kurt A. Christoff.
        p.   cm.—(The Scott, Foresman series in computers and
    information systems)
    ISBN 0-673-38081-5
    1. Management information systems.   2. Information services.
I. Title.   II. Series.
T58.6.C467   1990
658.4'038—dc20   90-30047
                                                              CIP

1 2 3 4 5 6—KPF—95 94 93 92 91 90

Commit thy way unto the Lord; trust also in him; and he shall bring it to pass.

Psalm 37:5

With gratitude.

PREFACE

The information center revolution has a lot in common with Martin Luther's "priesthood of the believer." In the early sixteenth century, Luther proposed a radical idea; people did not need priests to approach God for them. Instead, they could approach God directly. Likewise, the information center revolution began when technological advances allowed most computer users to approach data directly, without the help of the data-processing establishment.

Since the power structure of the sixteenth century was made up almost entirely of priests, Luther's radical proposal was not embraced with open arms—in fact, the church hierarchy sentenced Luther to death. In the same way, the mere existence of the information center pioneers irritated the data-processing establishment. Often, emerging information centers were greeted with criticism, doubts, and open hostility. The establishment was threatened, and the upstarts often risked the corporate equivalent of death sentences.

Both Luther's revolutionary idea and the information center concept are now firmly established; priests today serve more as pastors, and programmers serve more as consultants. Information centers are no longer considered radical or daring. They are simply another MIS tool in most organizations. By becoming part of the establishment, however—and by being seduced by the technology that has made them possible—information centers can easily lose sight of their initial purpose; getting information into the hands of decision makers to help them solve business problems.

Managing the Information Center is about information centers, not about technology. Obviously, technical innovations such as personal computers, interactive BASIC, and spreadsheet software helped information centers emerge, but the success or failure of information centers depends on their ability to help business managers make decisions. It is tempting to focus on the sophisticated technology that enabled the information center revolution, but the roots of the revolution lie in the ability of information centers to effectively solve business problems.

This text thus presents information centers from a business, not a technical, perspective. It is appropriate for upper-level undergraduate and graduate-level courses in end-user computing and information center management. An abundance of real-world examples on many topics—using a strategic planning cycle, selecting fourth-generation languages, and constructing data bases—show how information centers can be important tools for business managers. The examples have one purpose in mind; to challenge all beliefs or actions that make technology the master of business, not the slave.

Managing the Information Center begins with philosophical foundations. Chapter 1 provides a definition of *information center* that is used throughout the text. The second chapter explores this definition and looks at the forces that gave birth to the information center revolution. A "world view" of information centers, rooted in a firm understanding of strategic principles rather than technology, is introduced in Chapter 3.

The text then looks at the technological concepts and tools underlying information centers. Chapter 4 discusses a typical "tool kit" as well as effective methods to select tools that best serve an organization's business needs. Chapter 5 is an overview of one of the most critical skills for information center staff: the gentle art of data-base design. This chapter, while not vital to understanding information centers, provides a collection of techniques that can make the difference between a successful project and a failure. Chapter 6 extends the discussion of data-base design skills by looking at prototyping, a "blitzkrieg" approach to development.

Chapter 7 examines the concept of stewardship by asking who owns an information center's data and supporting technology. Having discussed this critical topic, Chapter 8 then looks at the issues that emerge when information centers try to connect all their tools together.

The final five chapters concentrate on management issues. Chapter 9 looks at training; what steps can information centers take to effectively prepare their customers for technological sulf-sufficiency? Chapters 10 and 11 discuss the ways in which information centers can develop a project orientation to avoid the siren songs that have lured many traditional MIS departments to destruction on the rocks of poor quality.

Information centers are only as good as their staffs, so Chapter 12 examines the process of attracting, training, and retaining a top-notch staff. Finally, Chapter 13 looks at audit issues, concentrating on possible risks and effective ways to manage them.

Suggestions for possible projects appear at the end of each chapter. These projects can be presented as student papers, panel discussions, or class discussions. The "right" answers for these projects, however, are not in the back of the book; there are no right answers about information centers, only right questions. *Managing the Information Center* provides techniques and methods to help readers ask the right questions and search for solutions to business problems. I hope that classroom discussions will be animated and lively. Successful information centers are possible only when complacency is challenged and enthusiasm abounds.

Kurt A. Christoff

CONTENTS

CHAPTER 3

Taking the Strategic View   33

CHAPTER **4**

Selecting the Tools for an Information Center   53

CHAPTER 5

The Neglected Art of Data-Base Design

CHAPTER 6

Prototyping

CHAPTER 7

Stewardship and an Information Center   119

CHAPTER 8

Connectivity

CHAPTER 9

Training and Education

CHAPTER 10

A Project-Oriented Information Center   181

CHAPTER 11

Quality and Ethics: The Realities of a Project Orientation

CHAPTER 12

Staffing

Managing the
Information Center

CHAPTER 1

What Is an Information Center?

1

Have you ever heard the story of three blind men encountering an elephant for the first time? The first man grabs the tail and concludes that an elephant is like a rope. The second, with his arms around the elephant's leg, determines that an elephant is like a tree trunk. The third places his hands on the elephant's side and announces that an elephant is like a brick wall. Each man's conclusion is valid within its own context but does little to explain what an elephant is really like.

If you listen to people discussing an information center, you will be reminded of the elephant story. Ask any five experts to define an information center and you get twelve different answers. To make matters even more confusing, many organizations completely ignore the term *information center*, choosing to use a synonym such as solution center, information technology center, decision support systems, end-user systems, or quick response team. Obviously, to discuss an information center intelligently, it is necessary to determine just what an information center is—that it means the same thing to everybody.

INFORMATION CENTER: A DEFINITION

Pause for a moment and write down your definition for an information center. When you are finished, use your definition to answer the following questions:

1. If a department is concerned only with personal computers, can it be considered a "real" information center?
2. Can a department be considered a "true" information center if it does not have technical experts on staff?
3. If a department writes programs for users, is it a "real" information center?
4. Can an end-user department create an information center that is independent of the traditional data-processing establishment?
5. If a department does not have a fourth-generation language or a data-base management system, can it be considered an information center?

Did you have trouble answering these questions? Perhaps your definition is based too much on technology. If you are a data-processing professional, you probably tried to cast your definition in terms of the hardware (personal computers, mainframes, terminals) and software (fourth-generation languages, data bases, spreadsheets) that are traditionally associated with an information center. However, looking at these and other questions, the technology-based definitions start to break down and what remains is a lack of understanding of the problem being examined.

Another way to approach the problem is to define an information center in business terms. Consider the definition on the next page.

An information center *is an organizational entity that facilitates the transformation of data into information that managerial, professional, and support staff can use to solve business problems.*

Notice how this definition avoids the questions that plague technology-based definitions. The presence or absence of a fourth-generation language is immaterial; the real question is how data becomes information. Likewise, it does not matter whether an information center reports to the traditional management information systems (MIS) group or to a user area as long as it facilitates the transformation of data into information. The following sections will examine in more detail how this definition captures the essence of an information center.

THE TRANSFORMATION OF DATA INTO INFORMATION

The distinction between data and information is a constant source of confusion. Distinguishing between these terms will help demonstrate how well the preceding definition of an information center works (see Figure 1-1).

Data: Facts in Context

Data is often defined as a collection of stored facts; by themselves, however, facts such as "123" and "789" are meaningless. Do they represent weights, account balances, or area codes? You don't know unless you also know the context in which the facts are defined. Therefore, it is more useful to define data as a collection of stored facts within a specific context.

This context may be thought of in terms of width and depth. *Width* refers to the different types of facts collected about a particular item; *depth* refers to the items about which facts are being collected. For example, a business may need to collect a number of different facts about employees—their addresses, birth dates, and employment dates. These different facts are the data's width. To be meaningful, a fact such as "04/21/52" must be placed in

---

FIGURE 1-1   Data vs. Information

Data is . . .	Information is . . .
• *stored* facts	• *presented* facts
• *inert* (it exists)	• *active* (it enables doing)
• *technology*-based	• *business*-based
• *gathered* from various sources	• *transformed* from data

context. If it is a birth date, it has one meaning; if it is an employment date, it has another meaning.

The concept of "depth" means that there are a number of occurrences of all data elements for a type of item. There will be many employees, each with the same collection of facts. The employees—the items about which facts are being collected—are the data's depth. A birth date of 04/21/52 belongs to a particular employee. In traditional terms, the "depth" dimension is referred to as the number of records, segments, or table rows within a given file or database.

To define data as a collection of stored facts in context means that each piece of data is a specific type of fact (width) about a particular item (depth). For a piece of data to be meaningful, a user must know what type of fact it is and the item to which it refers.

Information: The Meaningful Interpretation of Data

Consider a simple personnel system that will store 20 different facts about 100 employees. Simple arithmetic shows that with a width of 20 facts and a depth of 100 employees, this system will store 2,000 different pieces of data. To use this system to solve business problems, each piece of data must be put into context; it must become information.

Data becomes information when it is presented in a meaningful or actionable way. There are a number of different ways to make this transformation, including:

1. *Extraction*—selecting a certain number of occurrences (depth) or a certain number of facts for each occurrence (width).
2. *Capture*—storing new occurrences or new facts based on events in the real world.
3. *Analysis*—developing rules expressing the relationships among existing facts, or creating rules to combine facts to form new facts.
4. *Presentation*—arranging facts in a fashion that can be understood. This may change the order of the facts (sorting) or the format (graphics).

Different transformations can be performed in any combination to produce different types of information (see Figure 1-2). These transformations have very little to do with technology. In fact people performed these operations long before the advent of automated data processing. Two hundred years ago, census takers gathered facts about the population (data) that were assimilated into meaningful tables (information) through a tedious, manual process. The fact that data was transformed into information without the aid of computers points out again that an information center should not be defined by the technology it offers, but instead by the basic business processes it facilitates.

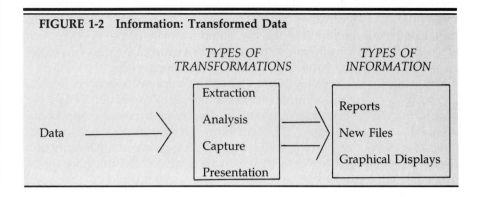

FIGURE 1-2 Information: Transformed Data

Facilitating the Transformation

The transformation of data into information has always been at the heart of data processing. Before information centers, a data-processing department's role was to create a collection of rigid, fixed transformations called standard reports or online screens. The available data-processing tools made these standard transformations highly error prone and exceptionally time-consuming to build. Thus the key to the present role of an information center is in its ability to facilitate a more efficient transformation of data by end users, rather than rigidly performing all data transformations in a single data-processing department.

The technology that emerged in the late 1970s allowed a transition from the traditional data-processing approach to a more spontaneous approach. Initially, the hardware changed. The computer moved out of its temperature- and humidity-controlled, raised-floor temple into the end-user department. First came the departmental minicomputer that could be installed without complex power and environmental demands. Right on its heels came personal-sized computers such as the Apple II. Within a few years, it became possible to have computer power at the desk-top level that previously had been available only with a large mainframe. Simultaneously, the capabilities of the largest mainframes grew exponentially. It was not uncommon for a company's available computing power to increase tenfold over a period of five years.

Second, the software changed. The first data-base management software was cumbersome and complicated, and required vast armies of technical wizards to keep it going. Within ten years, simple yet powerful data-base technology was available for every computer, from the smallest personal computer to the largest mainframe. Simultaneously, innovative products made entirely new data-to-information transformation possible. Fourth-generation languages allowed programs to be written by specifying the results rather than by using the step-by-step process required to create the results. Spreadsheets allowed users to concentrate on the relationships among the data itself rather than on the way to capture and store data. In sum, the explosive growth of hardware and software power enabled people to concentrate on the transformation of data into information instead of on the procedures used to implement the transformation.

Most important, these hardware and software innovations were accompanied by a change in attitude about the people who should control the transformation of data into information. Information center pioneers envisioned putting consumers of information directly in charge of its production. This vision was the critical step in the development of the information center. The transformation of data into information did not have to be rigorously defined in advance by technical wizards; it could be developed by end users with a little help from a new type of professional. The information center became a facilitator as the ability to create data transformations became directly available to end users.

MANAGERIAL, PROFESSIONAL, AND SUPPORT STAFF

Data transformations vary in complexity and scope, from simple data-capture screens to complex statistical analyses. Each type of transformation has a different effect on an organization. To examine this impact, it is helpful to divide the possible transformations into three categories on the basis of the business process underlying the transformation. These three categories include:

1. *Transaction Transformations*—processes that capture and manipulate data. They are the online entry systems, the batch-posting systems, and the extract/feeder systems that allow separate systems to work together. Their unglamorous role is to convert data from one format (written, screen image, or old file) into a new format (data-base, extract file, or application data).

2. *Control Transformations*—processes that allow us to monitor the behavior of transaction transformations. They show transactions in progress, posted and rejected transactions, control totals, and other information that allow a user to ensure that the transaction processes are behaving as planned. Control transformations concentrate on data that is in a transition state and include such items as traditional proof-and-control reports, audit-trail listings, and account statements.

3. *Analysis Transformations*—processes that provide the "big picture." These processes select, summarize, and sort data to allow a user to identify trends, design new business processes, and ensure that the business is meeting its objectives. These transformations rarely look at individual items of data, but concentrate instead on various

aggregations of data. Included in this group are trend reports, summaries, and exception reports.

Similarly, the users of these transformation systems can be divided into three categories:

1. *Support Staff*—the people who function as an extension of a manager or professional. Their goal is to maximize the productivity of others in the organization. Examples of this category might be data-entry operators, typists, administrative assistants, and maintenance staff.
2. *Professionals*—the people who possess special skills that an organization uses as resources. They include programmers, attorneys, accountants, and doctors.
3. *Managers*—the people who direct the resources of a business to meet organizational goals and objectives.

Traditionally, these distinctions were used to provide fairly rigid data-processing systems, as shown in Figure 1-3. For example, it was almost unheard of for a traditional organization to devise a system that would allow a manager to capture data directly. Instead, a transactions-capture system would be built for use by a support staff, that would then furnish reports to the manager.

There is an inherent problem, of course, in such inflexibility—it does not allow for potential changes in the needs or nature of a business or of its personnel. In the past, it was almost inconceivable that anyone outside the data-processing department might want to use a computer. However, with the advent of personal computers that gave every person the capability to analyze transactions, reports, and other information, the data-processing department was unable to respond because such machines violated its preconceived notions. This inability to respond to a new paradigm was one of the forces that gave birth to information centers.

FIGURE 1-3 Traditional Roles of Data Processing

	MANAGER	PROFESSIONAL	SUPPORT
Transaction Transformation	Almost no activity	Almost no activity	Transaction-capture systems
Control Transformations	Used to monitor performance of support staff	Limited activity; uses existing reports for special purposes	Validate transaction capture
Analysis Transformations	Traditional MIS systems; usually sorted summary reports	Almost no activity	Almost no activity

To meet the new demands, then, an information center must go beyond the traditional rigid rules. According to the previous definition, its role is to facilitate the transformation of data into information without regard for the type of transactions involved. The information center staff must feel equally at ease in helping a manager to develop a transaction-driven data-base application on a personal computer as in teaching support personnel how to use a fourth-generation language to get key management reports for their own tasks.

Notice also how this approach requires the relationship between an information center and a traditional data-processing department to be defined. Programmers and analysts are professionals just as accountants and market analysts are, and so should be viewed by an information center simply as users with business problems to solve. Thus, the relationship between a data-processing department and an information center, as with any other user, is one of client and consultant.

SOLVING BUSINESS PROBLEMS

Recall the definition of an information center presented earlier: "An organizational entity that facilitates the transformation of data into information that managerial, professional, and support staff can use to solve business problems." But what, exactly, is meant by "business problems"?

Problems or Troubles?

It is very important to distinguish "business problems" from "troubles." Many managers see themselves as solving "problems," such as labor unrest, machine breakdowns, or scheduling conflicts. These, however, are not problems but "troubles," and such managers may never actually realize the underlying business problems.

Consider a manager in a manufacturing plant who is facing a breakdown in a key machine. Without the machine, production will come to a halt, and the company's quotas will not be met. The "trouble" is solved as soon as the machine is repaired, but the business problem is much broader in scope. It involves such questions as: How often do machines break down? Is there a pattern to the breakdowns? Why is this machine so critical? Can the process be changed to make breakdowns less devastating? What are the effects of the breakdown on other parts of the operation?

Business problems transcend the immediate troubles and must be looked at from a new perspective—they must be expressed in terms of organizational norms and deviations from those norms. In the previous example, the business problem might be viewed in terms of a capacity norm: the operation should produce a specified number of products, and

---

FIGURE 1-4   Business Problem Definition

A good problem statement does not presuppose a solution. The problem is expressed as a deviation from a norm.

Bad: We need a bigger, faster computer. (Implies solution.)

Good: On-line response time is worse than standard three seconds. (Norm: three-second response time.)

Bad: I need to download data. (Implies solution.)

Good: The month-end analysis is taking three weeks longer than expected and requires too many people to enter the data. (Norm: expected completion, number of people.)

Bad: Give me this report. (Predetermined solution and delivery medium.)

Good: I can't monitor sales performance. (Norm: sales performance goals and actuals should meet targets.)

Bad: I want a new personal computer.

Good: I don't have enough status. (The norm need not be generally acceptable, as this example shows. However, once it is clearly and honestly stated, the solutions become easier.)

---

because of a machine failure, this expectation may not be met. Figure 1-4 illustrates this approach.

Notice how this new approach changes the manager's perspective. Repair of the machine is not the ultimate goal. The real business problem is now seen as ensuring a certain level of production capacity and the broken machine as a symptom of the larger problem. The manager must start to look deeper to analyze cause and effect and to identify long-term solutions. A manager whose time is devoted to resolving troubles will never be able to break free to seek solutions for the real business problems.

This distinction between trouble and business problem is essential to the role of an information center. Almost every "problem" that the user brings in to a consultant in search of a solution is not really a problem at all, but a trouble that seems to demand an immediate fix. Information centers have the tools to create quick solutions to these troubles that masquerade as problems and can become overwhelmed with urgent but unimportant demands. It is important to recognize that if an information center is to be truly effective, it must concentrate on the larger picture.

What role should an information center take in the solution of true business problems? The answer lies in the definition of a business problem as a deviation from the organizational norm. Solution of a business problem involves two possible alternatives: remove the deviation or change the norm. An information center can help in accomplishing either choice.

Removing the Deviation

To solve a business problem by removing the deviation, one must first accurately identify the deviation, and then analyze its cause. The following example shows how these two steps can be facilitated by an information center.

The management of a large bank is concerned that income from fees is not meeting expectations. This concern can be defined as a business problem because the expectation is a particular fee target and the deviation is the shortfall. The first step in solving this business problem is to define the deviation more accurately: Are all types of fees falling short of the goal? Is the problem limited to particular types of accounts? Is it limited to a particular geographic area? The information center's first task here is to help management quantify the deviation. This may be done, for instance, through reports using the fourth-generation language or with a spreadsheet on a personal computer. In this example, the results of the first step may show that there is a significant shortfall in fees for checking accounts in three geographic locations. Once the deviation has been accurately quantified, the first step has been taken toward solving the real business problem.

If the solution goes no further, however, it may concentrate on the wrong thing. The manager might decide to raise fees for checking accounts in those areas, whereas there are better solutions available. The information center needs to apply its tools once again to help the user analyze the causes of this deviation. In this example, additional queries might show that in checking accounts in those areas the fees for checks written with insufficient funds are waived automatically. Based on this analysis, various possible solutions emerge. The manager might provide training and "management counseling" to stop the practice of allowing customers to bounce checks without charge. Alternately, the automated account setup programs might be changed to require additional levels of authorization if fees are to be waived. But with either solution, notice how the information center's role has been to facilitate the transformation of data to information to solve the real business problem.

Cause-and-Effect Analysis

The last example deserves closer scrutiny. It was not sufficient simply to analyze the fees and identify the key geographic areas where the problem existed. The correct solution required that the information center become involved in helping the manager analyze the possible causes of the problem. This represents a significant departure from the traditional role of the MIS function.

Traditionally, the MIS has used cause-and-effect analysis to test programs and correct problems. If the program behaves incorrectly in a par-

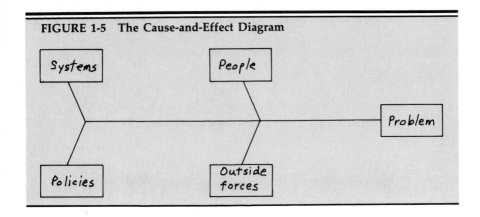

FIGURE 1-5   The Cause-and-Effect Diagram

ticular type of transaction, then the cause must lie in a specific program or routine. But the "facilitate" clause of the definition requires that the role of an information center extend into a partnership with the users as they analyze the causes that underlie a particular business (rather than technical) problem. It is interesting at this point to consider the nature of the cause-and-effect analysis that needs to be applied by an information center.

Most people want problem solving to be simple—find the cause of the problem and fix it. However, life is not that simple; there seldom is a single cause. In fact, even if a cause is identified, it may have its own causes. If an information center is to be successful, it must use a more structured method of cause analysis. One such method is based on the principles of quality control.

In a definitive text on quality control[1], Kaoru Ishikawa suggests that a fishbonelike diagram be used to analyze the causes of a problem (see Figure 1-5). In that diagram, each branch represents a type of causal factor. These factors depend on the nature of the process. For example, when analyzing manufacturing problems, Dr. Ishikawa suggests using "materials," "work methods," "equipment," and "measurement." In a service business, these factors might be "systems," "people," "policies," and "outside forces."

Once this framework is established, the analysis proceeds by brainstorming to identify every possible cause of the problem. Both users and information center staff participate in these brainstorming sessions. Each cause is represented pictorially as a line off the main branch (Figure 1-6). If an identified cause is sufficiently complex, it may have its own branches as well (Figure 1-7). No attempt should be made at this point to list only the "right" causes on the chart, but all possible causes should be included. An evaluation of each comes later.

---

[1]Kaoru Ishikawa, *Guide to Quality Control* (Tokyo, Japan: Asian Productivity Organization, 1968), pp. 19–28.

FIGURE 1-6   Cause and Effect for Bank-Fee Problem

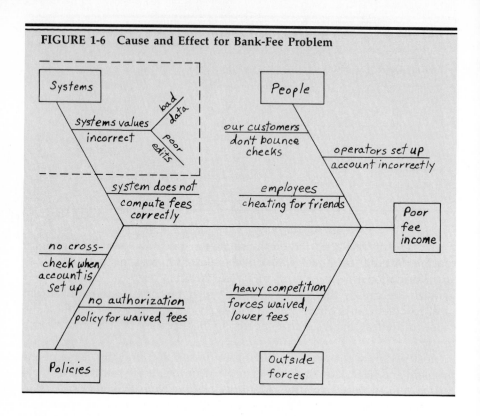

FIGURE 1-7   Detail of Cause-and-Effect Diagram

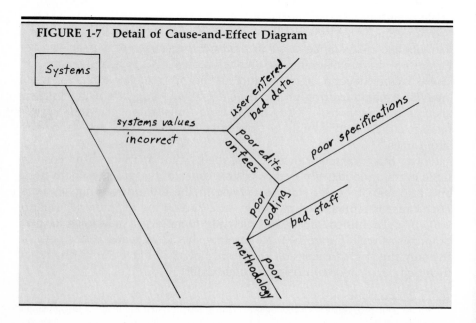

When completed, the diagram becomes a framework for investigation. Each of the potential causes can be tested for its effect on the problem. An information center and its users can work together, using the correct tools to identify and analyze the source of the deviation. And, as shown earlier, once the deviation is removed, the problem is solved.

Notice how this approach differs from the traditional systems approach. It is problem oriented, not operation oriented. It is cooperative, not departmentalized. It is structured from a business perspective, not a technological perspective. The technology is merely a tool to analyze and resolve a business problem. This is what the definition means by facilitating and solving business problems.

Changing the Norm

There is, of course, another solution to business problems—change the norm. In the bank example, perhaps the charges for bounced checks are being waived for competitive reasons, to keep customers from taking their business elsewhere. Thus, the best solution to this problem might be to change the norm so that the problem no longer exists. The bank's information center might become involved in building profitability models to allow bank management to try different fee scenarios. Modeling new norms places an information center in the role of facilitator of the transformation of data into information to solve business problems. Fixing troubles is fine, but solving business problems is the key to long-term success for an information center.

What is important here is to see the real role of an information center in the problem-solving process. That role is to offer alternatives—alternative views of problems, alternative procedures, alternative analysis methods, alternative tools. An information center should provide the means whereby a user can break out of the traditional constraints and begin to solve real business problems.

SUMMARY

This discussion starts with what appears to be an innocuous definition of an information center: an organizational entity that facilitates the transformation of data into information that managerial, professional, and support staff can use to solve business problems. Some of the terms in the definition are far more complex than they seem at first. Concepts such as *data* (stored facts in context), *information* (meaningful interpretation of data), and *business problems* (deviations from a norm) are critical to an understanding of what an information center really is. An information center is best defined by its results—not by the technology it uses.

SUGGESTED PROJECTS

1. Defend or oppose this thesis: Any large organization must have an information center if it is to be successful.

2. Consider the following situation: The sales manager for your company comes to the information center with the complaint that she never knows what her salespeople are doing until it is too late. She asks the information center for help. Discuss this request in terms of the distinction between *problem* and *trouble*. Use a cause-and-effect diagram to help identify some of the possible underlying causes of the real problem.

3. The text suggests that one way to classify transformations is by the terms *transaction, control,* and *analysis*. Develop your own classification scheme and discuss how it affects both the traditional data-processing view and an information center.

CHAPTER 2

Information Centers— Past, Present, and Future

Who discovered America? That is the subject of one of perhaps history's most provocative—and longest running—arguments. Traditionalists insist that it was Christopher Columbus who first sighted the New World in 1492 in his quest for a shorter route to India. Others argue that the early Vikings were the first to visit the North American continent. But to the native Americans who were here to greet those intrepid European adventurers, the question of which of them was first was merely rhetorical since they themselves had already "discovered" the continent many centuries earlier.

Thus it is with almost any aspect of the human endeavor. A bit of probing will show that seldom is any facet of history as cut-and-dried as the textbooks make it out to be. Only in very rare circumstances are historians able to point to a single event and definitively state: "That one was first."

The concept of the information center is not very different, with various conflicting sources taking credit for its development. Although each may have played a part, none can be singled out as the prime mover. In the final analysis, the history of the end-user computing movement must be told in personal terms, not in historical absolutes. Its underpinings are both technological and emotional, and encompass both personal and corporate forces. Accordingly, a definitive history of information center will not be presented here; instead, its history will be examined from a cultural perspective, looking at the changes that preceded its arrival, together with the forces that gave it life and those that will shape its future.

SETTING THE STAGE

Early business computers were big, dumb accounting machines. The more sophisticated took card input and generated even more cards and paper reports. Since vast armies of technically trained people were required to keep the systems going, direct interaction with the ultimate user was impossible. It was somewhere in the interim between those early days and the evolution of today's end-user computing environment that an obvious change occurred in the basic perceptions of technology. The computer had changed from a model based on accounting machines to one that made the technology an indispensable part of business itself.

Paradigm Shifts

Knowledge is rooted in paradigms—models that dictate perceptions of reality. Every person undergoes personal paradigm shifts; for example, a baby believes that when an object disappears from sight, it no longer exists. As children develop cognitively, they learn to recognize the permanence of objects outside of their own perception. The lost toy has not vanished completely but is merely someplace else.

People also go through collective paradigm shifts. For example, Martin Luther's assertion of the priesthood of the believer was a significant paradigm shift. Not only did this model alter the nature of religious thought, but it also freed the intellectuals of the time to explore other ideas that previously had been considered immutable. The prevailing concept of the nature of government, of artistic expression, and even of the planetary system were all altered once the constraints of the old model were lifted. Figure 2-1 lists other notable paradigm shifts in history.

An important characteristic of paradigm shifts is that their implications always extend past the original boundaries. What starts out as a change in the model that defines religious life, for example, soon affects the understanding of the nature of the universe. Newton's concept of gravitation was driven by the inadequacy of the existing model to explain a universe in which the planets moved around the sun in elliptical orbits. That heliocentric view of the universe was introduced by a Polish astronomer who was seeking a better way to compute the calendar in order to accommodate the church's need to mark the feasts of various saints. The establishment of such celebrations, in turn, was part of a movement to modernize church life initiated by the Council of Trent, in reaction to Luther's growing popularity.

Another important characteristic of these paradigm shifts is that each was not merely a new collection of knowledge but represented a fundamentally different way to think. Newton is not a significant historical figure because he saw an apple fall to the earth, but because he proposed that the earth was also attracted to the apple. That was a radical alteration of thought.

An information center is also the result of a paradigm change. The most interesting factor in its history is not the technology of end-user

---

FIGURE 2-1   A Sampler of Paradigm Shifts

WHO	WHAT
Martin Luther	Described a priesthood of the believer.
Thomas Jefferson	Said that government derives its power from the consent of the governed.
Copernicus	Described a heliocentric (sun-centered) universe.
Louis Pasteur	Said that disease is caused by microorganisms.
Albert Einstein	Said that matter and energy are interchangable.

FIGURE 2-2   Paradigm Shifts That Enabled End-User Computing

INTERACTIVE BASIC—TECHNOLOGY NEED NOT BE TECHNICAL
- English-like language
- Expanded access to computer
- Broad base of nontechnical users

Apple II—*TECHNOLOGY CAN BE LOCAL*
- Did not need a computer room
- Built on foundation of BASIC users
- Affordable computer on a desk

VisiCalc—*NONPROCEDURAL INTERACTIONS*
- New model for interaction: the spreadsheet
- Nonprocedural format: did not tell order of calculations
- Results driven by structure of numerical model, not program

---

computing, but rather the change in paradigms that are represented by certain key enabling technologies. How some of these enabling technologies (which are summarized in Figure 2-2) fundamentally changed the nature of computing is examined in the following pages.

One final word of caution is in order, however. Just like all paradigm shifts, these enabling technologies did not happen in isolation. In fact, the interrelationships among these developments are best thought of as a jigsaw puzzle such as Figure 2-3: Each piece fits into the other, none is sufficient in its own right, and the whole picture becomes clear only when the pieces have been properly assembled.

Interactive BASIC

Many observers might argue that the development of an interactive operating system was critical to the emergence of end-user computing, but, even so, that operating system was useless without a simple language that

---

FIGURE 2-3   The Enabling Technologies Jigsaw Puzzle

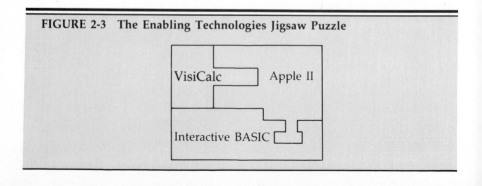

would open up access to the computer to the nontechnically trained user. The language that emerged for that purpose was BASIC.

The original BASIC was far from elegant: variables could be only two characters long, the scope of the language was severely limited according to today's standards, and its dependence on line numbers to control process flow was the source of much anguish. Nevertheless, BASIC allowed a programmer to write programs that looked a lot more like English than assembly language. In essence, it represented a very early attempt to provide computing power to nontechnical users.

Even more important; BASIC quickly became the language of choice, especially on university campuses. It may not have been pretty, but it was popular. In many universities, it was often the first language taught in the computer science curriculum. When the era of end-user computing finally became a reality, BASIC already had a broad base of followers. These users formed a natural constituency.

One way to understand the effect of this new language is to look at the results. The giant software company Microsoft began its operations with the development of a single product—BASIC interpreters. The default language for the first Apple II computers was a version of BASIC, and the first IBM personal computers were shipped with a version of BASIC hard-wired in their motherboards. The almost universal appeal of BASIC fore-shadowed the need to develop the computer into a tool for general use, and was instrumental in changing the established thinking about the role of computers in science, in business, and in everyday life.

The Apple Contribution

The earliest personal computers came in do-it-yourself kits. Armed with manuals and soldering irons, the faithful would retreat to garage or basement and painstakingly assemble the kit's components into a computer. Most of these early computer builders had an almost missionary zeal about their tasks, and would meet periodically to brag about their machines and the techniques they had developed. But for the most part, these pioneers had about as much impact on business as do amateur radio operators. They represented an electronic technology that was interesting but not useful.

With the introduction of the first Apple computer, however, the situation changed. Although it was not the first, or necessarily the best, of the nonkit computers to reach the market, it was clearly the most successful. As was the case with BASIC, the Apple computer represented the shift of technology away from the technicians. A nontechnical user could now command computing power at a reasonable price with the flip of an on–off switch.

Coincidentally or not, the language that came built into each Apple was BASIC. Thus hardware and software converged to make computing power more generally accessible. Again it should be noted, however, that the paradigm changes at work behind the emergence of end-user computing rarely proceeded in a straightforward direction. Instead, its development was marked by a number of paths that sometimes ran parallel and sometimes crossed at critical points. The combination of the Apple computer and the BASIC language represented one of those points, but there was yet another product that was to be a critical factor in the growth of end-user computing.

VisiCalc

As tradition has it, the students at a major university were struggling with their accounting problems. It seems that every simple change required that the results be carried through a number of related calculations, a procedure that often bore testimony to the availability of sharp lead pencils and good erasers. Then, the story goes, a friend of one of the students purchased an Apple computer, and the student proposed that there might be some way to use the computer to help simplify the classes' problems. The rest is history.

VisiCalc became the first commercially available spreadsheet and was almost an immediate success. The significant event here, though, was not the birth of the spreadsheet but the advent of the nonprocedural software that the spreadsheet represented. It meant that the user no longer needed to tell the computer what to do—all that was required was to express the relationship of the data elements. To a large degree, the popularity of most fourth-generation languages is an outgrowth of the nonprocedural roots planted by VisiCalc.

Although the creation of VisiCalc was in itself an important event, when viewed in the context of the other pioneer products in end-user computing, it is seen to represent an even more powerful symbiosis. Some people bought VisiCalc because it made their Apple computers more useful; others bought Apple computers so that they could run VisiCalc. Thus it was not any one product but a combination of products that formed the technological basis for a new approach to computing.

THE BIRTH FORCES: EMOTIONAL, NOT RATIONAL

It would simplify the discussion to be able to say that information centers came into being as the result of a carefully thought-out strategic plan by top management to take advantage of the various technological innovations. That, however, is not the case. The forces that gave rise to information centers were largely emotional; how these emotional forces combined with the technological forces to create information centers is examined in this

---

FIGURE 2-4   The Information Center Birth Forces

REACTIVE FORCES—THE USERS
- Traditional data-processing perceived as unresponsive
- Demand increased for information for business needs
- Shift to strategic information needs

PROACTIVE FORCES—THE DP ESTABLISHMENT
- Head off new technology and control it
- Offload development to somebody else's budget
- Set up a savior scenario where data processing could come in and straighten up the mess created by ignorant end users

BUREAUCRATIC FORCES—THE ORGANIZATION
- Needed slots on the organization chart for new managers or changes in existing managers
- Wanted to impress peer organizations
- Wanted to provide a safety valve to take pressure off of existing demands, problems

---

section. These birth forces are summarized in Figure 2-4 and are discussed in more detail in the sections that follow.

Reactive Forces: The Users

Advocates of information centers found a receptive audience among computer users in most organizations. These end users were simply fed up with the organizational problems that they encountered in dealing with the data-processing hierarchy. It seemed that every request for new features or functions was met with bureaucratic rigmarole, layers of management approval, and cost estimates measured in years and millions of dollars. The users were clearly ready for a revolution.

To a great degree, the difficulty was self-inflicted wound. In many organizations, the process of designing and delivering systems had become a nightmare. Among the problems that hindered the procedure were the following:

1. *Poor Design Methods.* In many development projects, the designers started out by assuming that the real solution to the business problems they were trying to solve would be found in the reports furnished by the user. They also believed that by requiring the user to approve written specifications that could run into hundreds of pages, they could stabilize the design. In reality, nothing could be further from the truth. By concentrating on the inputs, the process, and the output, these designers worked only on the apparent

problem and always seemed to be surprised when a new business need emerged. The delays and frustrations caused by rework were devastating to both the programmer and the user.

2. *Poor Management.* In many cases, the management of the systems development function was completely disorganized. This disarray often resulted when outstanding technical-staff members were rewarded by promotion into the ranks of management, where they might lack the overall skills necessary to manage a project successfully to completion.

3. *Hot-Button Approaches.* Because poor design required so much reworking and poor management only exacerbated the problem, many organizations found themselves taking a "hot button of the week" approach. The urgent projects would receive extra attention at the expense of the merely important. In an effort to make the target deadlines, quality and testing often would be sacrificed. The cost of maintenance programming became an increasing part of the development budget.

Some projects were well managed, of course, and responsive to the needs of the users, but these represented a minority of the development teams. In most organizations, the users had become very frustrated with the data-processing department and were ready for the changes that the new products and technologies promised.

However, there was yet another force that was driving the user community to react. That force was the changing nature of management, which had become much more quantitative. Each tier of managers, recognizing that there was a wealth of data available but a paucity of information, wanted to know "the numbers" involved in any management decision. Demands for new numbers analyzed in different ways were accelerating at a dizzying pace. Something had to be done.

Proactive Forces: The Data-Processing Department

These various developments did not go unnoticed by the data-processing establishment. They were aware of the restlessness of the users, as well as of the availability of the new user-oriented technology, and they were afraid of the results. They needed to head off the revolt before it could get started. In particular, they needed to:

1. *Control Personal Computers.* Each personal computer represented a further fragmentation of the organization's computing resource. The data-processing department had to find a way to manage this process for the benefit of the organization and to avoid piecemeal solutions that might serve in the short term but would not meet long-term requirements. Banning the new devices outright was a bad idea; any manager who wanted a computer badly enough could

figure out a way to obtain one. (Consider how many purchase orders were cut in those days for filing systems with monochrome monitors!) Devising an approach whereby the technology could be introduced into the organization in a controlled fashion was imperative.

2. *Off-load Development Activities.* Even though the users claimed to be dissatisfied with the process of systems development, they continued to add new requests to the queue at an alarming rate. Somehow that load needed to be shifted by giving the user a greater role in the development of systems. In fact, if the MIS department could pass off more of the uninteresting development activities (such as report creation) to the user, everyone involved would be happier.

3. *Be Able To Say "I Told You So."* Many MIS directors were sceptical that end-user computing would ever prove viable, but rather than openly oppose it, they chose to watch it push forward into new areas. After all, it would to their advantage to be able to rescue the users if things were to go wrong.

4. *Contain Costs.* Programmers were an expensive breed of employee. To perform all of the pending work would require more programming personnel and hence an increase in the salary budget of the data-processing department. For most managers, asking for a larger budget represented a career-killing choice. If more service could be provided without a corresponding increase in the budget, the MIS director would be a hero without risk.

Organizational Forces

With users ready to start using some of the new technologies and the data-processing professionals feeling compelled to control the growth of end-user computing tools, the only remaining step was to fight organizational inertia and actually set up an information center. That inertia was overcome in various ways, including:

1. *Organizational Upheaval.* In the life of any organization, corporate earthquakes occur regularly that result in the reorganization of the boxes on the company charts. In many instances, in the wake of one of these periodic upheavals, a manager on the way up, or a fallen hero on the way down, might end up in a box on the chart labeled "Information Center."

2. *Committee Roulette.* The typical organization had a steering committee made up of senior executives from all of the company's various divisions or departments. As the user community became more disturbed by the problems of the data-processing group, and as the data-processing group grew more defensive, an information

center often was created as an "experiment" to take some of the heat out of the committee meetings.

3. *Me-Too-ism.* As soon as one company formed an information center, others quickly jumped on the bandwagon. The underlying frustrations and demands might not have reached a state of crisis in those organizations, but corporate egos demanded that they not allow another company in the same community to establish a claim to superiority, either real or imagined.

4. *Carefully Weighed Response to Problems.* In a few, very rare situations, an organization might actually examine the problems of end users, as well as the tools available and the organizational structures needed to enable those tools to be used successfully. After this careful analysis, an information center was set up with a clearly defined charter and a clear directive from management.

5. *Corporate Schizophrenia.* Often, an organization would maintain that the information center was a carefully weighed response to problems, whereas it was really the result of organizational upheaval, committee roulette, or corporate me-too-ism, or a completely paranoid response to perceived or real problems. In those organizations, the information center was born out of knee-jerk reactions masquerading as a carefully weighed response to the problems.

In the final analysis, most information centers came into being owing to a combination of three forces: the users' demands, the establishment's proactive needs, and corporate upheavals. But however the information center evolved in a particular instance, it was almost always an emotional experience that the participants in its birth will never forget.

EARLY INFORMATION CENTERS

It is impossible to look at the early days of the information center phenomenon with complete objectivity. Talk to any of the pioneers in the movement and an overwhelming sense of passion comes through. They believe in what they did and found great personal satisfaction in the daily successes, and failures, of this new department. The dreams of those responsible for the concept of the information center will be considered, with special focus on their dual nature—the dreams that motivated the establishment of the early information centers also seemed to contain the seeds of failure.

Service Orientation

Many of the founders of early information centers were altruists who saw the new department as a way *finally* to serve the users. They had observed the frustrations involved with the traditional data-processing approach, and wanted to help the users do their jobs.

This service orientation was simultaneously an information center's greatest strength and its greatest weakness. On the one hand, it afforded an information center the opportunity to be of real value to the organization by attempting to meet information needs that had been unattended for years. On the other hand, it tended to foster a "Robin Hood" attitude on the part of the information center staff, which often saw itself as the means to free the users from the tyranny of the "wicked" traditional data-processing approach that had "oppressed" them for years. This attitude was not one that would foster confidence on the part of the MIS managers.

This service orientation proved to be a mixed blessing for fledgling information centers. In their rush to be helpful, the staff members found themselves either overcommitted (since they wanted to help everyone) or working on the wrong projects (since there was no easy way to determine who needed help the most). The dream may have started with an altruistic desire to serve the user better than ever before, but that dream quickly gave way to realism and the information centers were forced to ration their services or to extend their working day. As will be noted in subsequent chapters, the service orientation of the early information centers needed to be tempered by an understanding of strategic principles.

Power

Almost every young child dreams of having special powers and superhuman strength, and of being virtually invincible. The pioneer information centers were no different.

The information center's tools allowed one person to do in days what previously had required many months to accomplish. This was very heady stuff. Entire on-line systems together with all necessary reports could be produced over a weekend. Complex reports that once necessitated weeks of effort could be completed within hours. Impressive graphics could be created in an afternoon. The members of the information center staff felt power at their command.

The image of many information centers in those early days is similar to one depicted in the Disney classic *Fantasia,* in the segment entitled "The Sorcerer's Apprentice," starring Mickey Mouse. In that segment, the master sorcerer has gone away for the day, leaving Mickey, his apprentice, to fill a large tub with water. Instead of doing the task manually in the traditional manner, Mickey consults a book of spells and is able to charm a broom into life to do the work for him. The broom servant dutifully starts carrying the water up the stairs to fill the tub.

What makes this movie an outstanding metaphor for the early information centers was not the apprentice's use of the magic power in a new and productive fashion, but what happened next. The apprentice soon realized that although he had determined how to use the power to solve his immediate problem, he did not know how to control the power. No matter how he tried to stop the broom from bringing water, it stubbornly persisted. In fact, he only succeeded in making matters worse. What started out as an exercise in power soon evolved into a situation that was seriously out of hand.

In their intoxication with power, those early information center managers often failed to realize that they needed to establish a degree of control over the basic processes they were attempting to introduce. They could build systems overnight or develop dazzling graphics almost instantly, but what were the long-term ramifications of this power? What was missing was a sense of stewardship.

Computing Power and Decision Makers

Yet another common dream for early information centers was that they would enable nonprogrammers to develop complete application systems. Old-fashioned methods that required layers of users, analysts, and programmers would be replaced by putting computing power directly into the hands of decision makers.

For most early information centers, this shift in power meant training, and lots of it. Inexperienced end users had to be trained in the basics of data processing and in the fundamental skills the tools would provide. This need for training also meant that new facilities, including rooms full of terminals and personal computers, would be required, as well as curriculum materials and teacher aids. The revolution would not come cheap.

The personnel in most early information centers instituted the desired training procedures on schedule, only to encounter a new question: When, if ever, should an information center go beyond training and actually write code for users? This question soon became a major topic of discussion whenever information center managers gathered. Some would adamantly refuse to write code, citing contention with the traditional development group and a burgeoning maintenance problem. Others would argue just as vehemently in favor of occasionally writing code, citing lack of sophistication on the part of the users and the professional desire to make sure that the new applications were developed correctly. All, however, agreed that computing power should be placed in the hands of the end user—although their views as to how that power shift should be carried out varied widely.

The debate was never resolved, in part because early information centers were looking for universal rules when, in fact, there were no rules. The traditional data-processing department had survived for years by following a set of clearly defined rules of conduct. Analysts and programmers had their respective roles in the process and that lack of ambiguity was comforting. The transferral of these programming tasks to the end user obliterated the boundaries, leaving a void—a problem that will be discussed in more detail in Chapter 10.

EMOTIONAL BIRTH, RATIONAL EVALUATION

The preceding sections have provided a flavor of the early days of the information center movement. It was a confusing time marked by emotion, high expectations, and dreams—and the problems created by those dreams. The information center almost never came out of a rational, clearly thought-out plan; it was usually the result of an emotional reaction to a need. Unfortunately, within a few years the emotions had died and the information center was being evaluated on a purely rational basis.

The "Warm Fuzzies": Not Enough

The feeling that one senses when talking to people involved in those early days of information centers is primarily one of fun. Being in on the birth of the concept was a very heady experience. Most thought the good times would never end. They were wrong.

Sooner or later, every information center was called on to justify its existence to the organization. If it had concentrated on training, why was that route more effective than purchasing training from outside vendors? If its primary role was to control the implementation of personal computers, why was a separate department still needed once the personal computer population in the organization had stabilized? If it was a facilitator of end-user–developed systems, how could it show that those systems provided value for the amount of computing resource consumed? The emotional birth forces had given way to the rational forces of evaluation.

Figure 2-5 illustrates this concept. Notice that for each emotional birth force, there is an implied rational criterion that will be used to evaluate the

FIGURE 2-5 Emotional Birth—Rational Evaluation	
BIRTH FORCES	*LIKELY EVALUATION*
Reactive users	Ability to solve important business problems in an efficient and timely fashion
Proactive data-processing establishment	Control of environment and cost-effective delivery of services
Organizational forces	Ability to fit in with the rest of the corporation structure and strategy

---

FIGURE 2-6   Information Center Death Threats

YOU ARE REPLACEABLE
- By outside services
- By other internal resources

YOU ARE EXPENSIVE
- Hardware
- Software
- Liveware

YOU HAVE FINISHED YOUR TASK
- The information center was an experiment
- The information center was only a bridge to the new paradigm

---

success of the information center. For example, some information centers came into being in response to what was described earlier as reactive users. They were fed up with the existing organization and demanded change. In many cases, the mere act of creating an information center gave the users enough hope that the pressures stopped for a time. However, the ultimate success of an information center is not judged by how well it diffuses the reactions of users, but by its ability to meet the needs of the business in an efficient manner.

Unfortunately, many information centers could not pass the tests of these rational evaluations. In fact, in the late 1980s, it has become fashionable to decommission information centers—they have been receiving "death threats" from the very people who chartered them. These threats are summarized in Figure 2-6 and will be discussed in the following paragraphs.

A Replaceable Entity

Information centers whose managers insisted that they were only enabling forces have fallen on hard times. Once the critical mass of trained end users was in place, those information centers became superfluous. Such administrative functions as securing system sign-on authorization and passwords could be handled by the traditional data-processing personnel. The training function could be carried out via peer training or by purchasing outside training. Almost every service that the enabling information center provided was available from the outside, except for one important factor: organizational knowledge.

Once an information center decided to be a facilitator and not a hands-on provider of services, it lost a critical advantage. Although all of the functions could be provided in other ways, the information center staff could have furnished those services with an understanding of the strategic and political realities of the organization. Long-term success depended on the ability to be perceived by the organization as a strategically critical element. Information centers that did not make themselves an indispensable part of the corporate picture were soon headed for obsolescence.

An Expensive Undertaking

Running an information center entails considerable expense. There are the hardware costs for personal computers, terminals, printers, plotters, modems, and the various other devices that make up a modern information center. There are software costs for the spreadsheets, fourth-generation languages, data bases, project-control systems, and graphics packages that comprise an information center's tool kit. And there are the "liveware" costs for consultants, product specialists, managers, and support personnel.

Even worse, while the costs of an information center are easily quantifiable, the results are often difficult to delineate. Is it worth the expense to be able to make better decisions and to make them more quickly? What is the value of the strategic project that cannot directly demonstrate any measurable impact on the bottom line?

The next chapter, discusses a method of measuring the effect of an information center by looking at the strategic values of the organization. But for many information centers, this comes too late: they were perceived as a very expensive (and therefore expendable) operation whose only virtue was that they generated warm and fuzzy feelings among the computer users.

Mission Accomplished

Many information centers were commissioned for a single purpose, such as to control personal computers—a role that was usually assumed in answer to the reactive stance of the traditional MIS department. However, an information center that maintained this narrow focus was doomed to long-term failure.

The truth is that every single-purpose operation has its saturation point. If the purpose was to introduce personal computers, an information center essentially became obsolete once the maximum number of computers needed had been installed. Similarly, if the single purpose was to provide a temporary bridge from operational systems to information systems, once the MIS group began training its own staff, an information center was out of a job. As long as information centers were established to carry out a single purpose, they were likely to be disbanded once that purpose was accomplished.

The Secret of Survival

What are the differences between those information centers that have survived (and even thrived) and those that have been decommissioned? The secret starts with an understanding of the history.

The survivors are those whose founders understood that all of the enabling technologies and birth forces had very little to do with success. These information centers are the ones whose managers were able to look beyond the highly emotional birth and see its role as a true business function responsive to the changes in the computing paradigm.

The staffs at those information centers also understood that success depended on their ability to recast the birth forces into terms that supported the organization's strategic vision. They were able to establish rational criteria for their success that, although based on the birth forces, enabled them to look toward the future and to transform their technology and skills into tools that could solve real business problems. This ability to translate actions into strategic terms is critical and will be discussed at length in the chapters that follow. Not only did those who were unable to accomplish this objective fail to understand the lessons of history but their information centers themselves became part of that history.

SUMMARY

This chapter began with a look at some of the major cultural and technological changes that gave birth to the concept of an information center— birth forces that tended to be highly emotional in nature. It was noted that information centers pioneers came with a collections of dreams that contained the seeds of both success and failure. Finally, the problems that seemed to arise when the emotional birth forces were followed by rational evaluations were discussed.

The history of information centers should be viewed more as a cultural movement than as a technological change. Its founders were driven by a vision and its power came from pure emotion. What this lesson teaches is that it is not movements, by themselves, that ultimately succeed in attaining a goal. Long-term success comes instead from a broad-based understanding of the character of the organization to be served and from knowing how best to implement that service. The rest of this book discusses how an information center can accomplish this end.

SUGGESTED PROJECTS

1. The text states that major paradigm shifts that enabled end-user computing were VisiCalc, the Apple II, and interactive BASIC. De-

velop your own list of enabling technologies and defend your choices.

2. As a research project, survey a number of information centers. Develop a questionnaire to determine the following about each center:
   - How old is the information center?
   - Why does the current manager think the information center was founded?
   - How was the first information center manager selected?
   - Who were the initial client departments and why?
   - Does the manager think the information center will ever be decomissioned? If so, why will it happen?

   How do the results of your survey compare with the birth forces described in the text?

CHAPTER 3

Taking the
Strategic View

In a chapter titled "World Nations and People," *The People's Almanac*, takes an interesting approach to the earth's geography and the cultures it represents. For each country, it presents traditional material such as location, size, population, and history, but it also includes two additional sections: "Who Rules?" and "Who REALLY Rules?." For example, in describing the United States, the book lists the president, Congress, and state governments under "Who Rules?" but states that "Who REALLY Rules" are "the interlocking directorates of the major banks, corporations, and insurance companies, with the backing of the leaders of the military."[1] This approach recognizes a critical fact: an organization's "official" statements of its methods and objectives may differ radically from the way in which it actually behaves.

This, then, is the task for an information center: not only to identify what the organization says is important, but also to look critically at the values that are reflected in its actions. In this way, an information center can position itself to deliver the services that will make it indispensable.

AN IDEAL STRATEGIC PLANNING PROCESS

The number of words that have been printed on the subject of strategic planning is astronomical. Most of them are either too esoteric for the purposes of this discussion or describe a process that is too detailed to be of value here. Instead, the nature of strategic thinking in business will be considered as a four-step process that takes place at all levels of the organization from the first-line supervisor to the chief executive officer, not just in the domain of designated strategic thinkers.

Step 1: What Is This Organization?

The first step in the ideal strategic planning process is to formulate a clear statement of how the organization sees itself: What kind of business is it in? What market does it serve? What is the nature of its products? (The worksheet in Figure 3-1 illustrates this step.) Notice that Figure 3-1 emphasizes stating the answers in one sentence. Although this is an artificial constriction, its goal is to help in understanding the nature of strategic thinking. It is not to make a laundry list of the things the organization *does*, but to describe what it *is*. The difference is crucial.

However, limiting the response to one sentence does not preclude accuracy and honesty. Consider a major university as an example. It may

---

[1]David Wallechinsky and Irving Wallace, *The People's Almanac* (Garden City, N.Y.: Doubleday & Company, Inc., 1975), p. 464.

FIGURE 3-1   The Strategic Planning Process

WHAT ARE WE?

Describe in one sentence the nature of the products or services of the organization.

> *The information center facilitates the transformation of data into information to solve business problems.*

Describe in one sentence the market served by the organization.

> *The target market for the information center is the professional staff, support staff, midlevel managers, and top executive management.*

Describe in one sentence the management philosophy of the organization.

> *The management philosophy is based on these two principles: the competancy of the user and the concept of responsible stewardship for all resources.*

Describe in one sentence the nature of the competition.

> *The competition comes from two sources: internal (traditional MIS group, departmental experts) and external (retail computer stores, independent consultants).*

---

answer the first worksheet question as follows: "The university provides a superior education at undergraduate and graduate levels in academic disciplines." However, if the university is typical, it has omitted a major product in this answer: research. A better answer might be: "The university provides a superior education at undergraduate and graduate levels in academic disciplines while also seeking to conduct meaningful research in key fields." The first answer describes the university as it wants to be seen, but the second is a far more accurate description of its real nature.

This example also illustrates two key tenets of strategic planning. First, there must be almost brutal honesty. In these first steps, it is vitally important to see the organization as it really is. Second, the process must proceed iteratively, through a number of evaluations and revisions. Each successive attempt will elicit a statement that increasingly approaches one that best reflects the nature of the organization.

Step 2: What Changes Are Foreseen?

Once the nature of the organization has been accurately defined, it is time to look into the future. This step calls for intuition, research, and a good sense for trends. Here, the organization is asked to predict possible changes in products, services, markets, and competition. (Figure 3-2 provides a sample worksheet to illustrate this step.) The requirement for a single-sentence answer is relaxed in this phase as more than one change may be predicted.

FIGURE 3-2   The Strategic Planning Process

WHAT CHANGES ARE FORESEEN IN YOUR ORGANIZATION?

What changes will occur in the nature of your products or services?
- Increased emphasis on connectivity
- Standardized user interface on all hardware platforms
- Increased power and effectiveness

What changes will occur in the markets served by the organization?
- Flattening of management pyramid (few midlevel managers)
- Increased demand for information
- Decrease in staff support functions

What changes will happen in existing competiton?
- Weaker retail computer stores will fold
- Stronger retail computer stores will consolidate power
- Consultants will form strategic alliances with computer stores and vendors

What new competition will arise?
- Information centers in other corporations may start reselling their training and consulting
- Vendors may open local training and support offices

It is tempting to come up with self-serving predictions by basing the answers to the questions posed in this step on those obtained in the first step. In the university example, for instance, there might be the temptation to look at the markets and conclude that there will be increased demand for postgraduate programs (one of the areas in which the university has invested heavily). This is the route to disaster. If this step is to accomplish its purpose, the predictions must be made honestly and without bias toward any existing product, service, or market. Anything less skews the final results and may destroy the organization.

Step 3: What Should This Organization Be?

The results of step 2 should enable the creation of a clear picture of what the organization ought to be. Using the worksheet from Figure 3-1 as a guide, the questions should be answered as it is hoped they will be answered in a few years. This step is often the most difficult of all because it forces the organization to articulate a clear vision of what it must become. If the university in the example were to look at its markets and conclude that the potential student population would be decreasing over the next five years, it might choose to change its statement about products and services to add "nondegree skills training" to its traditional academic disciplines. Alternatively, it might choose to change its statement about markets to recruit applicants from a national, rather than regional, talent pool. Both alternatives are valid responses to the envisioned changes. Similarly, each predicted change should be reflected in a change in the nature of the organization.

Once again, brutal honesty is the key to success. Since the vision that emerges from this third step will guide the actions of the organization over the next few years, consensus among its leaders is critical. A clearly articulated vision of the future organization is essential to the final step in the idealized strategic planning cycle.

Step 4: How Will the Organization Get There?

If the first step has accurately identified the current organization and the second and third steps have developed an agreed-upon vision of the future organization, all that remains is to identify the actions that must be taken to reach that future. This step moves from the realm of strategic thinking into tactics.

In this stage, action-oriented goals are developed for each component of the strategic vision and their respective responsibilities and time frames assigned. In the university example, if the third step identifies a new vision for the markets that expands the potential student pool from regional to national, one tactic may be: "By the third quarter of this year, the Director of Alumni Affairs is to develop a list of qualified alumni to serve as regional recruiters." In an ideal strategic planning process, tactics should always be tied to the strategic changes identified in the first three steps.

Strategic Planning at All Levels

Do not assume that this idealized methodology is to be used at only the highest levels of the organization. Indeed, each operational unit can use the same approach to determine its activities. At the department level, however, there is usually a significant difference: the products and services may not be those that the organization as a whole offers, but may be designed only for internal use. The products and services offered by an accounting department, for example, are only rarely available outside the organization. However, if the department is to be successful, the controller needs to view it as if it were a business within itself, delivering products and services to customers who just happen to be other departments of the company. A strategic plan should be developed to show how the nature of the accounting system will change, and how the accounting department must change as well. Similarly, information centers need to develop a strategic business view toward their customers and activities.

THE REAL STRATEGIC PLANNING PROCESS

The previous section paints a picture of a superbly rational organization—
one whose managers honestly examine its current state, perceptively look
into the future, intelligently form a vision of where it ought to be, and
meticulously select actions that will help it progress from its current state to
its envisioned future. Unfortunately, the real world is never that rational.
Organizations may go through a strategic planning process, but their
leaders may lack the honesty or vision to develop a solid plan. In other
organizations, an accurate plan, may be developed but never executed
successfully. For still other organizations, an explicit plan is never developed at all, and they seem to move from one week to the next as if by
accident. If, an information center's success rests on delivering strategically
important services and products, how can the truly important be differentiated from the merely urgent without a clear vision of the organization's strategy?

As the authors of the *People's Almanac* discovered, there is often a discrepancy between what an organization says is important and what its
behavior indicates. It is an organization's behavior and not an official
position that reveals the most about its strategic vision. How, then, can this
behavior be used to help determine the strategic vision for an information
center?

Value-Driven Strategic Analysis

The problem of determining a strategic view is similar to what everyone
faces in interacting with other people. A person who claims to be a thrill
seeker but always manages to be elsewhere when the group lines up to
ride the roller-coaster obviously is exhibiting behavior that does not match
the boast. Similarly, one who professes financial conservativism but invests aggressively in hog-belly futures must be judged by the actions rather
than the words.

People behave as they do because of the values they believe in—values
such as recognition by others, achievement, financial security, religion,
stability, and control. Although almost everyone considers all of these
values to be of some importance, for each person, one or two of the values
will assume greater importance than the others and will become a driving
force behind that person's behavior. This is a lesson car dealers learned
long ago: determine the values of the potential buyer and emphasize the
automobile's features that best fulfill those values. To the analytical, the
dealer would stress engineering features; to the frugal, fuel economy; to
the adventuresome, high performance. By identifying a person's primary
values, one can predict the person's behavior. Thus, a product or service
that is described in terms of the primary value of a potential user is more
likely to be viewed as indispensable.

FIGURE 3-3   Corporate Values

The values for an organization might include:

- **Distribution**—the organization prides itself on its ability to get products and good from one point to another effectively.

- **Technology**—new technology is developed for the sake of innovation. Practical applications will come naturally later on.

- **Stable Products**—the products and services offered today will not differ much from the products and services tomorrow.

- **Market Driven**—the market determines new products and services and the organization reacts quickly to these needs.

- **Resource Conservation**—the resources used by the organization are scarce. Careful conservation of these resources means success.

- **Production Capacity**—the production capabilities of the organization are expensive investments. Keeping them operating is critical to success.

- **Size/Growth**—there is intentional behavior to change the size of the organization.

- **The Bottom Line**—the financial return of the organization is the final determiner of success.

Organizations also have sets of values, some of which are illustrated in Figure 3-3. As with human beings, the professed values of an organization often do not match its behavior. Consider a company that claims to be bottom-line oriented but nevertheless invests $2 million in product development. Or consider an organization that declares itself to be market driven, but whose products take three to five years to create. In both of these cases, the stated values do not match the behavior.

Before looking at how an organization's behavior reveals its values, two of the values shown in Figure 3-3 merit additional discussion. The first is "size/growth." Organizations that honestly claim this value are usually in transition. Growth for its own sake is not a long-term objective; normal growth is usually the natural result of some other value. The downsizing of a corporation is also usually a transitional value. Some other force such as a changing market or new technology has required the change and what appears to be an emphasis on size is really a transitional state.

Similarly, few organizations really focus on "the bottom line." Since all organizations exist to make money (or at least to break even), the fact that an organization maintains that it focuses on the bottom line does not provide much information about the organization's behavior. What is more important is how an organization behaves as it tries to improve the bottom line: Will it invest in new technology, develop new marketing programs, create new products, or open different distribution channels? An organization that continues to apply profits to the bottom line to the exclusion of all other activities is in a state of transition, making short-term decisions that are reflected immediately in the bottom line rather than long-term decisions that would sustain bottom-line growth. Sustained growth is always the result of some other value, not an obsession with quick profit.

The Dichotomy Question

The Bible (Mark 6:21) teaches: "For where your treasure is, there will your heart be also." This is the crux of analyzing the values of an organization. The choice of areas to which it devotes its resources provides a fairly accurate indication of an organization's values.

To determine an organization's values, begin by asking a series of questions that compare two alternatives. These dichotomy questions force a choice between two possible values. For example, one such question might be: If an organization were to receive a million dollar windfall, would the money be applied directly to the bottom line or would it be invested in a marketing campaign for a new product? A second question might be: In taking advantage of a new federal program that will provide the necessary funding, will an organization hire ten new research scientists or lease a new distribution facility for three years? By asking such questions, one or two values eventually will emerge as the primary forces behind the organization's behavior.

To whom should these questions be directed? It might seem that top managers would be the only people who could give accurate answers, but this is misleading. The problem is similar to that involved in analyzing an individual's values. An individual asked similar behavioral questions is likely to give answers that are tainted by a sense of "should be." The answers usually will be self-serving, rather than a true reflection of the individual's probable behavior. The most accurate answers will be obtained from the person's family and close friends.

Similarly, the people who can best answer questions regarding the values of an organization are not always the top managers. Instead, middle managers, and even the organization's competitors, can better assess the organization's behavior. Thus, it is these individuals who should be questioned since they are observers of the corporate behavior but are not charged with setting the direction of that behavior.

These questions do not allow for ambivalent answers—one of the alternatives must be selected. As the primary values are approached, the questions become more difficult to answer; that is, the organization is being asked to choose between two roughly equivalent values.

Value Clashes

The asking of dichotomy questions can help determine the primary values of an organization, and the same procedure can be applied to an organization's operational units. Interestingly enough, the values of the two need not match. For example, an organization may be primarily market driven, trying to react quickly to the changing needs of the marketplace by introducing new products at a breakneck pace. However, its accounting department may emphasize stability in its results and its data-processing department may concentrate on distribution, ensuring that the data and voice communications network are expandable and responsive. What are the implications of such discrepancies in primary values?

The fact that values differ can be supportive as well as a hindrance. If the stability of a market-driven organization's accounting system, for example, provides a consistent means of measuring the success of new products, then the difference is supportive. Conversely, a drive for stability that becomes overpowering may prevent an organization from being responsive to its marketing needs and may hinder the implementation of corporate values. If the company's data-processing department's emphasis on distribution provides a means to communicate better with the marketplace and the sales staff, the values support each other, but, if so much energy is expended in maintaining the communications network that the management information systems are unresponsive to the new products, then the values clash.

Unsupportive values almost always cause organizational changes. The MIS director may be replaced with one who will support the organizations values better; the unresponsive accounting software may be replaced with software that is more flexible. Different values are neither good nor bad—they are just different.

Value Sets and an Information Center

Understanding organizational values is essential to an information center's success. Most information centers started as enablers, seeking to teach end users how to use the tools to solve business problems. Classes in personal computer software packages and fourth-generation languages abounded. Yet many information centers that clung exclusively to the training role were eventually disbanded. The reason was that they were not perceived as supporting the corporate values.

Consider the question of cost justification. How can the expense of hardware, software, and the salaries of the people required to operate an information center be justified? What dollar value can be placed on providing information to enable quicker or more accurate management decisions, or on analysis that gives the organization a significant edge over competitors? Any values assigned to the benefits of an information center will be guesses at best. Information centers that were decommissioned may have assigned dollar values to their activities, and may even have convinced everybody that the numbers were accurate, but they failed to translate those dollars into terms that described the real value of the activities.

Developing better algorithms to compute an information center's value will not help. As long as the benefits are determined by dollars, an information center cannot justify tackling projects that have long-term strategic value. A dollar-benefit approach forces an information center to focus on short-term, high-payback projects.

The problem, then, is essentially one of values. Computing benefits on the basis of dollars saved is useful only if the primary value of the organization is "the bottom line"—an orientation that is rare and usually represents a transition state. Saving $200,000 for a market-driven organization has value only if the money can be used to determine market needs or to deliver a new product to the market faster. To be perceived as successful, an information center must provide services and keep score in terms that the organization can understand.

Consider a large hotel chain that has invested a significant amount of money in facilities and staff training. One of the questions asked as a part of the value analysis was: Which would you rather see on a given night, one hundred guests at $75 per room or seventy-five guests at $100 per room? When the response "one hundred guests" was chosen, further questions showed that one of the primary values of the organization was to keep the hotels running at peak capacity. The management was confident of its ability to deliver top-quality service even at peak capacity, and felt that each satisfied guest would generate additional business, which, in turn, would produce significant long-term results.

An information center at this hotel chain would be making a fatal error in judgment if it were to concentrate on teaching classes in word processing and utilizing spreadsheets. Dollar savings and counts of people trained might look impressive in status reports, but they would have no measurable effect on the primary value—full use of the production capacity. Unless an information center can express its values in terms of improved occupancy rates, it will be viewed as just another drain on the organization's resources.

Training and consulting are part of an information center's role, but they are not ends in themselves. Trainers must use examples that involve the primary values of the organization. After the training has been completed, they should follow up to see how the students have used their training to meet the needs of the organization. If they are not solving problems that relate to the primary values, the training program must be changed.

Similarly, when confronted with a number of projects for key user areas, an information center must select those projects that will afford the greatest return in terms of primary values. In an organization that emphasizes resource conservation, which project should receive top attention from the information center: project A, which will analyze the accounts receivable system to find ways to accelerate payments on late-paying accounts, or project B, which will analyze shop operations, identifying operations that produce the most rejected and scrapped products? Project A may identify thousands of dollars that can be saved; project B can be translated directly into resources saved. Both projects have value, but project B will have the greater strategic impact.

As another example, consider an organization that believes it is about to become the target of a hostile takeover. In an effort to avoid the takeover, it attempts to drive up its stock price by showing exceptional growth in the bottom line. This organization's values will change for a short period as emphasis is placed on bottom-line growth for its own sake.

The information center in this organization might be tempted to begin a number of projects that would yield measurable cost savings. Such projects clearly would support the current values of the organization and have a significant strategic effect. However, an information center that succumbs to this temptation is making a serious error. Even a relatively small information center of, say, three consultants, a manager, and an administrative assistant represents an overhead cost to the organization of at least $150,000. If the values have indeed shifted to an emphasis on the bottom line, the organization may see that overhead as unreasonable, even if the information center projects will save money for other departments. In a bottom-line-driven organization, saving money is not enough. The information center must make itself indispensable.

To become indispensable to such an organization, an information center needs to analyze the organization and determine who its scorekeepers are—that is, which departments or managers are charged with identifying unprofitable activities, products, and practices? It then must decide what products and services it can offer to the scorekeepers. By becoming indispensable to the scorekeepers, the center will become indispensable to the organization.

Both approaches support the primary values of the organization. By providing an indispensable service to a key part of the organization, however, an information center ensures that its contribution will be remembered long after the various cost-cutting projects have been forgotten. Strategic success not only requires delivery of the products that support the primary values, but also delivery of those products to the right markets. Figure 3-4 suggests the key departments and the types of projects that might be strategically important for some of the different values.

Value-Driven Evaluations

How can an information center's success be assessed? What scorekeeping device can be used to justify its existence? The answers here also lie in the organization's values.

FIGURE 3-4   Marketing Plans for Selected Strategic Values

VALUE	KEY DEPARTMENTS	POSSIBLE PROJECTS
Distribution	Shipping	End-point analysis
	Maintenance	Expert systems—best route selection
		Preventative maintenance scheduling
Technology	Research/Development	Data collection
	Engineering	Statistical analysis
		Computer-assisted design
Stable Products	Marketing	Statistical quality
	Quality Assurance	Quality
		Market potential analysis
Market Driven	Marketing	Market analysis
	Engineering	Connections to outside data bases
	Production	
		Computer-assisted drafting
Size/Growth	Corporate Planning	Financial models
	Finance	External data bases
	Audit	Portfolio analysis
	Executive Office	Expert systems to evaluate acquisitions

Quantitative measures are deceptive in considering the results of an information center's endeavors. What quantitative value can be placed on a project that identifies a potential means to sell other products to existing customers? Any quantitative valuation placed on this project will be arbitrary. Even worse, in trying to compare the benefits of this project with those of the next project, what is being compared may be two different units of measure. The old cliche of trying to compare apples and oranges seems to apply here.

Perhaps the answer is that the values of an information center should *not* be quantified, but be determined subjectively by how well it meets the organization's values. Instead of gathering numbers, the information center should keep a "scrapbook" of its projects, including memos from satisfied users, internal memos explaining the benefits of the project in terms of the primary values, and working notes for the project explaining how the unique skills and tools of the center made the results possible. The scrapbook's role is to express the success of an information center in terms that make sense in view of the organization's business goals.

Not only must an information center keep score in terms of the organizational values, but it must also communicate its success to the larger organization. Newsletters, status reports to top management, and attendance of information center personnel at corporate management meetings and their regular contact with senior managers are essential. An information center cannot afford to be passive. Good public relations goes hand-in-hand with scorekeeping.

STRATEGIC MANAGEMENT OF AN INFORMATION CENTER

Thus far, the discussion has focused on the nature of strategic planning and on how an information center's staff needs to understand the strategic forces at work in the organization if the information center is to be successful. The ideal strategic planning process identifies the current status of the organization and any anticipated changes, develops a future view of the organization, and determines tactics to move the organization from its present state to its envisioned future. It was shown that not only is this process valuable to the organization, but it could also be applied to each operational group within the organization.

In this section, an example of a simplified strategic planning methodology and its use in a case study to develop a strategic plan for an information center are considered. In this approach, the current state of the organization is examined by comparing its strengths and weaknesses, the future is forecast by identifying potential opportunities and threats, and the results are used to drive the tactical plan. This approach, called a SWOT[2] (Strengths, Weaknesses, Opportunities, Threats) analysis, will be used to develop the strategic plan for an information center, beginning with a self-assessment.

Self-Assessment: Strengths and Weaknesses

An ideal strategic planning process concentrates on what an organization *is* rather than what it *does*. The SWOT approach does this by asking an information center to identify its three most critical strengths and three

---

[2]The author was first introduced to the concept of using strengths, weaknesses, opportunities, and threats as a part of the strategic planning process at First Tennessee Bank in Memphis. The methodology presented in this chapter represents significant modifications of this approach by the author to meet the unique needs of an information center.

FIGURE 3-5   Strengths/Weaknesses

TOP THREE STRENGTHS
- Good understanding of business success factors
- Staff is experienced in using data
- For a given customer there is a lot of data available to solve problem

STRENGTHS, BUT NOT IN TOP THREE
- Staff has strong technical skills
- Staff is strongly committed to the information center
- Close cooperation within group
- Lots of contacts in production systems
- No preconceived notions. No one knows what the information center is supposed to be doing
- Staff is open minded when trying to solve problems

TOP THREE WEAKNESSES
- Lack of standards and policies
- Don't know how to measure success
- Lack of marketing skills. Doesn't know how to present itself to the rest of organization

WEAKNESSES, BUT NOT IN TOP THREE
- Information center is perceived as just another application programming group
- Long lead time until department actually becomes operational
- No easy access to corporate data dictionary
- No chargeout plan in place
- No agreed-upon data-base implementation methodology
- Unknown performance constraints of the information center tools
- Not enough education, expertise for staff

most important weaknesses (the SW of SWOT). As any information center obviously has more than three strengths and three weaknesses, it must start simply by listing all of its strengths and weaknesses. Once all possible candidates have been identified, selecting the three most important in each category becomes a relatively straightforward task.

In the following example, the information center is brand new. It has picked its team members from among the existing applications programming staff, selected its tools, and is about to open its doors to its first users. The marketing-oriented organization of which it is a part is fairly large and has decentralized its decision making into a number of autonomous units, one of which will be the sole client of the information center. The manager of the information center asks the team as a group to brainstorm to create a list of strengths and weaknesses; the results are shown in Figure 3-5.

In the group's lists, notice that some of the items identified as strengths overlap. This is not surprising since an organization's strengths manifest themselves in many contexts. In addition, although all of the identified strengths and weaknesses appear to be accurate evaluations of the current state, the SWOT process forces the group to identify the three most important in each category because the information center does not have the resources to cope with all of them. Instead, it concentrates on the strengths and weaknesses that are likely to have a significant effect on its success or failure. Moreover, choosing only three strengths and three weaknesses forces the group to confront its values as it struggles to weigh the alternatives.

Opportunities and Threats

The manager of the information center in the example then asks the team to identify the opportunities that are available to the center. An opportunity is defined as "areas of business or new activities in which the information center currently is not involved but ought to be." Additionally, the group is asked to identify the threats that the information center faces. Threats are defined as "forces external to the information center that might prevent it from meeting its goals." The results of these two exercises are shown in Figure 3-6.

The opportunities identified in this phase need not be profound or grandiose. Some of them represent fairly mundane changes, while others alterations to the nature of the business. Similarly, threats need not be sinister. They may represent the potential activities of a single person, a change in the nature of the organization, or a shift in the general economic system. However, if this part of the process is to be successful, the opportunities and threats must be linked to the primary values of the organization. If the organization is market driven, marketing opportunities and threats that will prevent the information center from supporting a marketing perspective should be identified. If the organization's values emphasize product distribution, opportunities to become a part of this business should be noted. An information center's vision of the future must be compatible with the organization's vision.

By the end of this stage, an information center should have developed a fairly good picture of itself through the SWOT analysis: It has, it is hoped, painted an accurate self-portrait that shows the strengths and weaknesses at the current time. It has identified a vision of where it would like to be in terms of the opportunities available. Furthermore, it has identified the threats outside of its control that might keep it from realizing its potential. And, perhaps most important of all, the staff of the information center in the example has gone through the analysis as a group so that the entire team has been able to contribute to the discussion and participate in the vision. The process so far has conformed nicely to the ideal. All that remains is to develop a tactical plan to define activities that must be undertaken to achieve the vision.

FIGURE 3-6   Opportunities/Threats

TOP THREE OPPORTUNITIES
- Provide access to outside data bases for marketing information
- Implement data administration function
- Sell data to outside—analysis of market trends, name and address listing

OPPORTUNITIES, BUT NOT IN TOP THREE
- Develop prototype for a corporate customer information system
- Implement public relations program to promote information center
- Publish catalog of available data
- Provide education in the software tools to end users
- Control/facilitate office automation
- Set company-wide standards for access, hardware, software

TOP THREE THREATS
- Users make bad business decisions using information center tools
- Budget cuts, realignment, or change in long-term management priorities eliminate interest in information center
- User expectations too high to meet; users get turned off

THREATS, BUT NOT IN TOP THREE
- System compromised by unauthorized data access—both internal and external
- Information center perceived by top management as too expensive, with too few benefits
- Unmanageable peak demands cause poor system response times
- Out-of-control user wastes resources
- Audit requirements turn off users

The Tactical Plan

To develop a tactical plan from the SWOT analysis, an organization or department should identify three or four actions it can take to exploit each of its strengths. These actions should be expressed in concrete terms so that it will be known unequivocally when that task has been accomplished. Furthermore, each action should be assigned a tentative completion date and an individual who will be responsible for that completion. Similarly, for each weakness, a list of three or four activities should be developed that will overcome that weakness. For each opportunity, the activities would take advantage of that opportunity, and for each threat, their objective would be to blunt that threat. (This process is summarized in Figure 3-7.)

Note especially the difference between weaknesses and threats. Since, by definition, threats are something that cannot be controlled, the aim can be only to blunt them at best. On the other hand, weaknesses can be

FIGURE 3-7   Tactical Planning Overview

STRATEGIC COMPONENT	DEFINITION	GOAL OF TACTICS
Strengths	Skills that allow the organization to perform its role in effective and efficient manner.	Determine ways to *exploit* each strategic strength.
Weaknesses	Items under control of the organization that keep it from fulfilling its role.	Determine ways to *overcome* each strategic weakness.
Opportunities	Areas of business or new activities in which the organization is currently not involved but ought to be	Determine ways to *take advantage* of each strategic opportunity
Threats	Forces external to the organization that might prevent it from meeting goals	Determine ways to *blunt* the impact of each strategic threat

overcome. Likewise, since strengths are currently in place, the goal is to exploit them, whereas since opportunities may or may not prove fruitful, the objective is to take advantage of them. Figure 3-8 illustrates some possible tactics for four of the strategies from the SWOT analysis. Once these tactics have been delineated, all that remains is to assign someone responsibility for the tactic and a date by which the action is to be accomplished. The strategic plan is anchored in a clear vision of the present and future and the major activities of the information center are now anchored in that strategic plan.

SUMMARY

Too often, an information center is portrayed in terms of its technology. As this chapter has shown, success really lies in understanding the strategic nature of the business. This strategic analysis is based on a process that identifies the current state of the organization, looks into the future, shows what the organization must become, and sets forth a plan of action to guide the organization to that future.

Unfortunately, this ideal process does not always work so easily. Often, an information center's staff must infer the real strategic plan of an organization from its behaviors. Having identified the primary values of an organization by analyzing the behaviors through dichotomy questions, an information center can express its own value to the organization in meaningful terms.

FIGURE 3-8   Tactical Plan Example

STRENGTHS AND WAYS TO EXPLOIT THEM
Staff is experienced in using data.
- Develop a service guide telling what's available, how to get to it, etc.
- Provide a dictionary/glossary of common business terms linked to specific data elements
- Provide a "guide service" to the data, modeled after that provided by fishing lodges

WEAKNESSES AND WAYS TO OVERCOME THEM
Don't know how to measure success.
- Conduct user satisfaction survey (formal feedback)
- Hold focus group sessions on state of information processing. Repeat in six months and compare
- Develop written, agreed-upon success criteria

OPPORTUNITES AND WAYS TO TAKE ADVANTAGE OF THEM
Implement data administration function.
- Develop database design methodology
- Publish catalog of files, field definitions
- Define automated method of integrating dictionary with appropriate tools

THREATS AND WAYS TO BLUNT THEM
Users make bad business decisions using information center tools.
- Develop security and control procedures
- Implement online glossary of business terms
- Develop standard benchmark reports to validate results of user reporting

---

A simplified strategic planning methodology has been developed for information centers that focuses on strengths (and how to exploit them), weaknesses (and how to overcome them), opportunities (and how to take advantage of them), and threats (and how to blunt them).

Real success for an information center is not defined by its technology. Good strategic vision even with mediocre technology will be judged far more valuable to an organization than will be the aimless implementation of the highest technological advances. After all, nobody likes a loose cannon.

SUGGESTED PROJECT

Select an organization with which you are very familiar, such as a corporation, a branch of the armed forces, a church, or a university. Then use your knowledge of that organization to complete the following exercises:

1. Develop a list of dichotomy questions that could be used to determine the values of the organization.

2. Using the list of dichotomy questions, determine the primary values of the organization.

3. Assuming you are establishing an information center for the organization, based on the response to the dichotomy questions, determine what strategic services would be required and how you might provide those services.

4. Develop a strategic and tactical plan for an information center for the organization using the SWOT technique and the results of the previous exercises.

CHAPTER 4

Selecting the Tools for an Information Center

Mechanics have a standard piece of advice for a colleague who is struggling to remove a particularly obstinate part: "You aren't using the right tool. Go get a bigger hammer." Data-processing professionals are often guilty of taking a similar approach: they merely get larger and larger system hammers until the problem has been beaten into submission. However, if an information center is to succeed, its developers must select its tools with a careful eye toward ease of use, ability to solve business problems, and the amount of user support that each requires.

As is the case with most information-processing endeavors, the tools of an information center are best considered in terms of hardware and software.

HARDWARE TOOLS

Perhaps the worst way to discuss types of computers is to consider them in the traditional categories of mainframes, minicomputers, and microcomputers. Consider, for example, the problem of how actually to differentiate among these classes of computers. This problem is much more deceptive than it would first appear to be.

The Problem of Measurement

Basic measurements such as MIPS (millions of instructions per second) are not adequate as they are based on the erroneous assumption that all instructions are created equal. This simply is not true. The instruction set of one computer is often radically different from that of another. What can be accomplished with a single instruction on one computer might require many instructions on a different machine. This is best illustrated by considering a special computer architecture called RISC (reduced instruction set computer).

The RISC architecture is based on the premise that greater throughput is made possible by dramatically reducing the number of instructions available while accelerating the rate at which the instructions are processed. The MIPS rating of a RISC computer is significantly higher than that of a similar computer using a more standard architecture, but the actual throughput may not be much different since the RISC machine must execute many more instructions to accomplish a task than its traditional counterpart. Processor speed alone is a poor measure of performance.

Even if some sort of standard measurement based on processor speeds could be developed, it would be too restrictive in light of the rapid changes in the technology. What was considered mainframe processor speed ten years ago is now found in a desktop computer. As price and performance continue to improve dramatically, and as expectations increase exponentially, arbitrary distinctions based on processor speed will become even less meaningful.

The problem really stems from the names of the categories themselves. Whereas "mini-" and "micro-" connote size, size alone is not the key. What starts out as a simple microcomputer can be used with a different operating system and can support a number of users better than can some minicomputers. Similarly, a so-called minicomputer might be dedicated to a single individual using sophisticated computer-assisted design software. In this application, the minicomputer is really functioning as a very large, very fast personal computer. Distinctions based on the processor itself will not work. What is needed is a fresh approach.

Recall the basic theme of this book: technology is not an end itself, but a means to address business problems. This approach also affords a better way to look at the hardware tools available to an information center, in which the computing resource is classified according to use (not its size) as *individual, departmental,* or *corporate.*

Individual Computers

Individual computers can be defined as the hardware that is used by only one person at any given time. This definition can refer to a traditional personal computer or to a minicomputer that is dedicated to a specific user for a specific purpose such as solving engineering workstation. Networked microcomputers, however, are not considered in this category but are a departmental computing resource. Individual computers are just what the name implies: devices used by a single individual with no shared resources.

Departmental Computers

A departmental computer can be considered to be a piece of hardware that is used by more than one person at a given time, but is not available to an entire organization. Thus, personal computers in a local area network are not viewed as individual tools but are seen in the aggregate. Similarly, minicomputers fall into this category if they are used by a small group of users, but not if they are the computing resource for an entire organization (e.g., a small business). This classification scheme is based on the premise that shared resources have different needs than dedicated individual resources and that resources shared by an entire organization are different from resources shared by a small working group.

Corporate Computers

Corporate computers are those that are available to the entire organization. This does not mean that everyone in the company routinely has access rights, but that anyone with a sufficiently good business reason to use the resource can do so. The same type of computer that is used by a marketing staff as a departmental computer might also be employed as a corporate computer by a small company. Once again, it is the business use that is important, not the size of the hardware.

By approaching hardware tools from the perspective of use rather than size, previously murky issues become clearer. For example, an information center is asked to help decide which printer is best to use with a personal computer. How should it go about finding the answer? If only the size of the machine is considered, the answer is unclear. However, once it is determined that the computer is linked to a local area network, solutions can be considered that will provide the capability for larger print volumes and faster printing times. The solutions to problems related to networked personal computers are likely to be similar to those for small departmental computers. Similarly, when a personal computer is connected to a network, the peripherals that used to be solid performers now become inadequate. The hardware has not changed but the use has. Hardware selection is not a function of size or speed, it is a function of the business use.

SOFTWARE TOOLS

It would be almost impossible to create a definitive list of software tools used by an information center; however, it would be safe to concentrate on three tools: fourth-generation languages, spreadsheets, and graphics packages.

Notice that the list does not include a data-base management system (DBMS). This omission is not an error; in fact, it illustrates an important principle in choosing software tools for an information center.

No Data-Base Software?

Consider a simple vending machine. A customer puts money into a slot and pushes a button, and out drops the appropriate product (usually). Almost everyone has used these machines but almost no one knows exactly what goes on inside of them. For all that is known, the machine might actually be teleporting the can of soda from a distant planet. However, to the user, the actual process is immaterial. All that is important is that the requested item is ejected when the proper request is made (by inserting money and pressing the button).

FIGURE 4-1 Sample Report Request

```
TABLE FILE EMPLOYEE
PRINT LAST NAME
      FIRST NAME
      DATE OF BIRTH
      DATE OF HIRE
BY    DEPARTMENT
END
```

Data-base software is very similar in nature. Users of the DBMS don't care what goes on inside, but are concerned only with the actual tools used to enter new data or request existing data. For example, consider the sample FOCUS (Information Builders, Inc.) report request in Figure 4-1.

In this example, a list of employees in each department obviously is being created. But ask this basic question: What DBMS was used to store that employee data? The request itself gives no indication of the underlying DMBS and, in fact, the same request would be used if the data were stored in DB2 (IBM), IMS (IBM), IDMS (Cullinet), or a simple sequential file. Just as the vending machine customer never knows the actual source of the soda, from the viewpoint of an information center, the underlying DBMS is equally immaterial. The important elements are the tool used to access that data and the data's fundamental logical structure (discussed in the next chapter).

Consider another example. Previously, to obtain information about a customer required COBOL statements that resembled Figure 4-2. If, however, the traditional indexed file is replaced with a relational data base such as DB2 (IBM), the COBOL program is changed to resemble Figure 4-3. The data-base change is not as significant as the change to the code: a READ statement has been replaced with embedded SQL statements. In fact, if the COBOL compiler could have been revised to translate the READ into SQL as needed, even the coding changes might not have been required.

This does not mean that no one in the organization need be concerned with the actual workings of the DBMS. After all, somebody has to stock

---

FIGURE 4-2 Traditional Files and COBOL

```
MOVE CUSTOMER-ID TO CUSTOMER-KEY.

READ CUSTOMER-FILE
     INVALID KEY MOVE "INVALID CUSTOMER" TO ERROR-MESSAGE.
```

FIGURE 4-3   Using Relational Data Base and COBOL

```
MOVE CUSTOMER-ID TO CUSTOMER-KEY.

EXEC SQL
    SELECT NAME, CITY, ZIP
    INTO :CUST-NAME, :CUST-CITY, :CUST-ZIP
    FROM CUSTOMER
    WHERE CUSTKEY = :CUSTOMER-KEY;
END-EXEC

IF SQLCODE NE 0 MOVE "INVALID CUSTOMER" TO ERROR-MESSAGE.
```

---

and maintain the vending machine. The technology is certainly important, but it must be considered in its proper perspective. Most users (including applications programmers) never actually see the data-base system itself. All they see is the tool used to access the data, such as SQL or FOCUS.

All of this illustrates a key point that must be considered when examining the software tools of an information center. That point is that the technology itself is immaterial to an information center. What really matters is that the technology tools, such as fourth-generation languages, spreadsheets, and graphics packages, operate on the data to solve business problems.

Software Tools as Transformations

Chapter 1 introduced the concept of transformation—a means of changing data into meaningful information. It was suggested that there are at least four different types of transactions: extraction, analysis, capture, and presentation. So instead of rehashing the basic characteristics of each of the major software tools, it will be more instructive at this point to view them in terms of the transformations they perform.

Fourth-Generation Languages

Figure 4-4 presents the major transformations that a fourth-generation language (4GL) must be able to provide. This list is not meant to be exhaustive, but its value becomes obvious when trying to wade through the marketing hype for 4GLs.

For example, in most of the literature and advertisements, SQL (Structured Query Language) is touted as the ideal data language and the salvation of all information processing. But is it really a 4GL? It certainly

---

FIGURE 4-4   Fourth-Generation Languages

	REQUIRED	*OPTIONS*
Extraction	Able to extract data from at least one type of data base	Able to extract data from many different data bases
	Set-at-a-time processing (whole file orientation)	Processing many sets at a time
	Able to create new files in sequential format	Able to create new files in many formats
		Able to extract data from one type of hardware to another e.g., departmental to individual
Analysis	Able to create new data fields from existing ones using arithmetic and logical operations	
	Able to use simple statistical operations to create new data	Able to perform complex statistical operations
Capture	Able to update at least type of data base	Able to update many different data bases
	Able to capture data from simple sequential transaction files	Able to capture data from files, screens, or other data bases
Presentation	Able to sort data regardless of actual key order	
	Able to provide special report formatting such as headings	Able to provide graphic display of data

---

meets the basic requirements for EXTRACTION and CAPTURE (although it misses some of the optional transformations). It is able to do the simple statistical operations such as COUNT and MAX. However, it seems to lack most of the presentation functions, as well as the ability to create new data items easily from existing ones.

In fact, most SQL vendors find they need to supplement their implementation of SQL with other products IBM, for example, provides a tool called QMF (Query Management Facility), which actually formats and displays the data extracted using SQL. Similarly, the capture of data from a sequential file is not performed by SQL; instead another product (DXT) is required to capture data in one format and load it into another. As

FIGURE 4-5   Graphics Packages

	REQUIRED	*OPTIONS*
Extraction	Be able to extract data from sequential files	Be able to extract data from a number of different files or data bases
		Be able to work in conjunction with other products to provide full functioned extraction
Analysis	Be able to convert from "Raw" data to percent	
	Perform simple statistical analysis such as simple regression	Perform more complex statistical analysis such as smoothing
Data Capture	Allow direct entry of data	Provide edit functions to validate data
		Provide scripting (e.g., macros) for entry
Presentation	Provide basic graphic formats: bar, line, pie	Provide more complex formats such as bubble charts, 3-d
	Provide output on screen, printer, or plotter	Provide output in other formats: video facsimile, etc.
		Provide animation
		Allow mixed graphics and text

indicated in Figure 4-4, simple SQL is not a 4GL (or at least not a very good one), but when it is combined with other tools (QMF, DXT), it is able to fulfill the required 4GL transformations.

Graphics

The development of a list of required transformations for a spreadsheet is left as an exercise for the reader. However, Figure 4-5 shows the transformations required by graphics packages. Once again, this list is not meant to be definitive.

It should be noted that certain tools may be able to support transformations for more than one type of product. For example, Lotus 1-2-3 may have been purchased to meet the needs of a spreadsheet, but a look at Figure 4-5 will show that it also can support all of the required, and many of the optional, transformations indicated there. A product can easily fit into a number of categories once the transformations that the tool provides become the prime consideration rather than the technology behind that tool.

Another benefit that can result from thinking of software tools in terms of transformations is illustrated by a large money-center bank that each week put together a book including approximately seventy-five graphs displaying the key performance factors of its major products. This book was used at weekly meetings of the bank's executives to identify problem trends before they became critical. A management team from a smaller bank was so impressed with this approach, that it decided to establish a similar program, one that initially would concentrate on thirty graphs on a monthly basis. In this case, the results were far from impressive. Instead, the book generated resentment and frustration in return for only marginal results. Why didn't the approach work for the smaller bank as it did for the large money center?

For its book, the money-center bank used production graphics software. The data was automatically captured from the production information systems and fed into the graphics system. The graphs were produced on large-capacity plotters or high-speed laser printers. Almost no manual intervention was required to provide the graphs on a weekly basis. At the second bank, however, the graphs were produced by various individual departments using personal computers and six-pen plotters to present data gathered manually from printed production reports. Since color copiers are prohibitively expensive, ten originals of each graph had to be produced each month. Informal studies showed that each graph required an average of forty-five minutes to gather data, thirty minutes to enter the data into the graphics package, and sixty minutes to plot the required ten copies—or nearly ten days of effort each month to produce the 30-graph books used at a two-hour meeting.

Thus, whereas the results ostensibly were the same, the basic transformations were quite different. In the money-center bank, there were no data-capture transformations; all the data was extracted from existing systems. The presentation transformations took place without operator intervention and were directed to an appropriate output device capable of making numerous copies. In the second bank, the data had to be captured, rather than extracted. The nature of the transformations dictated the choice of software tools. Since no data capture was required, the money-center bank was able to use tools, such as TEL-A-GRAPH, that were able to concentrate on large-scale extraction and presentation; the second bank's need to capture data forced it to consider a different (and less efficient) set of tools.

Tool Selection

The lesson to be learned from these examples is obvious—to select the best tool, first identify the transformations that will be needed. But several questions then arise. How can the needed transformations be determined for a particular type of product? How can an information center evaluate new technologies fairly? How can it use these evaluations to select the right tools?

EVALUATING NEW TECHNOLOGIES

As some of the examples showed, using the wrong tool for a task can be disastrous. How, then, can an information center evaluate emerging technologies and new tools to find the best way to solve business problems?

Using Outside Sources

Perhaps the simplest way to keep up with the trends is to rely on outside sources to provide the expertise. For example:

1. *Trend Analysis.* A number of consulting companies provide weekly or monthly analyses of the trends in information technology. The Gartner Group and the Yankee Group, for instance, have been providing accurate analyses and predictions for many years.
2. *Product Evaluations.* Specialized services (such as DATAPRO and DATA SOURCES) and selected trade journals (such as *PC* magazine) pride themselves on furnishing accurate and fair evaluations of various products according to well-defined criteria. Some even survey current users of a product and include the responses with their evaluations.

No matter how helpful these outside sources may be in providing analysis and direction, the final responsibility for introducing new technologies in an appropriate fashion rests on the information center. In carrying out this responsibility, the conscientious information center needs to develop strategies to review the literature critically and to evaluate the new trends that may lead to solutions to the organization's real problems.

Keeping Up with the Literature

Success in any rapidly changing field requires constant reading. This applies to managers of information centers as well, but they have special problems. They have no definitive source for product information. At best,

---

**FIGURE 4-6   Subject Areas To Be Monitored in the Reading Program
(and Suggested Sources of Information)**

Personal Computers
PC magazine, *PC Week, Info World, MAC World*

Product-Specific Journals (IBM, DEC, etc.)
IBM Systems Journal, FOCUS Systems Journal

General Computer Trade Press
Computerworld, MIS Week, INFO Week

Data-Processing Management
Datamation, Infosystems

General Business Press
Wall Street Journal, Business Week, Forbes

Industry-Specific Journals (Banking, for example)
American Banker, Bank Systems and Equipment, Banking Software Review

Information-Center-Specific Publications
Information Center magazine, *Managing End-User Computer* newsletter

---

there is a litany of conflicting expert opinions, product announcements, press releases, and advertisements. Then there is the sheer volume of publications that must be covered. More than twenty-five different publications are dedicated to the individual (micro)computer alone, and this is but a small part of the tool kit. How, then, can information center professionals even hope to keep up with the new developments, let alone try to evaluate them? The answer lies in the phrase "team effort."

The first step in a team approach is to select a manageable subset of publications stratified according to subject area. As a starting point, consider the list in Figure 4-6.

It will be noted that a key characteristic of that list is that it is not made up exclusively of technical journals. Because an information center's success is as much a function of business knowledge as it is of technical expertise, it is important for an information center professional to be aware of the trends in general business and the current hot topics in the company's particular area. This broad-based knowledge is especially critical in those industries that are undergoing dramatic transitions, such as deregulation, corporate downsizing, or a flattening management pyramid.

With Figure 4-6 as a guide, the list presented there can be adapted to an information center's group reading program. First, the two or three most definitive publications in each category are identified—for example, under "general business," *The Wall Street Journal* and *Forbes* might be selected, or perhaps *Fortune* and *Business Week*. The actual selections are a matter of personal judgment; all that matters is that the information center's manager believes them to be the most definitive in that category.

Having selected the subset of publications, the next step is to divide the labor. Each publication should be assigned to two staff members, one as primary monitor and the other as backup monitor. The work load should be distributed evenly, with each staff member, including the manager, having approximately the same number of pages to monitor each week.

What exactly is meant by the phrase "monitor the publications?" In hospital trauma rooms (as well as in reruns of the old TV series "M*A*S*H"), incoming injured are divided into three groups: those whose injuries are not life-threatening, and who can wait for treatment; those whose injuries are life-threatening, and who will die without immediate treatment; and those whose injuries are so severe that they are likely to die even with treatment. This process is called "triage" (from the French word *trier*—to sort). The process of monitoring publications is very similar—the role of the "triage officer" for a given publication is to divide the articles, advertisements, product announcements, and columnists' prognostications into three groups, as follows:

1. *Critical.* These items represent essential information. They describe the new strategic products, the known flaws in existing products, or the insightful analysis that will alter strategies. These articles are to be copied and distributed to the entire team at once, as well as filed for future reference.

2. *Important.* These items represent the "second wave." They are the follow-ups to new-product announcements, tips and techniques, or interesting (but not critical) analysis or explanations. They need to be disseminated to the team, but at a more leisurely pace. Routing slips can be attached to these articles so that they can be circulated through the rest of the team.

3. *Noise.* The rest of the material may be very nice, and perhaps even occasionally useful, but from the point of view of the reading program it is noise that can be ignored.

Although this team approach dramatically reduces the amount of reading required of each team member, to be really effective, it needs periodic reviews and adjustments to ensure that the reading load remains equitably divided and that the "triage officers" are correctly classifying the material. However, properly managed, the approach provides the mechanism to gather the raw information from the literature. The next question is: How can this information be evaluated?

Evaluating Trends: The Simple Approach

There are many complex methods that can be used by information centers to evaluate technological trends, but the best approach is quite simple. To evaluate trends, all that is needed is to answer three basic questions: What is the literature saying about a trend? What is the literature *not* saying about that trend? Finally, what is really needed to solve the business problems?

To illustrate this approach, consider the history of the technology of artificial intelligence. Once, the phrase "artificial intelligence" seemed to be almost a magic incantation that gave power to any product. Hardly a week would pass without some product announcement invoking that phrase. The prices of the tools of artificial intelligence, most notably compilers and decision-processing software, seemed to continue to drop dramatically while their availability increased exponentially. Everybody wanted to be the first kid on their block to install artificial intelligence in something.

So much for what the experts and trade press were saying. What was *not* being said? Plenty.

What was being overlooked was that artificial intelligence is more than the software tools. Rarely did anyone consider the actual design that must provide the basis for any expert system. Putting knowledge into the form of explicit rules requires significant training and expertise; it is not just simple coding. The entire discipline of knowledge engineering (the science of determining and structuring expertise) was being bypassed in the enthusiasm to "have" artificial intelligence.

Even assuming that an organization had the expertise to design the rule base for an artificial intelligence application, what was the real business need? Who would use the system? What level of confidence would the organization place in the system?

If an expert system were developed, consider the possible users. First would be the naive unsophisticate, who would accept the results of the system without any question. At the other extreme would be the genuine experts, who would not use the system at all since their knowledge is already internalized and they have no need to consult an outside authority. Between these two groups would be the up-and-coming experts. They would be likely to use the expert system to validate their decisions and as a reference in difficult situations.

These groups have radically different needs for the expert system and it is likely that no one system would fit all of these needs. But unless an information center manager looked past what the experts were and were not saying to the target audience and the real business needs, even the most diligent systems-development effort was doomed. Artificial intelligence systems not only involve technology, but they require an organizational culture that will accept them and integrate them into its daily business activities. Otherwise, the system will prove a dismal failure. In most organizations, artificial intelligence has been utilized as a solution in search of a problem.

The key, then, to evaluating trends in new technology is to answer the three questions posed earlier: What are the experts saying? What are the experts *not* saying? What does the organization really need? The answers will provide an information center with the tools to lay the groundwork for its future success—or failure.

INFORMATION CENTERS AND STANDARDIZATION

If an information center is keeping up with the literature and evaluating the new technologies, it seems only logical to have it develop standards for all of the end-user computing tools in the organization. Or does it?

The Pros of Standardization

There are some very valuable reasons for an information center to set standards for end-user computing. Consider, for example, the issue of cost/benefit. By selecting a standard set of products, an information center can save a significant amount of time and money for the organization. First, it avoids having users "reinvent the wheel" as they decide which tool is best to solve their problem. Tool selection becomes a simple act of choosing from a small list of "authorized" products. Not only do standards simplify selection, but they afford an advantage in purchasing since larger orders can be used to bargain for better pricing. The savings that are to be gained from standardization are important considerations in the standardization debate.

A second, highly selfish reason for standardization is that it is easier and more effective for an information center to support a limited number of products. A center cannot be expected to answer questions about seven different word processors, nine data-base management systems, and six spreadsheets. Standards enhance the ability to meet user needs effectively.

Third, standards promote solution sharing among users. The biblical Tower of Babel was never finished because each of its builders spoke a different language. Similarly, if each group of users develops solutions using a different tool, they will be unable to share valuable algorithms or data structures. Each user group will be isolated from its peers and much work will be duplicated because there is no standard means of sharing results.

The Cons of Standardization

If all of these savings are possible, what could be wrong with allowing an information center to set corporate standards? The answer is: a great deal.

The United States is one of only a few countries that has not adopted the metric system. It isn't that the metric system doesn't make good sense—it's a lot easier to compute that there are 100,000 centimeters in a kilometer than to determine the number of inches in a mile. Moreover, the metric system has been in use for over 200 years and is the standard throughout most of the world. Why, then, has the United States steadfastly refused to convert to the metric system?

There are two reasons, both of which also apply to the question of information center standards. The first reason is human resistance to change—people have become used to the old standard. As new products emerge and the standards change, an information center must make the transition very attractive or the resistance to change will undermine any hope of implementing them.

In addition to the fact that people resent change, the metric system has been a failure in the United States for purely economic reasons. The transition would require very expensive changes that would affect almost every facet of American life. Every tool would need to be replaced, every speed-limit sign changed, every scale in every store converted from pounds to kilograms. The cost would be tremendous. So, also, is the cost of changing from one information center standard to a new version. If an organization has purchased 1,000 microcomputers at an average cost of $5,000, there will be significant reluctance to adopt any new standard that will suddenly make $5 million worth of equipment obsolete.

There is a third disadvantage to setting standards, unrelated to the metric-system example, that should also be discussed. Standardization can cause an organization to use improper tools to solve a problem. If a new type of problem emerges for which there is no standard solution, one of three things will happen: the problem will go unsolved until a standard is determined; a current standard tool will be used, even if it is not the best tool; or the standard will be ignored (remember the tower of Babel). Obviously, none of these alternatives are very attractive.

Standards: The Conclusion

Who wins the debate about the value of the standards? The "pros" indicate that a number of benefits can be gained by selecting a standard set of tools. However, according to the "cons," the process of setting and managing standards must also be responsive to changing business needs and provide a simple path to migrate from old standards to the new.

Both sides of the debate have merit, but in the final analysis, the vote goes to standardization. When all of the arguments have been presented, a simple truth emerges. That truth is that unless a set of well-defined standards is in place, an organization runs the risk of developing isolated pockets of technology. In the absence of standards, each area will be free to pursue its own course until that fateful moment when it needs data from another area. Unless all areas are using a common set of tools, coherent strategic data will be impossible to obtain. To some, standards may be a double-edged sword, but they are indeed necessary.

DEVELOPING TOOL-SELECTION CRITERIA

For the correct tool to be selected, the parameters of a business problem must first be identified. The real question cannot be: What is the best 4GL for an organization? It must be: What are the business problems the organization faces and what can be done to solve them?

Putting the Business Problem First

A standard tool set can be developed through a three-step process. The first step is to identify the business problems that the proposed tool set is to solve. As pointed out in Chapter 1, the way to express business problems is as a deviation from a norm. Therefore, a business problem should not be stated as, for example, "A standard spreadsheet is needed," but as, "The organization has no way to analyze a number of key financial variables over time." Notice the difference. The first version begs the answer, "Select ABC as the standard spreadsheet." The second version allows the consideration not only of spreadsheets, but also of 4GLs that provide data-analysis capability as well as a number of sophisticated statistical packages.

Once all of the business problems, phrased as deviations from the norm, have been listed, the six or eight most critical problems must be selected from this list. Then for each of these critical problems, a list of no more than three tests must be developed that can be used to evaluate a product's capability to solve the problem. Figure 4-7 gives an example of an evaluation worksheet based on this approach.

Quantifying the Criteria

As not all of the tests listed will have equal value, a means must be developed to weigh their importance. Similarly, as each product is graded using these criteria, the temptation to employ elaborate grading schemes must be avoided while still providing something a little more meaningful than pass/fail.

One approach might be to assign an importance weighting of *low*, *medium*, or *high* to each criterion according to the following scale:

1. *Low.* This criterion is not important at all. Even if a product meets this criterion, it will have only a minimum effect on the business problem.
2. *Medium.* This criterion is important to the solution of the business problems. However, scoring well on this criterion does not guarantee a successful solution of the problem.
3. *High.* This criterion is a "show stopper." If it cannot be met, the business problem is likely to go unsolved.

FIGURE 4-7   Product Selection

In this example, the process for selecting the correct spreadsheet is considered. Based on the approach in the text, the following table can be developed for the key business problems and the associated tests.

Product Name _____

Problem: Analyze key financial variables over time
   Tests:
      • Simple means of expressing time series
      • Standard financial functions readily available

Problem: Integrate information from multiple systems
   Tests:
      • Capability to receive data from external systems
      • Ability to provide data to other systems in standard format

Problem: Decision makers are too removed from actual analysis tools
   Tests:
      • Provides intuitive command structure
      • Provides analysis alternatives such as graphics, statistics
      • Supports alternative user devices (mouse, digitizing pad)

Each product would then be rating according to its ability to meet each of the criteria, as follows:

1. *Low.* The product has little or no ability to meet this criterion.
2. *Medium.* The product is not able to meet the criterion fully, but provides alternatives to deliver the required functionality.
3. *High.* The product is fully able to meet this criterion.

Notice how simple and straightforward this approach is compared with traditional grading schemes such as rating from one to ten. In using this approach, the evaluator does not have to wrestle with such thorny questions as the difference between a "six" and a "seven" rating, but focuses solely on functionality.

Evaluating the Results

The foregoing scale can now be used to evaluate the products. First, any product can be discarded that was rated *low* on a criterion with *high* importance (remember the definitions of high importance, low ability). Second, point values are assigned to both the criteria and scores as follows: high = 3, medium = 2, low = 1. The score of a product for a given criterion is determined by multiplying the importance by the raw score. (see Figure

---

FIGURE 4-8   Product Selection

This example considers the process for selecting the correct spreadsheet. Based on the approach in the text, the following table can be developed for the key business problems and the associated tests:

	PRODUCT NAME	_Wiz Calc_
	Importance	_Ability_
PROBLEM: Analyze key financial variables over time		
TESTS		
• Simple means of expressing time series	_M_	_M = 4_
• Standard financial functions readily available	_H_	_M = 6_
PROBLEM: Integrate information from multiple systems		
TESTS		
• Capability to receive data from external systems	_L_	_M = 2_
• Able to provide data to other systems in standard format	_M_	_H = 6_
PROBLEM: Decision makers are too removed from actual analysis tools		
TESTS		
• Provides intuitive command structure	_H_	_H = 9_
• Provides analysis alternatives such as graphics, statistics	_M_	_M = 4_
• Supports alternative user devices (mouse, digitizing pad)	_L_	_L = 1_
		_32_

4-8). The total of the scores can be used to arrange the products in order of ability to solve the business problem.

Notice that it does not immediately follow that the product with the highest score is automatically the best product. If the resulting list does not match your visceral feelings about the products, then the criteria may have been assigned incorrect weights, the evaluation of the products' capabilities may be incorrect, or you have been seduced by market hype, looking only at the product's glitter and not its ability to meet the business needs. It is perfectly acceptable to readjust the importance scales or the product ratings, as long as it is done honestly. This approach is not meant to be a replacement for judgment; it is merely a means to ensure that some rigor is applied to the standardization process.

The Role of Cost/Benefit Analysis

In the preceding discussion, no mention was made of the cost of the products, nor was any attempt made to justify the selection of a product on the basis of the ratio of the cost to anticipated benefits. Just how important is this concept in the selection process?

Traditional operational systems are easy to discuss from a cost/benefit perspective. For example, as a result of implementing a new receivables collection system, there will be a certain number of clerks who no longer will be needed, there will be an assumed improvement in collection efficiency, and the system changes required will drop by a known percentage because of the user-selectable options of the new package. Both the benefits and the costs can be easily quantified and compared.

But consider the problem of an information center trying to evaluate a fourth-generation language. The cost side of the equation is easy to determine: the vendor supplies it with the product brochures. However, what about the benefit side of the equation? What value should be placed on a decision that can be made faster or better? What dollar value can be placed on analysis that can change the strategic direction of an organization?

The cost/benefit approach is based on the very simple assumption that both the cost and the benefit to an organization can be measured in a common unit. In the case of the operational systems, this common unit is dollars. When evaluating information center tools, however, this approach breaks down. As noted previously, the real value of an information center and its tools must be expressed in terms of the organization's strategic values. It is poor mathematics to compare dollar cost with strategic value.

The problem is similar to determining the costs and benefits of advertising. The cost is simple to determine (there are development costs, media costs, and other agency fees), but the benefits are much harder to quantify. Obviously, increased sales indicate that the advertisements have had some benefits, but the ability to tie a specific ad or a specific campaign to a specific sale has never been a straightforward proposition. Advertising agencies have tried to provide a quantitative answer through surveys and studies that are analyzed by arcane mathematics, but the cost/benefit relationships that have been derived are tenuous at best.

Yet organizations continue to advertise even if they cannot ascribe a pure cost/benefit ratio to the results. Why? They do so because they understand that advertising supports an organization's strategic direction. They set their goals and try to purchase the best advertising values that fit those goals within their resource capabilities.

The tools of an information center need to be considered in a similar fashion. Their benefits are no more quantifiable in terms of dollars than are those of advertising. And, as in the case of determining the correct advertising tools, the process needs to start by identifying the business needs and then determining the best values among those tools that fit the goals within the resource capabilities. Cost is a tie-breaker, not a primary decision factor.

DESELECTING TOOLS: WHEN THE STANDARD CHANGES

In discussing the pros and cons of selecting standard tools for an information center, one point that emerged was the enormous problems associated with moving from one standard to another. If a center chooses to standardize, how will it manage the problems of changing the standards?

In an article in the May 1987 issue of *Information Center*,[1] Floyd Kemske outlined some basic strategies for deselecting a standard product, as paraphrased in the following:

1. *Don't Ever Deselect a Product.* Any product once selected as a standard will always be a standard. Natural attrition will eventually kill off the old products in favor of the new ones. However, selecting this strategy means significant support headaches for an information center as the staff tries to help users with all of the older products, as well as the newer ones.

2. *Subsidize the Changes.* If a product is to be replaced by a new standard, offer financial aid to make the new product attractive. If the previously standard data base is being replaced by a new product that costs, say, $495, perhaps the information center could absorb part of the costs, offering the new product for $295. In the long run, this subsidy might prove less costly than maintaining expertise on both the new and old products. Alternatively, if an information center charges for its services, it could price support for the old product significantly higher than support for the new product. Differential pricing of services can prove a strong financial incentive to change products.

3. *Provide Individual Attention.* Through a series of personal contacts, show users and their management the value of migrating to a new product. One-on-one demonstrations appeal to the enlightened self-interest (as well as the ego) of the users, making the transition easier.

4. *Order the Users to Change.* In an arbitrary and totalitarian fashion, simply order the users to change from the old standard to the new. This is a short-term strategy that will cause significant damage to the trust relationships upon which an information center is built.

Regardless of the strategy chosen, it is clear that the presence of any strategy is better that no strategy at all. To allow the anarchy that results

---

[1]Floyd Kemske, "On the Deselection of Software," in *Information Center* (May 1987), p. 21.

when there is no deselection strategy is to place an information center in a fire-fighting mode from which it might never escape.

SUMMARY

This chapter has discussed the types of tools available to an information center, and has also considered the issue of standards and whether the benefits they confer outweigh the problems they create. A semirigorous model was developed that can be used to evaluate products from a business perspective. In that model, cost/benefit analysis is put into its proper perspective, as the tie-breaker among products that equally meet strategic needs. And finally, some alternatives were suggested that can be used to deselect standard tools.

What must be made clear, however, is that the tools of an information center are designed to solve business problems. The selection of these tools must always ensure that they meet the needs of an information center as defined in Chapter 1:

> An information center *is an organizational entity that facilitates the transformation of data into information that managerial, professional, and support staff can use to solve business problems.*

Unless its tools solve business problems, an information center is not doing its job.

SUGGESTED PROJECTS

1. The text states that the DBMS itself is almost inconsequential to an information center. Defend or oppose that statement.
2. Figures 4-4 and 4-5 show the transformations that define a 4GL and graphics packages. Develop a similar chart for a spreadsheet. Be prepared to defend your choice of transformations as well as the designation of *required* or *optional*.
3. Develop the analysis for the following case study.

Background

The Betchure Life Company is a medium-sized insurance company. All data processing is centralized at the corporate headquarters. The systems installed are predominantly packages purchased from a variety of vendors and include both online and batch processing.

Recently, the chairman of the company, George Fenniman, commissioned a study of the data-processing department to try to leverage the large investment in traditional applications development into a strategic advantage. The conclusions of this study were:

a. The applications systems of the Betchure Life Company should be migrated to a DBMS. In particular, the consultants recommended one of the leading relational DBMSs in which the consulting firm has extensive experience.

b. An information center was recommended to provide training for end users in reporting facilities available under the DBMS. They would also be responsible for ensuring that the mainframe-to-micro link was available for any user wishing to download data for inclusion in spreadsheets.

The Problem

Your boss, the director of MIS, has asked you to review the recommendations of the consultants and to report on the following: Which DBMS should be selected (careful, this is a trick request)? Which mainframe-to-micro communications link should be used? Which spreadsheet should be supported for this project?

Develop an evaluation tool for this project using the methods discussed in the chapter. Make any assumptions you feel are necessary, but be prepared to defend them.

CHAPTER 5

The Neglected Art of Data-Base Design

Data-base technology—to many, the phrase conjures up images of so-phisticated software with the flexibility and power to meet any business need with just a few simple keystrokes. Hasn't it been touted as the solution to the corporate world's data-processing problems? Isn't anybody without a data-base management system (DBMS) hopelessly behind the times? The bitter truth is that any executive who believes all this hyperbale has been suckered. As many have found out, the data-base technology that looked so simple in the advertising brochures and trade journal articles never seems that easy when they actually try to "do data base" in their own environment. What makes the difference?

The source of the problem lies in the term *data-base technology*. Success in a data-base environment has almost nothing to do with technology. In-stead, it lies in a clear understanding of the underlying nature of the business itself. In this chapter, a simple, yet effective method for designing data bases is proposed that starts with the assumption that a clear un-derstanding of the nature of the business is the foundation of any data-base system.

But the subject of this book is managing an information center. What does data-base design have to do with the role of a manager? The answer is: plenty.

This book discusses a number of topics that contribute to the success of an information center. Many of them are philosophical, others are strategic in nature, and a few are somewhat technical. Data-base design is one of those technical topics, and its implementation represents the most critical factor in the success of an information center.

In Chapter 4, it was pointed out that the DBMS software itself is not that significant to an information center, but that the logical structure of the data is more important than the technology used to store it. And, although it is beyond the scope of this text, a very good argument can be made that there are actually very few differences among the competing DBMS alternatives. From the information center's viewpoint, the actual DBMS is not significant, but the underlying structure of the data is the key factor for accurate and timely responses to business questions.

This chapter will provide a "crash course" for information center mana-gers on this critical technical topic so that they can develop an awareness of the design process that must precede any successful project.

THE PRIME DIRECTIVE

In the television series and movie *Star Trek,* the mission of the captain and crew of the starship *Enterprise* was to venture boldly into the universe and seek new life forms, but in doing so, they often found themselves constrained by Starfleet's prime directive: Do not interfere with other cultures. The technology available to the *Enterprise* was not to be introduced prematurely into primitive cultures since such an action could impede the local cultural development process.

Similarly, good data-base designers must also enforce their own prime directive of noninterference: The inputs and outputs of the system should not be allowed to interfere with the design process. Introducing reports, input screens, interface files, and the like into the process too early biases the design and constrains thinking in ways that result in inflexible data structures.

Generations of systems professionals were trained to use the IPO (input, process, output) method of design, in which the designer looks at the outputs that are needed for the system, determines what inputs are required to create these outputs, and develops processes to convert the inputs into outputs. In the days when each application system stood alone, this approach may have made sense as it allowed the designer to develop single-purpose systems. However, the IPO approach has a fatal flaw: with each new system request, one must again start at the desired outputs, find inputs, and develop transformation processes. And if the inputs that worked for the other processes do not work now, the designer must try to add files or fields to accomplish the task. Each new business need requires the systems designer to reinvent the proverbial wheel. In a data-base environment, the IPO approach fails miserably.

As an example, consider the plight of these end users struggling with their first data-base system. They simply want to track the sales of widgets. Thanks to the end-user computing revolution, they can purchase a sophisticated piece of software that promises to perform any possible operation they will ever need. But what will they do about data-base design? Most often, such end users opt for simplicity—one record of their data base bears a remarkable resemblance to a line of the report they had in mind. Essentially, they automate each report line as a data-base record.

This procedure might work well for awhile, but eventually a second question will arise about the sales of widgets: What are the sales *per region* over time?. The user now faces a dilemma—whether to create a new data base to handle the new request or to rewrite the old system to accommodate the new request. The first choice virtually ensures that the results from the two data bases will disagree; the latter represents a duplication of a sizable amount of work that went into the system the first time.

THE PENALTY OF POOR DESIGN

The previous example underscores the deceptive nature of data-base systems. Such systems look easy to use when a fast-talking salesperson or consultant demonstrates them. But without a semirigorous approach, a data base creates more problems than it solves.

Poor Performance

If a data base is designed with one set of outputs in mind, some of the characteristics of those outputs become imbedded in the structure of the data. For example, the data may be sorted to match the sort order of the envisioned report. Alternatively, if the desired output is based on quarterly numbers, data will occur in multiples of four, one for each quarter. However, business needs change rapidly and the "required" reports of today become the scratch paper of tomorrow.

When needs change, it is natural that the developer might resist making changes to accommodate those new needs—the more effort that is invested in a system, the harder it becomes to discard it. Rather than change the data base, the developer is tempted to force the old design to work. The result is more sorting, many more calculations, and a lot more code as the developer tries to take a data base that was designed for one type of output and make it produce another set of reports. The price of output-oriented design is almost always poor performance.

Instability

Every data-processing professional dreads the words "file conversion." It is not that it is difficult to write programs to convert the old format to a new one; such programs are fairly simple. The problems develop as the conversion team tries to find all of the programs that used the file. Each of these programs must be changed to accommodate the changes to the basic structure of the file. Even worse, programs that previously had been dependable and stable suddenly develop an almost schizophrenic personality as they try to use the new structure. No matter how hard the conversion team tries to prevent it, any change to the nature of the file destabilizes every component of the system.

Poorly designed data bases always seem to require reorganization. New data elements are needed, new data structures have to be created from the old ones, and every program that uses the data bases must be changed. With each change in the data base, stability seems farther and farther away. True data-base systems should isolate the application program from new fields or new data structures, but poorly designed systems continually frustrate the attainment of this goal.

DATA-BASE DESIGN: THE RIGHT WAY

If poor design can result in problems of instability and poor performance that affect the end users as well as the data-processing professionals, how

---

FIGURE 5-1   University Registrars' Office Entities—Initial List

STUDENTS

FACULTY

DEPARTMENT

COURSES

---

can data-base designers avert such problems? First, recall the prime directive: inputs and outputs are not to interfere with the design. Start by looking at the nature of the business and its needs.

Entities—the Nouns of Data Base

Classic grammar defines a noun as "a person, a place, or a thing." Similarly, the *entities* of a data base can be defined as the people, places, or things that are used in the business. Consider, for example, the problem of automating the registrar's office of a university. What "things" are of interest in this business function?

This list of "things" or entities might look something like Figure 5-1. Notice a few important characteristics of this list. First, consider the nature of the items listed. The designer should not be concerned about the actual data that will be collected. For example, the list does not include "student name," even though this will be something that must be tracked in the system. "Student name" is not a "thing"; it is a fact about a "thing," STUDENT. In this first step, the process begins in a top-down fashion. Second, the list is not complete, but omits a number of important entities. However, the incompleteness should not be disturbing at this point. Data-base design must be an iterative process.

According to Greek mythology, Pallas Athena emerged from the head of Zeus in full armor. Too often, data-base design is viewed as taking the same leap into full-fledged maturity. The designer expects to produce a complete, fully detailed design on the basis of user interviews (BEHOLD!). As the rest of the chapter will demonstrate, data-base designers need to approach the process of design with a "rough draft" mentality. They must begin by listing the main ideas, and then clarify the design through a series of specialized techniques. Data-base design always proceeds iteratively, improving with each step.

Attributes—the Adjectives of Data Base

Classic grammar defines an adjective as a word that modifies a noun; that is, it tells something about that noun—for example, a "blue" moon, a "tall" tree, or a "boring" book. Thus, whereas the first step in data-base design identifies the "things" (entities) of the business problem, in the next step, the designer must determine the facts that tell something about each of the entities. These facts are called *attributes*.

Consider Figure 5-2, which lists some of the attributes of the entities in Figure 5-1. Once again, the list is not meant to be comprehensive. In fact, it

FIGURE 5-2   University Registrars' Office Attributes—Initial List

```
STUDENTS
      Student Name
      Address
      City
      State
      Zip Code
      Student Number
      Year of Planned Graduation
      Date Entered
      Courses Taken
      Faculty Advisor Name

FACULTY
      Professor Name
      Degrees Held
      Department Name
      Classes Taught
      Office Number
      Office Phone
      Home Phone

DEPARTMENT
      Department Name
      Department Head
      Department Secretary Phone Number

COURSES SECTION
      Course Name
      Course Number
      Section Number
      Sponsoring Department
      Teacher
      Schedule
      Students Enrolled
```

is seriously flawed as a number of these attributes may have been inadvertently associated with the wrong entities. But this is the way the real world operates. It is seldom tidy; first drafts are often filled with errors. In the following chapter, notice how the design becomes more correct and more intuitively obvious at each step.

Identifiers—Differentiating Among the Entities

At almost every sporting event, there seems to be the proverbial program vendor shouting, "You can't tell the players without a scorecard." Considerations of proper grammar aside, there is truth in that claim. In order to differentiate football players, for instance, they are assigned different numbers that appear on the backs of their jerseys. However, members of the opposing team may also wear the same numbers, and so to identify a particular player, the color of that player's jersey must also be known. Moreover, it is required that each combination of color and number be unique—no two players in the league can wear the same color jersey with the same number. Thus, a 34 on the back of a navy jersey on a football field, indicates that the player is Walter Payton.

Similarly, every entity in a database will be identifiable by one or more attributes. The role of attributes as identifiers is essentially the same as that of the colors and numbers of the football jerseys: to differentiate one occurrence of that entity from all other occurrences of that entity.

What are some of the characteristics of an identifier? First, it must be unique. Two navy jerseys, each bearing the number 34, would create chaos; so also would two occurrences with identical values for an identifier. In the list in Figure 5-2, "student name" would be a poor identifier for student as a number of students might be named John Smith. Notice also that an identifier need not be a single field. In the football example, it is not required that the player number be unique, but that the combination of player number and jersey color be unique.

Second, an identifier must be unchanging. Since the identifier is the way in which occurrences are differentiated, every reference to an occurrence of that entity is likely to include the identifier. Any change in the identifier can set the stage for serious instability.

The requirement that the identifier be unchanging has an important corollary—it also must be completely devoid of information content. In the sports example, the choice of the numbers on the players' backs is not completely arbitrary—numbers under 40 designate running backs, numbers over 80 designate receivers, and numbers between 60 and 80 designate linemen. Normally, this scheme does not cause any problems, but in certain formations, a lineman might be in a position to be eligible to catch a pass or run the ball. The rules state that in such cases the player must inform the officials so that they know that the number on the back of the player's jersey does not accurately reflect the player's role. Alternatively, a lineman who decides to change jobs permanently and become a linebacker must be assigned a new number, requiring that thousands of programs be reprinted. Thus, when an identification scheme also includes further information about the identified subject, additional rules need to be imposed to ensure clear understanding. Just as important, changes in the scheme that are required to reflect changes in status become expensive and cumbersome to implement.

Consider another example. A county assessor's office has developed a system for keeping track of the property on the tax rolls. As a part of the system, an eight-digit parcel number is determined by using a two-digit district number, a two-digit ward number, a two-digit block number, and a two-digit sequence number. This parcel number is used to track the tax history of a property, and to determine current ownership and tax liability. What could possibly be wrong with this design?

Notice, first, that this numbering scheme places arbitrary limits on the number of parcels. Even though an eight-digit parcel number could potentially identify one hundred million pieces of property, the first high-rise condominium would exhaust the possible list of parcel numbers. All units in the high rise would be in the same district, ward, and block, and there easily might be more units than could be accommodated by the two digits of the sequence number. The inclusion of information content in the identifier greatly diminishes the usefulness of the identifier because of the artificial constraints that it places on the possible values.

Second, consider the problems that would be caused by redistricting. With new districts and wards, new numbers would need to be derived for each piece of property. As many data-base systems will not allow changes to the identifier, every old property would need to be deleted and reentered with the newly derived parcel number. But even if the data-base system allowed changes to the identifiers, there are still significant problems that could arise. Each of the tax history records would have to be changed to show the new property number so that a clear history could be obtained for each property. In addition, the ownership records would have to be changed to reflect the new parcel numbers. Finally, a conversion table would have to be maintained relating the old parcel numbers to the new ones to accommodate inquiries using either number. By employing an identifier made up of changeable information content, the designer has ensured that changes to the underlying information will create chaos throughout the system.

Considering that the identifier for an entity must be unchangeable and devoid of information content, examine Figure 5-2 and determine the best identifier for each entity. The results should look something like Figure 5-3. Notice that one of the entities, COURSE/SECTION, needed two attributes to identify it. Course number alone is not sufficient as CIS201 may have a number of sections; the section number is also needed uniquely to identify the course/section. Notice also that some of the entities did not have attributes that were unchangeable and free of information content, and so

---

FIGURE 5-3   University Registrars' Office Identifiers

STUDENTS
          Identifier: Student Number

FACULTY
          Identifier: Faculty Number

DEPARTMENT
          Identifier: Department Code

COURSES
          Identifier: Course Number, Section Number

---

new attributes, such as DEPARTMENT CODE and FACULTY NUMBER, had to be created. If there are no attributes qualified to be the identifier, the designer must modify the original design to include new attributes. The process of refining the design has begun.

NORMALIZATION: IS EVERY ATTRIBUTE IN THE RIGHT PLACE?

As the last section showed, the identifier is used to differentiate one occurrence of an entity from another. This means that once an identifier is known, it should be possible to determine all of the facts about that entity in an unambiguous fashion. However, this will happen only if the attributes are correctly assigned to the entities.

Assume, for example, that in the course of a school year, Professor Smith marries Mary Jones and is now Professor Smith-Jones. According to the design in Figure 5-2, the attribute PROFESSOR NAME needs to be changed for the former Professor Smith. But if the process ends there, the data base will be left in a highly inconsistent state. All of the students who have Professor Smith-Jones as an advisor now have an incorrect value for the attribute FACULTY ADVISOR NAME. Furthermore, if Professor Smith-Jones is the department chairman, the DEPARTMENT entity is incorrect, as are the records for each of the classes the professor has taught. Apparently, not only must the professor's name in the FACULTY entity be changed, but all references to the former name in all of the entities must be found and changed to show the correct new value. There must be a better way!

This example illustrates some of the potential problems caused by not having attributes assigned to the proper entites. The process by which attributes and entities are correctly aligned is called *normalization*.

Classic normalization theory is couched in the language of the mathematics in which it is based, as the following examples show:

The only functional dependencies in any table will be of the form $K \rightarrow F$, where K is the primary key and F is some other field.[1]

A relation scheme R is in the third normal form if there does not exist a key X for R, a set of attributes $Y \subset R$, and a nonprime attribute A of R not in X or Y, such that:

1. *$X \rightarrow Y$ holds in R,*
2. *$Y \rightarrow A$ holds in R, but*
3. *$Y \rightarrow X$ does not hold in R.*[2]

As these illustrations indicate, classic normalization categorizes entities in a rigorous language by examining the relationship between each attribute and its identifier. On the basis of these relationships, the entity may be considered to be in first normal form, second normal form, and so forth, up to the "ultimate" fifth normal form. These are progressive levels of rigor so that an entity that is in third normal form is automatically in both first and second normal form, and so on.

The underlying mathematical model and the classic data-base design theory derived from that model are well beyond the scope of this book. What is needed is a simplified approach to normalization that can be utilized by an information center and its users in a straight forward manner. To meet this need, the following simplification is proposed:

An entity will be considered sufficiently normalized if two conditions are met:

1. *Every attribute occurs only once for a given occurrence of an entity.*
2. *There are no indirect attributes.*

In the following, each of these conditions is considered in some detail.

No Multiples

Consider the COURSE entity in Figure 5-2, focusing on the attribute STUDENTS ENROLLED. This entity will contain the student number of each student who has signed up for one of the sections of the course. It may safely be assumed that more than one student will enroll in a given course, and so this attribute represents a multiple occurrence. What problems can result from this design?

First, notice the somewhat obvious question: How many occurrences of STUDENT NUMBER should be allowed for a given class? The registrar may promise that under no circumstances will more than twenty-five

---

[1]C. J. Date, *A Guide to DB2*, (Reading, Mass. Addison-Wesley Company, 1984), p. 288.

[2]J. D. Ullman, *Principles of Database Systems*, (Potomac, Md.: Computer Science Press, Inc., 1980), p. 187.

students ever be placed in a class, and the designer who is naive enough to believe this will build a data base that has twenty-five occurrences of STUDENT NUMBER. This data base may even prove sufficient for quite a long time. However, it is inevitable that someday, some class will have twenty-six students enrolled. The result will be the necessity to make significant modifications to the data base and to all of the programs that have been built on the false assumption that no more than 30 students would be enrolled.

This example leads to the following observation about multiple attributes. No matter how adamantly the organization claims that no more than N occurrences of a given attribute will ever be required for an entity, eventually there will be a case requiring $N + 1$ occurrences. This rule may be restated as follows: More than one occurrence of an attribute for a given entity must be treated as if there were infinitely many occurrences of that attribute.

There is a second reason why the rule against multiple attributes makes sense. Suppose that the data base allows for twenty-five student numbers for each course and someone asks whether student number 23456 has taken a particular course (see Figure 5-4). To answer this question, a program must examine each occurrence of student number to see whether it is the desired number 23456. Since student 23456 might be found in the third occurrence in one class but in the sixth occurrence in another, the logic looks something like Figure 5-5.

Even worse, as the inevitable happens and the design needs to be changed to accommodate thirty students per class, code that looks like Figure 5-5 needs to be changed in every program in the system to accommodate thirty different IF statements. Of course, there should be no problem in finding all of these programs and making these changes in a timely fashion, right?

Multiple attribute occurrences do two things to a data-base design. They make the design highly unstable, requiring intervention to reorganize the data with every slight change in the nature of the business. In addition,

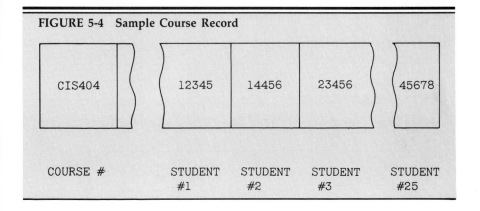

FIGURE 5-4   Sample Course Record

CIS404		12345	14456	23456		45678
COURSE #		STUDENT #1	STUDENT #2	STUDENT #3		STUDENT #25

FIGURE 5-5   Logic for Multiple Occurrences

```
IF STUDENT(01) = 23456
OR STUDENT(02) = 23456
OR STUDENT(03) = 23456

   o o o

OR STUDENT(25) = 23456
```

they create cumbersome logic where it seems that simplicity and elegance should prevail. What, then, should be done about problems of multiple occurrences?

Multiples almost always indicate the need for another entity. Remember that more than one occurrence of an attribute for a given entity must be treated as if there were infinitely many occurrences of that attribute. In the case of the multiple student numbers in the entity COURSE/SECTION, the new entity would be called ENROLLMENT. This new entity would have as its identifier the course number, the section number, and the student number, and there would be one occurrence for each student in each class (see Figure 5-6).

Note how this approach has simplified the design. First, there is no upper limit on the number of possible students in a class. A class with fifty students is accommodated just as easily as a class with two students. The

FIGURE 5-6   The New Enrollment Entity

COURSE NUMBER	SECTION NUMBER	STUDENT NUMBER
CIS404	2	12345
CIS404	2	14456
CIS404	2	23456
CIS404	2	45678

former will have fifty instances of an enrollment entity, and the latter will have two instances.

Second, the logic has become streamlined. Now all that needs to be done is to query the data base for all enrollment records where the student number is 23456. The logic has become focused on the business problem of finding enrollments instead of trying to write cumbersome IF logic. This new entity also plays a special role in relating STUDENT and SECTION that will be discussed later in this chapter.

No Indirect Attributes

The goal of data-base design is to store data about a particular entity only once. Examine Figure 5-2 again and count the number of times the name of a given professor might appear in the system. It would appear once with each student who had that professor as an advisor. It would appear once in the department if that professor were the chairperson. It would appear once with each class/section taught by that professor. And, finally, it would appear once in the occurrence of FACULTY that referred to that professor. If, as suggested earlier, Professor Jones marries and becomes Professor Smith-Jones, an unmanageable number of changes will have to be made. If even one of these changes is missed, the result is internally inconsistent data stored within the data base. This, then, is the problem caused by indirect attributes.

The truth is that the name of the professor is not really a fact about all of these entities. It is only a fact about one occurrence of the FACULTY entity. The name of the advising professor is not really a fact about a student. However, the faculty *number* of that professor is a fact about the student. Notice the subtle difference. When the identifier of FACULTY is an attribute of STUDENT, there is no problem. After all, by definition, the identifier is an unchanging attribute that uniquely determines *which* professor. Once only the professor's identifier is stored in the STUDENT entity, the name change is isolated to a change in the FACULTY entity. The change in the real world (something has changed about a faculty member) is reflected in the data structure (a change to only the FACULTY entity). On the other hand, a change in the advisor's identifier means that the student has transferred to another advisor. In this case, facts about the advisor have not changed—it is the advisor who has changed. Once again, the change in the real world (something has changed about a student) is reflected in the data structure (a change in a STUDENT entity).

To take another example, assume that the name of course GEO121 has been changed from "Introduction to Geology" to "Basic Concepts in Geology." If the university offers five sections of the course, this change requires updating five separate instances of the COURSE/SECTION entity. Once again, the name of the course appears to be only indirectly related to the COURSE/SECTION. In fact, the course name is really a fact about the

---

FIGURE 5-7   Revised Course, Section, and Enrollment Entities

```
COURSES/SECTION
       Course Number
       Section Number
       Teacher Number
       Schedule

COURSE
       Course Number
       Course Name
       Sponsoring Department

ENROLLMENT
       Course Number
       Section Number
       Student Number
```

---

course. As the design so far does not have an entity called COURSE, another entity must be added. Similarly, the identification number of the sponsoring department is not directly related to the COURSE/SECTION; it is also a fact about the COURSE. The result of this new entity is shown in Figure 5-7.

Notice how the design in Figure 5-7 reflects much clearer thinking. The facts seem to be aligned with other facts to which they are directly related. Now if the course name changes, the only required system change is to update that particular occurrence of the COURSE entity. The corresponding COURSE/SECTIONS are not changed at all, but now show the correct name because they are linked to the course through its identifier.

Indirect attributes are often called *transitive* attributes, based on the transitive property of mathematics: If A = B and B = C, then A = C. In the mathematical property, *A* and *C* are related because they are linked to a common entity, *B*. Similarly, transitive attributes creep into a design when the designer inadvertently imbeds foreign data into an entity when what actually was required was only the identifier to relate the two entities.

Conclusions

A design, then, may be considered sufficiently normalized if there are no multiple occurrences of an attribute and no indirect (transitive) attributes. (See Figure 5-8 for the normalized design to this point.) If a design meets these criteria, then each attribute has been correctly associated with the appropriate entity. But how can it be proved that all of the entities have been included?

FIGURE 5-8   Entities and Attributes After Normalization

STUDENTS
    Student Number
    Student Name
    Address
    City
    State
    Zip Code
    Year of Planned Graduation
    Date Entered
    Faculty Advisor Number

FACULTY
    Faculty ID Number
    Professor Name
    Department Code
    Office Number
    Office Phone
    Home Phone

DEPARTMENT
    Department Code
    Department Name
    Department Head Faculty Number
    Department Secretary Phone Number

COURSE
    Course Number
    Course Name
    Code of Sponsoring Department

COURSES/SECTION
    Course Number
    Section Number
    Teacher Number
    Schedule

ENROLLMENT
    Course Number
    Section Number
    Student Number

ENTITY RELATIONSHIP MODELS

Again, data-base design is an iterative process. The first few steps developed a rough draft that found a list of entities and their associated

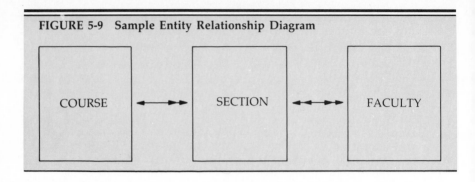

FIGURE 5-9 Sample Entity Relationship Diagram

attributes. The process of refining the design was then initiated by determining an appropriate identifier for each of the entities and by applying the rules for normalization. The design in Figure 5-8, which incorporates these refinements, is a much better design than the rough draft in Figure 5-2. However, the design is not finished. Up to this point, the process has concentrated on ensuring that attributes are associated with the appropriate entity. Now it is time to evaluate the list of entities itself.

The "correctness" of the list of entities will be evaluated by using a notation that expresses each entity as a labeled box. The relationship between two entities will be depicted as a line connecting the two boxes, and the type of relationship indicated by either a single- or double-headed arrow. Consider Figure 5-9 as an example of this technique. This diagram should be interpreted as follows:

1. COURSE-SECTION. For each class, there may be many different sections (the double-headed arrow means "MANY"); but each section always represents only one class (the single-headed arrow means "ONE"). This says that a particular section is never used to refer to two different classes.
2. SECTION-FACULTY. For a given section, there may be more than one faculty member. This means that the university allows team teaching for certain sections of classes. Furthermore, each faculty member may be assigned to many classes.

Notice that there is no arrow connecting CLASS and FACULTY. There is no direct connection between these two entities; instead, faculty members are associated with particular classes only because they are assigned to teach one of the sections.

These relationships may be categorized by the types of arrows they use as follows: *many-to-many* (e.g., SECTION-FACULTY): *many-to-one* (e.g., CLASS-SECTION); or *one-to-one*.

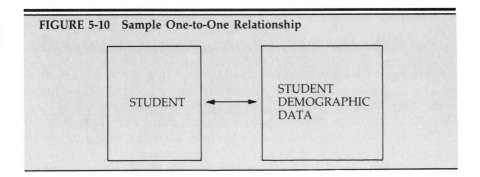

FIGURE 5-10   Sample One-to-One Relationship

One-to-One Relationships

Consider the example in Figure 5-10. Notice that there are two entities—one that contains basic student data, and one that contains demographic data about the student, such as income, race, and age. The one-to-one relationship means that for each student, the data base stores at most one set of demographic data and that each set of demographic data applies to a particular student.

One-to-one relationships usually indicate that there is a flaw in the design. The two entities described should be a single entity. As all of the attributes on the demographic data entity are really facts about the student, from the logical design viewpoint, probably only one entity is needed.

However, there are times when the designer should allow a one-to-one relationship to exist in the data-base system. For example:

1. *Performance.* If some of the attributes are to be used only rarely, then it may be better to segregate the lesser used attributes into a separate entity. By keeping the entity size smaller, the DBMS will be able to retrieve the commonly used data much faster.

2. *Security.* In most such systems it is far easier to control access to the data at an entity level than at an attribute level. By placing all of the sensitive data in a separate entity, security is simplified.

Notice that neither of these two reasons has anything to do with the logical design. Both are important only when moving from pure logical design into physical implementation.

Many-to-One Relationships

The many-to-one relationship is the ideal relationship in data-base design. It is easily implemented in all of the data-base architectures and requires no special steps by the developer, except to note its existence and move on to the more complex many-to-many relationships.

Many-to-Many Relationships

Many-to-many relationships, such as SECTION-FACULTY in Figure 5-9, represent a flaw in the data-base design. Consider the problem of implementing such a design. As noted later in this chapter, these relationships are implemented by making the identifier of one entity attributes of the other. If the identifiers of the faculty members are to be attributes of SECTION, this breaks the prohibition against multiples. Similarly, to include the identifier of the sections taught by a given professor as attributes of the FACULTY entity also violates the rules regarding multiple occurrences. Any attempt to relate these two entities seems to break the rules for normalization.

For example, where shall information regarding responsibilities for the class be stored? For a certain section, Professor ABC may be responsible for the lecture and Professors DEF and GEH may lead discussion groups. This attribute (responsibility code) cannot be a fact about SECTION as there may be a different value for each professor assigned to that section. It also cannot be a fact about FACULTY, as a professor may lead discussion groups for one section and give lectures to another. The attribute "responsibility code" has no entity to which it may rightfully belong.

This discussion points to the way that the designer must handle many-to-many relationships—that is, they must be decomposed into a new entity and a pair of many-to-one relationships (see Figure 5-11). Notice the composition of the new ASSIGNMENT entity. It has as attributes the identifier of a particular faculty member and the identifier of a specific section. (Remember, section has a two-part identifier.) This new entity has the role of relating a specific section to a particular professor.

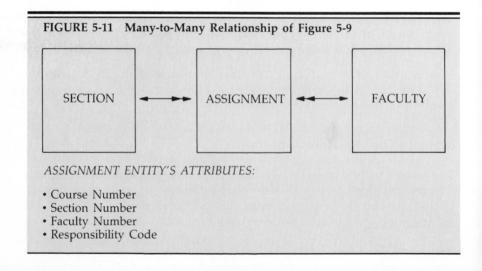

FIGURE 5-11   Many-to-Many Relationship of Figure 5-9

SECTION ◄——►► ASSIGNMENT ◄◄——► FACULTY

ASSIGNMENT ENTITY'S ATTRIBUTES:

• Course Number
• Section Number
• Faculty Number
• Responsibility Code

Intersection Entities

The new ASSIGNMENT entity is referred to as an *intersection entity*. Its role is to capture the facts about the interaction of two other entities (PRO-FESSOR, SECTION), which makes it the ideal place to store the responsibility code discussed earlier. The responsibility code is not a fact about either the professor or the section, but instead is a fact about the relationship between the two.

There has also been another intersection entity in the design so far. Recall the discussion about ENROLLMENT. This entity was created as a part of the normalization process when it was discovered that multiple student numbers could not be stored with the SECTION entity. It functions as an intersection entity between STUDENT and SECTION, holding data about the relationship between the two, such as the student's grade. As was the case with responsibility code, the student's grade is not a fact about the SECTION, as there is a different grade for each student. It is not a fact about STUDENT, as the student has a different grade for each section in which the student is enrolled. Grade is a fact about the relationship between the two, now shown as the intersection entity ENROLLMENT.

Intersection entities are very easy to miss in the initial stages of design. However, they begin to appear as the designer looks at normalization and entity relationships. It is important to use both techniques in the design process. In this way, careless thinking that might be overlooked in one step can be caught in the other. Consider the attribute list in Figure 5-7. Notice that the attributes for COURSES/SECTION include the faculty member's number. This is perfectly acceptable from a normalization viewpoint. However, upon reaching the entity relationship stage, the designer ought to realize that many faculty members might be associated with a given section. Even though the attribute seemed to be a single occurrence, the business case that was identified in the relationships rightfully exposed faculty code as a multiple occurrence. The two techniques complement each other.

IMPLEMENTATION

The final version of the entity relationship model for the example is shown in Figure 5-12. Depending on the university, the results may differ slightly. This design, for example, does not allow a course to be sponsored by more than one department (notice the "one" arrow going from COURSE to DEPARTMENT). Notice also that only the direct relationships are shown. There is no connection between DEPARTMENT and SECTION. These are related only through a COURSE, indicating that all sections of a particular course are sponsored by the same department. The final list of attributes for these entities is left as an exercise for the reader. It is finally time to begin implementing the data-base system.

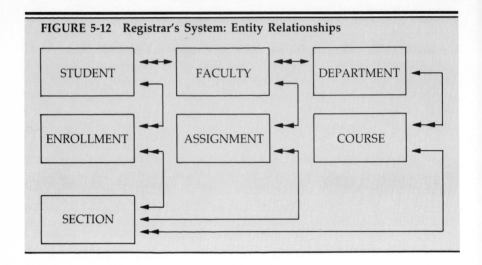

FIGURE 5-12   Registrar's System: Entity Relationships

An Overview of DBMS Architectures

A comprehensive discussion of data-base architectures is well beyond the scope of this book. However, as a basis for discussing implementation, brief definitions of the two computing approaches are needed.

1.   *Relational Data Bases.* A *relational* architecture captures the data as a collection of tables, each resembling a spreadsheet. Each row represents what is traditionally called a record and each column represents a traditional field. These tables are combined using special opperations such as JOIN or INTERSECTION to create new temporary tables when data is needed from two tables.

2.   *Network/Hierarchical Data Bases.* A *network hierarchical* data base predefines relationships between types of data in a structure that often resembles an organization chart. (See Figure 5-14 for an example.) Each box on the chart (called a segment) corresponds to a traditional record and the relationships between the boxes are expressed in geneological terms—the lower box is said to be the child of the upper. "Dotted line" relationships are also allowed, relating two segments that are not in the same structure (e.g., COURSE and DEPARTMENT in Figure 5-14). These dotted-line relationships are called *logical* parent–child relationships.

Armed with this very brief overview, the entity relationship model of Figure 5-12 can now be translated into a real data base.

The Relational Approach to Implementation

The first step in implementing the logical model in a relational data-base system is to ensure the integrity of the *foreign keys*. That is, the identifier of entity A, when used as an attribute in entity B, is referred to as a foreign key in entity B. For example, the department head's faculty number in the DEPARTMENT entity is a foreign key, as is the department code in the FACULTY entity. As a final integrity check, the designer must use the entity relationship diagram to make sure that the design is implemented correctly.

To use the entity relationship diagram, the designer must examine each relationship and ensure that the following rule is met: The identifier of the ONE side of the arrow must be an attribute (and hence a foreign key) of the MANY side of the arrow. To do so, the designer must ask the following types of questions:

1. Is the identifier of FACULTY an attribute in STUDENT? (Yes. It is called the advisor's code.)
2. Is the identifier of COURSE found in SECTION? (Yes. It is actually a part of the identifier of SECTION.)
3. Is the identifier of DEPARTMENT found in COURSE? (Yes. It is called sponsoring department code.)

Once these questions have been answered satisfactorily (or the list of attributes changed if necessary), the design is essentially complete. Each entity will be represented as a separate table in the system. In this case, seven tables will be created. See Figure 5-13 for an example of how one could use IBM's DB2® to create one of the tables.

One key feature is illustrated in Figure 5-13. Notice the clause NOT NULL following the student number. As part of the table definition, the designer is requiring that some value be provided for the identifier. This is a reasonable requirement given the role of this special attribute. Without a value, there would be no means of differentiating one occurrence from another. If the definition process does not incorporate the capability to make sure that the identifier is always present, then the application must programmatically ensure the unique presence of an identifier.

FIGURE 5-13   Implementing the Design in DB2

```
CREATE TABLE STUDENT
      (STUDENT#       CHAR(5)      NOT NULL,
       SNAME          CHAR(40)     ,
       ADDRESS        CHAR(40)     ,
       CITY           CHAR(25)     ,
       STATE          CHAR(02)     ,
       ZIP            CHAR(10)     ,
       GRADYR         INTEGER(02)  ,
       ENTERED        INTEGER(6)   ,
       ADVISOR#       CHAR(5)      );
```

The Network/Hierarchical Approach to Implementation

The network/hierarchical approach is based on the premise that there are two types of relationships: one reflects inherent ownership and the other reflects mere association. The inherent ownership is reflected in a parent–child relationship (e.g., COURSE-SECTION in Figure 5-14), whereas the associational relationship is referred to as a LOGICAL PARENT (FACULTY-SECTION in Figure 5-14). In moving from the logical model to the actual implementation under a network/hierarchical approach, the designer should heed these guidelines:

1. The ONE arrows imply parentage and the MANY arrow implies children. The parentage might be either physical (parent–child) or logical (pointer).

2. Physical parentage implies that the child has no existence except as a part of its parent. The child cannot be transferred to another parent, but must be deleted from one parent and added to the other separately.

3. Intersection entities will be implemented as the physical child of one of the related entities and the logical child of the other. Determination of the correct physical placement should be based on update patterns.

4. Physical children cannot be updated without the identifier of their parent. If updates must be done without knowledge of the parent key, then the parent–child relationship must be implemented as a logical relationship.

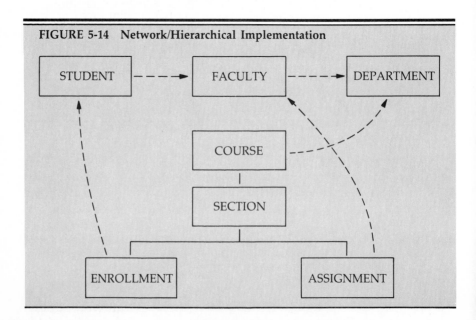

FIGURE 5-14   Network/Hierarchical Implementation

Figure 5-14 shows the network/hierarchical implementation of the logical design based on these rules. Observe the following:

1. Each entity relationship is reflected in the hierarchy as either a physical parent–child relationship or a logical relationship.

2. The hierarchy for courses reflects an intuitive feel for the business problem. A section cannot be added until the course has been added, nor can students be enrolled in the course or teachers assigned until both the course and section have been established.

3. If a course is removed from the catalog, all sections, enrollments, and instructor assignments will also be removed.

4. The advisor relationship between student and faculty has been implemented as a logical, not physical, relationship. The student will be allowed to change advisors. Similarly, the relationship between faculty and department is also logical. As new departments form or dissolve, professors may be transferred.

Intersection entities create an interesting dilemma. Consider once again the relationship in Figure 5-11. The two relationships would have ASSIGN-MENT the child of both FACULTY and SECTION. How should this be reflected in the hierarchy?

The intersection entity will be placed as the physical child of one of the two related entities and as the logical child of the other. Since the entity model is well served either way, the only other consideration should be based on the designer's willingness to require knowledge of the parent key to gain access to the intersection entity. In the case of ASSIGNMENT, the final implementation could allow it to be the child of either FACULTY or SECTION. As Figure 5-14 shows, the latter option has been chosen, but the alternative should be considered equally acceptable.

For those entities that are joined by a logical relationship (e.g., COURSE-DEPARTMENT), the same rule as used in the relational model must apply. The identifier of the ONE (now the logical parent) must be an attribute of the MANY (now the logical child). As an example of the network/hierarchical approach, Figure 5-15 shows the data-base design using FOCUS® (Information Builders, Inc.). Notice how the segment definitions match the logical (Figure 5-12) and hierarchical (Figure 5-14) designs and how the identifiers of the logical parents (student and faculty identifications) are attributes of the logical children.

FINALLY: REPORTS AND INPUT SCREENS

Remember that the prime directive is that outputs and inputs are not to interfere with the design process. Only after the design is complete should the designer start to examine the reports or online programs that will be required. These inputs and outputs provide an excellent way to validate

---

FIGURE 5-15 Implementing the Design in FOCUS

```
FILENAME=COURSES, SUFFIX=FOC, $
  SEGNAME=COURSE, SEGTYPE=A1, $
    FIELD=COURSE NUM    , ALIAS=      , FORMAT=A6     , $
    FIELD=COURSE NAME   , ALIAS=      , FORMAT=A30    , $
    FIELD=DEPT CODE     , ALIAS=      , FORMAT=A5     , $
  SEGNAME=SECTION, PARENT=COURSE, SEGTYPE=A1,  $
    FIELD=SECT NUM      , ALIAS=      , FORMAT=I3     , $
    FIELD=DAYS AVAIL    , ALIAS=      , FORMAT=A8     , $
    FIELD=TIME          , ALIAS=      , FORMAT=A8     , $
  SEGNAME=ENROLL , PARENT=SECTION, SEGTYPE=A1,  $
    FIELD=STUDENT ID    , ALIAS=      , FORMAT=A5     , $
    FIELD=GRADE         , ALIAS=      , FORMAT=A1     , $
  SEGNAME=ASSIGN , PARENT=SECTION, SEGTYPE=A1,  $
    FIELD=FACULTY ID    , ALIAS=      , FORMAT=A5     , $
    FIELD=RESP CODE     , ALIAS=      , FORMAT=A1     , $
```

---

the system. If the data-base design, working along with a fourth-, or even third-, generation language (see Chapter 4), can support the required programs and reports, then the design is successful. However, if reporting needs or online activities arise that are not easily supported by the design, then the developer knows that there is a flaw in one of two places. For one thing, the designer may have overlooked a critical entity, attribute, or relationship. Such flaws are relatively easy to repair as adding new entities or attributes is a fairly straightforward task. Or the discrepancy may indicate fuzzy thinking on the part of the user or the developer. The designer must be careful to avoid automating the absurd because "it's always been done that way."

This last point is critical. Many systems have evolved from years of fuzzy thinking. Codes have taken on ambiguous or inconsistent meanings, awkward procedures have become standard, and an entire underground culture has developed around those few individuals who can make the systems work. The designer must avoid the temptation to allow the data base for the new information system to reflect the poor design of the past.

SUMMARY

This chapter began with the bold statement that data-base design has almost nothing to do with technology. Even more damning, the previous chapter stated that the DBMS itself is not terribly important, but that a clear vision of the underlying logical structure of the data is. The critical step is the act of expressing the business needs in a semirigorous format so that the system is dependable, consistent, and stable. As this chapter showed, the design must pass through an iterative process that starts from the top (entities), works downward through the attributes, and then proceeds through a series of validation activities, including normalization and entity relationship modeling. Only after the logical design has been developed can that design be implemented with the technology of choice.

SUGGESTED PROJECT

You have been called upon to develop the data-base design for a project-control system. The system must take into account the following:

1. A project is made up of many tasks.
2. A task may be worked on by one or more persons.
3. Projects are sponsored by departments.
4. Time is tracked on a weekly basis by each person who worked on a given task.

Some of the business questions this system is to answer are:

1. How much time did each person spend on each task this week?
2. What other projects are being sponsored by each department?
3. What projects include programming time?
4. How does each task in a project compare in actual time and estimated time?

Develop a logical design for this system, including attributes, entities, and an entity relationship model.

CHAPTER 6

Prototyping

The Gothic cathedrals of the fourteenth century were truly marvels of human creation. Grandiose in scope and awe inspiring in execution, they required the efforts of hundreds or thousands of people over periods as long as fifty years. The original designers and sponsors of a project often did not live to see it to completion. Data-processing systems can be very much like these cathedrals in the building, but the results rarely are as inspiring. Most of the time, the final product is a patchwork quilt of programs that somehow get the job done in spite of themselves.

The frustrations inherent in the traditional systems-development process forced developers to consider whether there might not be some better way. One common response was to move toward a prototyping approach that produced tangible results in a very short time, reducing the distance between problem and solution. Since prototyping has become a standard part of the information-processing tool kit, it is important to understand how it fits into the vision of an information center.

WHAT IS PROTOTYPING?

In view of all of the verbiage and misconceptions that have accompanied the introduction of prototyping, it is useful to define what the term actually means:

> Prototyping *is a process by which information systems are rapidly developed in a user-oriented fashion through multiple iterations.*

Figure 6-1 illustrates this definition.

FIGURE 6-1   Prototyping: A Definition

DEFINITION

> *Prototyping* is a process by which information systems are **rapidly developed** in a **user-oriented** fashion through **multiple iterations.**

Rapidly Developed
- Is less resistant to change
- Provides instant gratification

User Oriented
- Users usually can't articulate real need at first
- Group-oriented approach works better
- Emotional ownership is shared

Multiple Iterations
- System is never right the first time
- Each version is better than the previous one

Rapid Development

Some of the greatest bronze statues start out as plaster models; each new car body begins as a lump of clay. Artists and designers have been using prototypes for hundreds of years. Since the initial version of the product is created using materials that are easily changed and easily discarded, the artist is able to try out ideas quickly and inexpensively.

But what if the automobile designer were constrained to work with the same material as would be used in the final production version? The designer would still be able to provide preliminary models before final production. However, it would take so long to form sheet steel into a one-time model that the designer might be tempted to settle for the results of a first attempt rather than go through the process again.

This is also a basic problem in developing information systems. Before the introduction of end-user computing tools, programmers and analysts had very few choices. At best, they could write specifications for how the system should behave and then meticulously write code that matched those specifications. Only after months of effort was a product finally available—and, much as would be the case with an auto-body designer, that product had taken so long to develop that it was usually proclaimed finished without even considering changes.

For prototyping to work, the speed with which a concept progresses to a tangible model is critical. The more time and effort a developer invests in a system, the more resistant that system becomes to changes. The longer a developer works on a system, the more the developer's ego and prestige become a part of the system. True prototyping should allow a developer to move from concept to results in hours or days rather than weeks or months.

Another benefit of rapid development is instant gratification. Teachers realize that a good grade given soon after the work is completed is much more satisfying to a student than the same grade given later. Teachers try to catch students doing something correctly and praise them for it immediately. The same principle applies to systems development. A tangible result after a week of work is far more gratifying than a result after months of work. The instant gratification provided by the rapid pace of a prototyping project becomes a powerful inducement for the development team.

User Orientation

Traditional systems development has often been compared to the rituals used in many primitive religions. When a tribe member goes to a shaman with a request, the shaman listens carefully and then retreats to a sacred cave, mountaintop, or magic tent to commune with the spirits. After a long period, the shaman returns and tells the tribe member whether the spirits have granted or denied the request.

In the development life cycle, users initiate a request and occasionally answer questions during the analysis phase of the project. Once developers feel they have an idea of what the system requires, users are only marginally involved until they are asked for their approval or the final result is ready for testing. Users are expected to know exactly what they want from the beginning, and to articulate that need completely and accurately. Furthermore, this approach assumes that the specifications developed in the early stages of the project can be cast in concrete once the initial analysis is completed.

The traditional development process would have users explain their needs to systems analysts, who, in turn, would develop specifications for programmers to use in the creation of a system. In the prototyping approach, users are assumed to have at best only a fleeting vision of what they really want and to be able to express their needs only through direct ongoing involvement in the development process. Prototyping insists on a group-oriented approach that blends user, analyst, and programmer into a team with the common goal of developing a system that reflects the real needs of the users.

Not only does user involvement improve the ability of the system to meet the real business needs, but it also changes the emotional ownership of the system. In traditional systems in which users are virtually ignored in the detailed design and coding stages, they see the system as belonging to the MIS department since it has been designed by MIS, coded by MIS, tested by MIS, and installed by MIS. Accordingly, any errors in the system result in an "us–them" argument: "Your system isn't right."

By involving users in the prototyping process, ownership of the system is shared among all of the participants in the development process. The system is neither "yours" nor "mine"; it is "ours." Emotional ownership is always a product of involvement, and by adopting a user-oriented approach, the results will be jointly owned.

Multiple Iterations

In Chapter 5, it was observed that the Greek goddess Pallas Athena is said to have sprung from the head of Zeus fully grown and in complete armor. Too often, the systems development process is viewed in a similar light— the designers hope that the design will spring from their heads fully grown. Sadly, in the real world truth usually arrives slowly and takes time to develop.

The prototyping approach takes as a guiding principle the fact that a system is never right on the first try. It assumes that a number of consecutive systems need to be developed, each one better that the previous one, until the system really does capture the solution to the business problem. This is the approach that was advocated in the discussion of data-base design in Chapter 5, and it can now be extended to the entire development process. Iteration alone is not sufficient, however. If this iterative process is to work, it must include two other components. First, the iterations must be developed in rapid succession. It will simply not do if the time between successive iterations can be measured in months rather than days. Second, the users must be directly involved. Without direct user involvement, there is no way to evaluate how well each new iteration meets the business needs.

Definition of Prototyping

The classic user lament about a new system is that it may be exactly what the user asked for, but is not what the user needs. The prototyping approach tries to overcome this problem in a number of ways. It takes into consideration that the final product may bear only a passing resemblance to the initial request, and that the definition of what is needed develops over time. As users see each iteration of the system, their own vision of the problems and the solutions become clearer. Furthermore, it is the capability to produce a new iteration of the system quickly (in days rather than months) that makes the prototyping approach effective. Finally, by combining these factors, a high-energy, responsive approach to systems development is realized.

PROTOTYPING AND QUALITY

With this emphasis on rapid iterations, it would be easy to assume that prototyping means "slapping together any old thing and seeing how it works." That assumption is completely wrong. The quality of a system is not a feature to be added after the prototyping is complete, but it must be built in from the beginning.

Design: A Critical Element

Design is a value-laden word that means something different to each system developer. For the purposes of this discussion, the term is taken to mean an orderly representation of the structure and functions of a business as reflected in the system. Two types of design are important as a part of the prototyping process: data design and process design (Figure 6-2).

   Data design is the process by which a structure is developed for the data that accurately reflects the structure of the business. In data-base design (as discussed in Chapter 5), first the "things" (entities) that will be tracked in the system are identified. Then the facts (attributes) about each of the "things" are established. Third, the identifier for each "thing" is determined, making sure that the proper facts are associated with the proper

---

FIGURE 6-2   Design Issues in Prototyping

DATA DESIGN
- Develop a clear list of the entities and attributes of the system (see Chapter 5)
- Develop a clear understanding of the relationships among the entities

PROCESS DESIGN
- Develop a common appearance for all system components
- Develop standards and naming conventions for internal use
- Develop a standard logic flow for system
- Develop error message standards

"things." Finally, the relationships among the "things" are examined to identify anomalies or fuzzy thinking.

This data design process is a critical part of the prototyping cycle and needs to be the first step, preceding any code. Good data design also fits into the model of prototyping, in that it is developed rapidly in a user-oriented fashion through multiple iterations. More important, good data design sets the stage for the other prototyping activities. Without a solid (but not necessarily perfect) data-base design, all of the other prototyping activities are doomed to failure.

Process design is concerned with the aesthetics of the system. All of the online screens need to have a common appearance, with common function key usage, and all reports need a standard header and footing. Spending time on the front end of a project standardizing these common elements will ensure the success of the prototyping process since user frustration is minimized by a common command set. Furthermore, the speed of the prototyping process is improved since each programmer does not have to grope for screen and report formats. Process design need not be elaborate, but might be as simple as creating a standard template for online programs and one for reports. However it is done, process design is the key to prototyping a *system* rather than quickly developing programs.

The User/Machine Dialogue

Perhaps the biggest error that is made in developing new online systems is seeing the process as the creation of a collection of programs. An online system is really a dialogue between the user and the machine and it is the role of prototyping to make sure that the dialogue is clear and understandable.

One of the major functions of an online system is the validation of entered data. After all, isn't it easier simply not to allow invalid data into the system from the very beginning? How, then, should the online system treat invalid data?

Perhaps the worst way is to display the error message "INVALID DATA." This message may be wonderful computer-eese but it is a bad dialogue: What data is invalid? Why is it invalid? What must the operator do to correct the problem? The answers cannot be determined because the system has done a terrible job of keeping up its side of the conversation.

Perhaps a better system response would be "INVALID ACCOUNT TYPE CODE." At least now it is clear that the account type code is incorrect and that value can be corrected. The conversation can be made even clearer with the message "ACCOUNT TYPE MUST BE 01, 04, OR 08." Not only does this indicate that the account type is wrong, but it also gives some hint as to the correct value. The computer has made the conversation much easier to comprehend for both itself and the user.

Thus, not only must the prototype try to capture the functionality of the system, but a dialogue must be developed that will be used between the operator and the system. Building a dialogue approach from the beginning is a lot easier than trying to add it after the system is complete.

MAKING PROTOTYPING WORK: A METHODOLOGY

In a broad philosophical sense, then, prototyping must be rapid, iterative, and user-oriented. Moreover, quality must be built in from the beginning through data and process design. Finally, the output of an online system should be viewed as a user-machine conversation rather than as a series of error messages. The following describes a simple, yet responsive methodology (Figure 6-3) that will implement the organizational changes necessary to make prototyping work.

Step 1: The Prototyping Project Team

Not all systems professionals—or users—can adapt to the use of prototyping. Prototyping requires a completely different approach—one that is centered on teamwork, tolerates vagueness in initial stages, and proceeds in iterations rather than in a straight line. This is significantly different from the traditional systems project.

Despite all of the lofty sentiments to the contrary, the systems development process has never been a very cooperative process. Developers may be divided into teams, but the process of creating systems is still highly individualistic. In fact, ego is often the fuel of successful projects.

Prototyping seeks to replace the ego of the individual with the ego of the team. The most successful developers in this approach will have very strong egos; however, the object of pride will not be themselves, but the

FIGURE 6-3   Prototyping Methodology

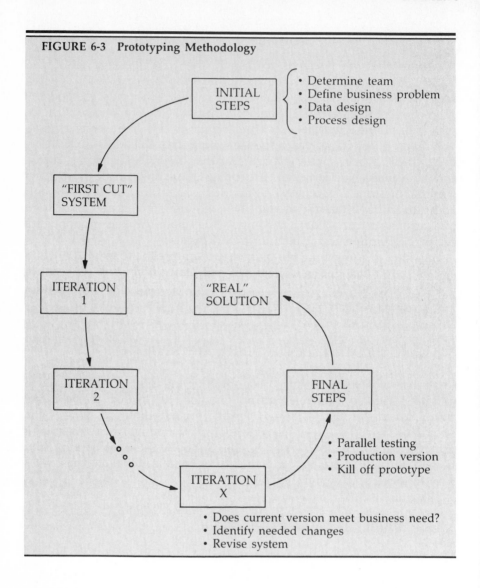

product and the team. Many systems developers will never be able to make this transition.

More than attitude changes are required. Traditional systems usually move through a well-defined series of phases. First, functional specifications are developed, followed by the development of detailed programming and system specifications, and finally by the completion of the actually coding. Prototyping, on the other hand, moves almost immediately from business problem to code, only to begin a series of iterations of coding and testing. Prototyping thrives on vagueness, with each

---

FIGURE 6-4   Traditional vs. Prototype Roles

	TRADITIONAL	PROTOTYPE
USERS	Request	Identify business problem
	Respond	Design
	Wait	Test
	Approve	Approve
		Manage business details
		Solution to problem
		Costs and benefits
DEVELOPERS	Interview	Identify business problem
	Design	Design
	Code	Code
	Test	Manage technical details
		Define standards
		Prototype death cycle

---

iteration, it is hoped, getting closer to the truth. In contrast, the traditional model requires that the functions of the system be fully defined before moving on to the next step. Some developers, and some users, will never be able to make this transition either.

Thus, a prototyping project always begins as a team effort. Users and technicians are on equal footing. Management of the team must emphasize the product, rather than the people, and must not expect perfection on the first, second, or even the tenth iteration. Success comes through recognition that each iteration is better that the previous one.

Finally, if the team is to be successful, it must be composed of people who are not afraid to break out of tradition. Figure 6-4 illustrates some of the role differences created by a prototyping approach. For the approach to work, the developers must be willing to give up some of their power to the users. Both design and testing become shared responsibilities, and even the management of the project is shared. Each group is responsible for managing the portion of the project it knows best, but they must work together to ensure success.

The developers must be willing to give up some of their traditional power, and the users must be willing to accept that transfer of power. Unless the users on the project team become full partners in the process, the results will be very disappointing. All of the participants must agree to shed their old roles and take on new ones.

Once the team has been selected and the expectations made clear, how should a prototyping project proceed?

Step 2: Business Problem Definition

A recurrent theme of this book has been the need to see business problems as deviations from a norm. How then does the team progress from the business problem to the first version of the system? For an example, consider the business problem articulated by the sales manager in a large financial institution: "I cannot tell with any level of confidence how the sales department contributes to the organization's profits." Notice how this fits the business-problem model: there is a deviation from the expected norm of being able to determine the profitability of an activity. What should be the next step?

A process of functional decomposition is begun in which the business problem is examined, and a limited number of questions asked, the answers to which either would remove the deviation or change the norm. In the case of the sales manager, these questions might be:

1.   What current and future income will be realized from sales?
2.   What sales incentives and commissions have staff members received?
3.   How can the income value of existing sales be maximized?

This step can be taken through one more iteration by decomposing each of the questions into a series of smaller questions that are easier to answer. For example, question 3 might lead to the following questions:

3a.   What customers should be called on to ensure that their business is retained?
3b.   What additional products or services can be sold to existing customers?
3c.   What are the characteristics of the company's customers?
3d.   Where can more people like the current customers be found?

This process can be continued through many layers of questions until a set of questions is reached that can be considered "answerable"; that is, can be expressed in terms of the data required to obtain an answer. This leads to the next step in the methodology.

Step 3: Data Design/Process Design

Once the system needs have been expressed as a series of answerable questions, it should be possible to develop a data-base model as discussed in Chapter 5. The process design discussed earlier in this chapter also can be developed on the basis of these questions. Each question implies the data needed and the process required to transform that data into information.

It is important to note that at this stage of the prototyping methodology, not a single line of code has been written. Even though every data-processing instinct is crying out to do something, the temptation to do so must be resisted until the proper groundwork has been laid.

As pointed out earlier, prototyping does not absolve the system developer of the responsibility to do good design. Even more important, since good design is done iteratively, the developer must be prevented from investing too much time in one attempt, but rather to discard that attempt if it does not appear feasible and try another. Paper-and-pencil designs, written business problems, and lists of questions are far more disposable than code. Only after the problem has been defined, the preliminary data structure delineated, and the process made clear can an effective prototype be developed.

Step 4: "First Cut" Coding

The basic philosophical premise of prototyping is that once the data and process are defined, the code itself is almost a trivial matter. In many cases, a code generator can be employed to create an initial version of the application; in other cases, the initial version is created by cloning shell programs and filling in the appropriate places. What should the goal of the first version be?

Since the code is likely to change after the user sees the first attempt, only minimal efforts should be invested in data validation. Each organization should set up clear guidelines that identify the appropriate level of data validation for this first attempt (e.g., the only validation in the first version of the prototype is to ensure that numeric fields contain only numerals). These clear rules are designed to make sure that the developer does not waste time on unproductive coding and that the user understands the "roughness" level of the prototype.

In this initial phase, a developer may be able to take advantage of a number of commercial products that actually generate code based on the data-base definitions. These applications generators may provide an effective shortcut to the first-cut code, if they meet the following conditions:

1. *Creates Modifiable Source Code.* The best role for the application generator is to create a code base for subsequent iterations. If the code generator does not generate modifiable source code, the developers will be severely handicapped.

2. *Can Match Process Design.* The process design sets up the common appearance and dialogue for the system. If the application generator cannot support the process design of the system, it will create more work than it saves.

3. *Have an Acceptable Internal Structure.* The generated code must be arranged in a structure that matches the organization's standards.

The logic flow, the coding structures, and the naming conventions should conform with generally accepted practices for clarity and maintainability. If an application generator fails to meet any of these criteria, it is likely to be a source of frustration and additional work. However, if it follows these general rules, a generator may provide a simple method to move quickly from design to the first iteration.

One of the real problems of a prototyping approach is that a user's first, and probably lasting, impression of the system is based on the initial version. Therefore, potential users' impressions and expectations must be carefully managed. This can be done in two ways.

First, the initial screen of the system should prominently display the phrase "PROTOTYPE—DEMO VERSION." Software developers have taken this approach for years, labeling prerelease versions as "beta test" or "demo version." The simple phrase identifies to a user that the product is not finished, and at least starts to manage the user's expectations. This labeling also has a second purpose that will be discussed later.

Second, the developer, not the user, should operate the initial versions of the system. The system is not "bulletproof" enough to let a user take control. The developer should offer guided tours, noting the comments of users regarding functionality and aesthetics. Direct user access comes only after the results of these user review sessions have been incorporated into the system along with a few more data element edits.

Step 5: Coding Iterations

After the initial version has been reviewed by users, the iterative prototyping process begins in earnest. In each iteration, the goal of the system designer is to:

1. Modify the system to resolve open issues from the last review cycle.
2. Increase the data validation checking as the process becomes more solid. No attempt should be made to add all validations in the second iteration; instead, they should be delayed until a particular screen and process have become fairly well defined.

After each coding iteration, a user review session needs to be held. With each successive iteration, the user can begin to take more responsibility for the direct operation of the system. At each session, the developer must listen to the needs expressed by the user and identify changes that need to be made to solve business problems. Figure 6-5 summarizes the differences between the first and subsequent iterations.

As the process runs through its iterations, the developer needs to avoid a cardinal sin of prototyping: invested ego preventing intellectual honesty in

---

FIGURE 6-5 Iteration Differences

ITERATION 1

Characteristics
- Data design stable
- Process design stable
- Few or no validations in system

Purpose
- Check basic functionality
- Check dialogue flow
- Check aesthetics, usefulness of process design

ITERATION 2—n

Characteristics
- Validations added for stable portions of dialogue
- Increased "buttetproofing"
- Previous iterations shortcomings resolved

Purpose
- Review functionality
- Ensure ability to meet business needs
- Provide foundation for integration into business operations

---

problem evaluation. With each iteration, more of the developer's ego is invested in the system. The developer is tempted to ignore or gloss over new business problems rather than change the system. Revisions become more difficult with each iteration because the developer can't bear the thought of changing the code again. If the iterative process is to achieve maximum effectiveness, all parties must subscribe to almost painful honesty until all of the business needs have been identified and met.

The last sentence is the key to avoiding an endless loop. Unless there is a clearly labeled stopping point for these coding iterations, the process will continue *ad infinitum, ad nauseum.* The stopping point is actually quite simple to recognize; the process is stopped when the system is able to answer the business questions identified in the first step. (Alternatively, the process may also stop if it is determined that the problem will never be solved or that the solution is not worth additional time or effort.) The list of business questions may also change in the course of the project, but management approval of these changes is required. The point of control for a prototyping project is not dictated by the amount of code, the number of hours, or the number of people involved. Prototyping controls the scope of the process by controlling the business questions that are to be answered.

Step 6: The Final Version

After the final iteration when it seems that all the business questions can be answered, there is a temptation to declare the project complete. However, it is not quite time to break out the champagne. Until the prototype has gone through a lengthy operational testing period, only after which can it be considered the "final" version.

How is such testing carried out? It is not sufficient to force-feed data into the system to see if something breaks. Testing must identify the right set of data needed to exercise every piece of code in the system, predict the results, and then compare the expected results with the actual results. Anything less is not testing; it is playing around. For prototyping, testing means two things. First, a set of test data must be developed to make sure that every section of code—every IF clause, every validation, every piece of logic—is tried to see whether the anticipated results emerge. Actually, this approach should have been employed at each iteration in the process, without waiting until the final version to start testing.

If the procedure has been followed carefully, then the final version will meet the business needs according to expectations. The next test, then, is to "pretend" that the system was actually in production. This test is known as the parallel test.

A parallel test requires significant commitment from the user area. It requires that the normal activities of the department proceed as usual *and* that the system be run as if it were actually in production. This might mean a double work load for the department—processing business in the old way, and then performing whatever is necessary for the new system, as well. No wonder this step is so often neglected or glossed over.

The parallel test has three purposes (Figure 6-6): First, it identifies activities that the designers may not have considered. The "once a month" transaction that everybody forgot will show up on the parallel test. Second, it measures a system's ability to handle the volume of requests. By paralleling the daily activities, it may be possible to identify places where a system's performance can be refined. Third, the parallel test can provide the basis for user documentation.

No matter how dedicated the effort, system documentation never seems to meet the need. Operators read it once and then put it on the shelf. As they continue to use the system, however, they tend to create their own documentation. Those yellow sheets of paper with notes about system operations that can be found taped to the sides of the terminals or stowed in desk drawers at any work station are the real system manuals. Unlike the formal instructions in the books on the shelves, such notes are written from a user perspective, identifying what the user finds difficult and what is considered trivial. At the end of the parallel testing period, these hand-written notes—which represent the single most effective source of information on how to use the system—should be gathered up and utilized to create or modify the documentation.

FIGURE 6-6 Parallel Testing Purposes

COMPLETENESS
- Have all transaction types been tested?
- Can the system solve unanticipated problems?
- Does the system blend well into the daily activities?

STRESS TESTING
- Are there key times in the day that performance degrades? Why?
- Are there conflicts when two operators try to update the same record?
- Are the response times and batch-processing times meeting expectations? Why?

USER DOCUMENTATION
- Can the operators use documentation to handle new situations?
- What commands are found on "cheat sheets" that point out documentation weaknesses?
- What "intuitively obvious" features aren't?

Step 7: The Production Version

After the "final" version has passed its parallel test (or if it has failed, has gone back into coding iterations until it does pass), it is time to move to the production version. The design team needs to be able to answer two basic questions:

1. Will the prototype version move intact into the production environment or will it need to be rewritten in a more efficient language or to use a better online access method?

2. Will the data gathered in the parallel test be used in production or will the system start from empty files?

In reality, these questions need to be discussed early in the prototyping process in order to better manage user expectations. If the user believes the prototype will move intact into a production state but the systems group plans to convert the 4GL code into COBOL, no one will leave the project with warm and fuzzy feelings toward each other. The ground rules for moving the system from testing into production must be a topic of discussion throughout the project.

What actually is the difference between "test" and "production" systems? Figure 6-7 presents the characteristics of each. Notice how the nature of a system changes as it moves from test into production. In making this transition, it ceases to be a project and becomes an asset of the organization. It is critical to understand that unless the transition from prototype to production system is clear, the conflicting expectations will destroy the potential of the approach.

FIGURE 6-7   Test vs. Production Systems

	TEST SYSTEMS	PRODUCTION SYSTEMS
DATA PROTECTION	Data, by definition, is test data. Backup and recovery are only to prevent lengthy reentry to resume testing in case of problems.	Data represents real business events and activities. Data must always be recoverable in the event of problems. Backup up and recovery procedures are critical.
CODE CHANGES	Code changes are made frequently, often by a number of individuals. Any controls on the change process are only to prevent simultaneous conflicting changes.	Code changes must be controlled to ensure system stability. Changes must be authorized, and must provide for the capability to restore the previous version of the code if necessary.
DATA ACCESS	Since data does not represent actual business relationships, data security is not a concern. However, once system moves into parallel test, data may be sensitive and require additional safeguards.	Data has become a corporate asset, representing information about the nature of the business. Access to the data must be controlled using the stewardship principles discussed in Chapter 8.
CODE PROTECTION	The code is under constant change and must be backed up to protect the investment in development.	The code has become an integrated part of the business activity. It must be backed up and protected to ensure the business functions can be performed.

Final Step—Killing Off the Prototype

The producers of soap operas often face the dilemma of how to manage the expectations of their viewers when an actor quits or is fired. They usually adopt a simple solution—they adjust the plot so that the character can be killed off. The audience knows the actor is now permanently off the show and can adjust its expectations accordingly.

Similarly, if the transition from test to production is to become reality, the prototyping team must "kill off" the prototype. There must be a definitive date when the label "PROTOTYPE—DEMO VERSION" is removed and all of the ground rules of production systems apply. Much like

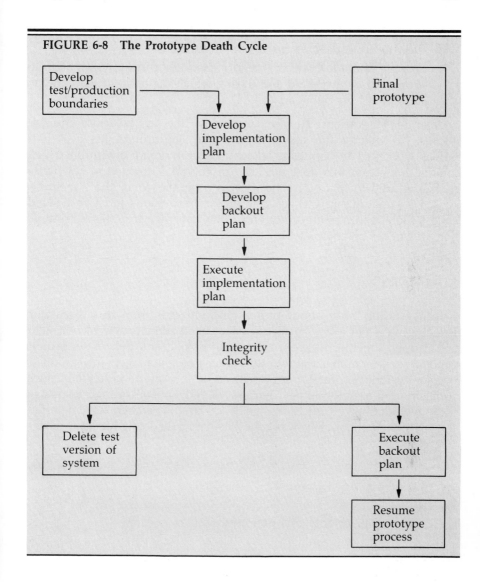

FIGURE 6-8 The Prototype Death Cycle

the process of killing off the character in the soap opera, everybody involved needs to be aware of the death of the prototype so that they can adjust their expectations accordingly. A sample system "death cycle" is illustrated in Figure 6-8; it includes the following key elements:

1. Clearly defined boundaries between test and production systems. Figure 6-7 illustrated some of differences those boundaries must protect.

2. A carefully prepared transition plan that outlines how data is to move from test to production versions, what system changes will be required in the move, and who will be responsible for each change.

3. A written backout plan, detailing the steps to be taken if the transition to production status is not successful.

4. A well-defined period of integrity checking, during which all functions will be inspected and during which the backout plan may be invoked if problems arise.

Coleridge's "Ancient Mariner" accidently killed an albatross and was doomed to wander the seas with the bird tied around his neck as a punishment. Just the opposite is true in a prototyping environment. An information center that does not kill a prototype is doomed to having the system around for eternity. The process is simple—once the system has passed its final integrity check, the prototype versions must be deleted. Unless there is that point of no return, the transition from test to production will never be complete.

SUMMARY

One overriding truth about prototyping emerges from this discussion: Prototyping is not a free-spirited, uncontrolled process by which systems are slapped together to see if they will work. It is a deliberate, rational process in which uncertainty, through careful management, gradually becomes certainty. Prototyping insists on design, attention to the business problem, and a methodology that moves deliberately through test stages into a well-defined production stage. It is a carefully crafted set of iterations that will deliver not only what the business asked for, but also what it needs.

SUGGESTED PROJECTS

1. Defend or oppose this premise:

    It is appropriate to use prototyping for all systems development projects.

    Cite examples to support your position. Provide any guidelines or policy statements that might be necessary.

2. The text (especially Figure 6-7) states that there is a significant difference between *test* and *production* systems. How does this principle apply to the activities of an information center? What policies or procedures would be needed to apply this principle? Be sure to discuss the implications for 4GL queries, spreadsheets, and other ad-hoc user-oriented products.

CHAPTER 7

Stewardship and an Information Center

Any organization that is characterized by a reasonable degree of automation has an automated general ledger system that performs the organization's accounting functions. *Question:* Who actually owns that system? Possible answers are (1) the accounting department, (2) the MIS department, or (3) none of the above.

Before choosing an answer, consider the implications of each. In the accounting department, the general ledger is "fed" from a host of other departments, including personnel, payroll, manufacturing, inventory, and sales. If the accounting department is considered to own the system and it refuses to provide any information from the general ledger to any of the other departments, it has the right to do so. After all, it owns the system and can furnish or deny information as it sees fit. Yet isn't there something about this behavior that doesn't seem fair?

If the system is considered to be owned by the MIS department, then the following scenario might be typical: Although there is an overwhelming demand for a new set of reports from the general ledger, the MIS group has a three-year backlog of work requests. The staff chooses to focus its efforts on setting up a new integrated manufacturing system, and so assigns a junior staff member to start to develop the report package in his spare time. As the owner of the system, the MIS department has the right to assign its staff to projects as it sees fit, but once again, it somehow doesn't seem right.

What these examples show is that "ownership" of information systems is a very slippery concept. No matter how one tries to define it, there always seems to be the potential for an arbitrary decision that runs counter to the needs of the organization. Selecting either the first or second answer seems to lead to possibly absurd results, leaving the conclusion that "none of the above" must be the correct answer.

A guiding premise for this chapter then might be: ownership of information-processing resources never rests at the departmental level; those resources are always considered to be owned by the entire corporation. This approach has been popularized by the slogan, "Data is a corporate resource." By itself, however, that slogan is not sufficient for establishing responsibility for the information resources of the organization. One more concept is required—stewardship.

STEWARDSHIP: A DEFINITION

In ancient societies, wealthy people assigned a servant to be steward of their property. The steward's role was a simple one—to protect the master's assets, to promote the growth of those assets, and to be sure that the assets were used in the master's best interests.

FIGURE 7-1   Stewardship Definition

DEFINITION
   The information assets of a corporation are always to be considered
   corporate assets. However, the organization will **appoint,** either by
   explicit direction or by unspoken expectations, various distinct
   individuals (stewards) to protect those assets and to ensure they are
   used in the **best interests of the entire organization.**

Corporate Asset
   • All computers (including personal computers) are corporate assets
   • May be paid for by department
   • May reside in department

Appointed Stewards
   • Appointed explicitly or implicitly
   • Clearly established lines of authority

Best Interest of Organization
   • Localized authority but corporate viewpoint
   • Responsible to corporation, not department
   • Corporate, not parochial viewpoint

Applying this concept to an information environment produces the
following guiding principle (summarized in Figure 7-1):

*The information assets of a corporation are always to be considered as corporate
assets. However, the organization will appoint, either by explicit direction or by
unspoken expectations, various distinct individuals (stewards) to protect those
assets and to ensure they are used in the best interests of the entire organization.*

Information Assets as Corporate Assets

That all information assets are corporate assets is a fundamental statement
of direction that has profound implications for a corporation. Personal
computers, departmental computers, and the mainframe computers and
the systems that run on them are to be considered corporate assets. The
funds to purchase these systems may come from the budget of an individual department, the applications may be dedicated to the functions of
a particular department, and all of the activities of that system may relate
only to one department, but the resources are still to be considered corporate, not departmental.

This is not just philosophical semantics. No information system is purely
local. Even the simplest and most direct system may have components that

eventually may be required by another part of the organization. Unless it is clear that any system is to be considered a corporate system, the organization will be doomed to redundant, conflicting data that is viewed as the private property of a specific department. If the organization is to have a successful comprehensive information system, corporate ownership is a necessity.

Appointment of Stewards

Simply considering the information resources of the organization as corporate resources is not sufficient because the lines of accountability are too ill-defined. If the data in a particular system is incorrect, who is going to accept the responsibility for correcting the system? Saying it is a corporate problem will not motivate anyone to set the system right. It is only when responsibility for each component of the information environment is clearly defined that the integrity of the information resource is secure.

In many cases, this responsibility is not explicitly delegated but is assumed according to the nature of the structure. For example, in most organizations, the accounting department takes responsibility for the contents of the general ledger system, and the data-processing-operations department by definition is responsible for caring for the tape library. These are both fairly straightforward illustrations of how everyone in the organization understands a particular department's role in protecting a portion of the information resource. These are the "unspoken expectations" of the definition.

Other responsibilities are not as clear, however. Who is to authorize access to a particular file for information center reporting? Should it be the user area, the MIS department, the information center, or the data security department? The concept of stewardship requires that the lines of responsibility be clearly established.

In the Corporation's Best Interests

Unless the definition of stewardship includes the clause "used in the best interests of the corporation," an organization quickly moves from the position that "data is a corporate resource" to "data is a corporate weapon." Meetings can quickly degenerate into arguments over "my numbers" versus "your numbers".

Simply put, this clause means that although each designated steward has responsibility for what appears to be a fairly localized portion of the information resource, the steward must always understand that any resource is always to be seen from a corporate perspective. A parochial view of data such as traditional user ownership will not do (see Figure

FIGURE 7-2 User Stewardship vs. User Ownership	
USER STEWARDSHIP	USER OWNERSHIP
Corporation owns all resources.	User department owns its respective resources.
Each resource is assigned to a specific user.	Each resource is assigned to the department that owns it.
Access and use based on corporate self-interest.	Access and use based on parochial self-interest.
Access and use based on business decisions. Decisions can be appealed through normal "chain of command" procedures.	Access and use can be selfish and arbitrary. No appeal possible since user *owns* resource.

7-2). How, then, does stewardship work in the various parts of an organization?

THE REALMS OF DATA

The lifeblood of an information center is data. It is, almost by definition, the starting point for all of the 4GL reports, spreadsheet analyses, and ad-hoc projects with which an information center becomes involved. But whose data is it?

According to the principle of stewardship, data is a corporate resource—it does not belong to the information center, the MIS department, or the user area; it belongs to the corporation. The organization, then, must appoint someone to serve as steward of that data to protect it, to ensure its integrity, and to make sure that it is used wisely in the best interests of the corporation. In particular, the roles of a data steward are as follows:

1. *Access Control.* The steward is to be the ultimate authority in determining who is to have access to the system's data. This access is not just limited to reports using a fourth-generation language, but also includes determining who is to be granted the privilege of reading the data online, who is to be able to create transactions in the system, and who is to receive the production reports from the system. The steward is to grant access by balancing the responsibility to the corporation to protect the data with the responsibility to ensure that the data is used in the best interests of the corporation.

2. *Integrity Assurance.* The steward is to ensure that the data itself is correct. This does not mean that the steward is to personally

supervise each data-entry operator, checking each change to the system. Instead, the steward must determine that the process is sufficiently well controlled to prevent erroneous data from being entered, and so must take a very active role in the implementation of any software change, lest the change affect the integrity of the data. In this role, as well, the data steward must periodically examine the contents of the system to see that old information has been purged correctly and that internal references are consistent (e.g., that the customer numbers in the invoice file reflect numbers of actual records in the customer data base).

3. *Continuity Assurance.* Since the data is an integral part of the daily functions of the corporation, the data steward must make sure that the flow of data is uninterrupted. In most systems, this means that the data steward must see that adequate backup procedures are in place and are being executed. Simply making backup copies periodically usually will not fulfill this responsibility since the data changes rapidly (e.g., data collected from an automated teller machine). In those cases, the steward must also ensure that a copy of each transaction is made as it is applied to the data so that an up-to-the-minute copy can always be reconstructed using the back-up and all of the applied transactions.

These roles are summarized in Figure 7-3.

Some of the foregoing activities (such as backup and access to data), of course, have been data-processing activities for years. The point here is, however, that they are *not* data-processing activities, but stewardship activities carried out on behalf of the corporation. Although the data-processing group may have traditionally assumed these roles, it has been as an implied steward rather than by inherent right. If an organization chooses to appoint a different steward (for example, placing data security

---

FIGURE 7-3   Data Stewardship

GOAL	POSSIBLE STEWARDSHIP ACTIVITIES
Assure integrity	Approve all changes to application systems that affect data.
	Check file contents for accuracy and consistency.
Assure continuity	Monitor backup procedures.
	Monitor transaction-recovery procedures.
Access control	Authorize (or deny) information center use of data.
	Review authorization rules on monthly basis.
	Monitor use of downloaded data.

decisions into the hands of the user), the data-processing group must take care to avoid resentment over the "loss" of one of its functions. Once in place, this concept of stewardship has the potential to alter dramatically an organization's existing power structure.

The question now is, how can these principles of data stewardship be applied to the common problems facing an information center?

Controlling Data Access

One of the oldest problems that an information center faces is how to determine who should be allowed to access a given data base. It is a problem only because it is a decision that an information center should not be making. Access to the data is the responsibility of a steward, not of an information center.

For example, the staff assistant to one of the executive vice-presidents of an organization wants to use the fourth-generation language to read the corporate budget files and the general ledger files in order to create reports that will help manage the budget process. If the information center considers itself the arbiter of access, it must evaluate whether this request is reasonable and justified. Unfortunately, it has no means of accurately making this determination and it is forced to make its decision somewhat arbitrarily. If the access decision is to be made intelligently, it must be made by the steward, who is better equipped to evaluate the request. It is the steward who understands the system and the business requirements.

Suppose the manager of the finance department has been designated steward of the budget and general ledger systems and approves access for the staff assistant. It then becomes the role of the information center to implement that access permission and to help the staff assistant get the correct information. If the manager of finance denies permission, the information center must so advise the staff assistant and then step out of the decision process. To try further to gain access, the staff assistant must go back to the vice-president and to the manager of the finance department and work with them until an agreement is reached.

The value of this approach is that the decision to allow access is not a technical decision, but a business decision. By letting the steward decide who has access, the decision is made on the basis of the business case. Similarly, the appeal is handled in a fashion similar to that of any other business decision: the respective management structures attempt to make their case objectively (or, in some organizations, subjectively). Only after the access decision is made by the parties directly involved in the business aspects should the information center actually implement the decision.

The granting or revoking of access, in turn, assumes the existence of a data security system that will prevent unauthorized parties from looking at the data. This security system must minimally control data at the file level (a user may either see the general ledger file or not), but ought to include

FIGURE 7-4   Sample Data Stewardship Policy

POLICY:	Access to Data Policy Number: DA-0029
PURPOSE:	To define the responsibilities for the secure and effective access to data.
RELATED POLICIES:	DA-0021 Data stewards
POLICY STATEMENT:	Each appointed data steward (see policy DA-0021) shall be responsible to grant or deny access to data according to the following guidelines:

- Data access cannot be denied solely on the basis of the requestor's department, job title, or rank. These factors may be considered in the decision, but cannot be the sole reason for denial.
- Data access is to be granted only to solve business problems. The steward may withhold approval until the requestor has demonstrated the need for the data.
- Security of the data is paramount. If the data is of a confidential nature or if disclosure of the data might result in legal action, the steward has the responsibility to ensure that the requestor will be capable of maintaining the security of the data once access is granted. Access may be denied for insufficient security.
- The decision of the steward is final. However, the requestor may appeal the decision by meeting with the steward and appropriate management in an effort to present the business case that justifies access. However, if after these meetings the steward believes that access is not consistent with his/her responsibilities, the decision to deny access will stand.

the capability for record-level or field-level security as well (access to the general ledger file is permitted but the user may only see certain cost-center records). Without such a system, maintaining ignorance is the only means by which a steward can fulfill the responsibility to protect the data. (See Figure 7-4 for a sample policy that supports this approach.)

Production Data vs. Extract Data

In the early days of information centers, no access was allowed to production data. Copies of the production files were made periodically and all information center activities centered around the copies of the files. This ground rule fulfilled all of the requirements for good data stewardship (particularly in isolating the production data from the more unpredictable information center processing), but at the cost of significantly increased disk storage and the additional operational overhead required actually to make the copies.

The principles of data stewardship in action can be illustrated by another policy (Figure 7-5) that could serve as well. Under this policy, any data that is stored on tape would not be available for information center users, unless a disk copy of the tape were made. This rule is not necessarily based on any of the stewardship principles, but is based instead on respect for the changes in operational work load that demand reporting would bring if tape files were allowed. This policy also would not allow information

---

FIGURE 7-5   Sample Data-Use Policy

POLICY:	Data Sharing Policy Number: DA-0037
PURPOSE:	To define the policies that govern the sharing of data between operational systems and end user computing.
RELATED POLICIES:	DA-0010 Data migration DA-0029 Access to data
POLICY STATEMENT:	A given data base or file may be used by both the online network and end-user computing subject to the following rules:

- All access to the data, either by the online network or through end-user computing, will be done only with the approval of the appointed steward (see policy DA-0029) and governed by the corparate data security software.
- Any file or data base not allocated to the online network may be used directly for end-user computing purposes. Copies of these files and data base are not to be made unless the structure of the data is such that end-user access becomes highly complex.
- Any file or data base stored on tape cannot be directly assessed by end-user computing. These files are to be copied to disk for a limited time only and with the special consent of the designated steward.
- Any file or data base allocated to the online network is not to be used for end-user computing. These files are to be copied to disk periodically with the special consent of the designated steward.
- When tapes or online files are copied for end user computing, the stewardship responsibility for the resulting files remains with the original steward. (see policy DA-0018).

center access to any file used in online processing. Copies of those files would be created periodically for information center users. This approach is mandated by both the integrity- and continuity-assurance principles since the steward should not permit any behavior that might adversely affect the online portion of the system. Finally, as long as access rules can be enforced with sufficient vigor, direct access to the production versions of all other files should be allowed.

This approach meets the guidelines for good data stewardship in that the data is protected because access is permitted only with sufficiently vigorous security software and so the production data is secure from inadvertent changes or deletions. Moreover, data integrity is actually enhanced by this approach. Each extract provides one more place in the operations where errors can be introduced. By permitting direct access to the production files under controlled conditions, the same source of the data is utilized for both production and ad-hoc reports. Finally, the continuity value of the data is also enhanced. If the production data needs to be recreated for some reason (processing errors, hardware failure), no additional steps are required to make certain that the extract data is also recreated. The information center data is at least as up-to-date as the production data.

Every organization needs to determine which files need to have extracts created and which can allow direct access. This decision, however, should be based on the principles of stewardship, not on blind obedience to tradition.

Data Migration

One of the more interesting developments of the information center era is the easy migration of data from one computer system to another. *Downloading* is the process by which data moves from a larger computer to a smaller computer; *uploading* moves data from the smaller computer to the larger one. Either process may involve corporate, departmental, or personal computers. (Data migration will be described more fully in Chapter 8, with the present discussion focusing on its data stewardship aspect.

The guiding principle of data migration can be described as follows: the permission to read data automatically implies the permission to download data; the permission to update a file automatically implies permission to upload data. If a user is able to display data from a file on a screen (READ access), then software may be purchased or built to capture that screen image and save it to a file. If that same user is able to use online screens or an editor to update a file, software can be purchased or built to emulate the keystrokes that would have been used to update the file manually. Data migration becomes a very real problem once any access to data is permitted.

Who, then, is to be the steward of downloaded data? Since the guiding principle of data migration implies that sooner or later someone with READ access will download data, an organization needs to develop very explicit rules regarding its stewardship. There appear to be two options: stewardship of downloaded data is the responsibility of the original steward, or the individual who performs the download is the steward of the newly created file. The first option is virtually impossible to implement since the guiding principle says that data could easily be downloaded without the knowledge and approval of the original steward, and the only way a steward could fulfil the responsibility to protect that data after it was downloaded would be to deny everyone access.

The second option makes more sense. An organization's established policy should be that once data is downloaded, the stewardship responsibilities for that data fall on the person who downloaded it. In addition to the stewardship responsibilities that any data impose, stewards of downloaded data must also play another role: they must protect the data as the initial steward would protect it. If the source data is not to be accessible to a particular individual, then it is the new steward's responsibility also to keep the copy secure. The most prudent policy might be that if person *A* downloads data for a specific purpose, then that downloaded data should only be by *A* for that purpose, then destroyed. If person *B* wants that data also, they must download their own copy. This is clearly the most restrictive policy. In any event, corporate policies must be very clear: the consequences of any data security violation regarding the downloaded data will fall on the downloader.

This suggested data-migration policy (Figure 7-6) has one other implication. In granting access to the data, the steward of the source data must also consider the risks that possible downloading may create. Does the person to whom access is being granted understand the stewardship rules of data migration? Can that person be trusted to abide by those rules? An information center's role in this decision is purely advisory. It may confirm that the intended user has been educated in the responsibilities of stewardship, or it may advise that the intended user has not sufficiently demonstrated responsibility with data use. The final decision, however, remains that of the steward, not of the information center (see Figure 7-4).

THE REALMS OF SOFTWARE

The software component of the information environment is another area in which the concept of stewardship applies. Two of the important factors here are test/production border and the need for stability in the underlying tool kit.

FIGURE 7-6   Sample Data-Migration Policy

POLICY:	Data Migration Policy Number DA-0018
PURPOSE:	To define the responsibilities for data as it is copied.
RELATED POLICIES:	DA-0021 Data stewards DA-0037 Data sharing PR-0030 Termination offences
POLICY STATEMENT:	Data copied from its original source is still considered a corporate resource. Stewardship responsibility for the extract file will be assigned according to the following policy:

- Copies of data made under the data sharing policy (DA-0037) will retain their original steward.
- For all other copies of data, stewardship for that data will become the responsibility of the copier.
- The steward of the copy of the data is not allowed to grant any other individual access to the downloaded data without the explicit permission of the original steward. Copied data is to be used only by the individual who copied it.
- Violation of this policy will be considered a serious offense under the termination policy (PR-0030).

The Test/Production Border

One of the driving forces behind the end-user computing rebellion was a frustration with the bureaucracy of the traditional systems development procedures. There always seemed to be a mountain of paperwork that needed to be signed, software changes that could only go into effect on certain days, and a tremendous amount of coordination required among the development group, the computer operations group, and a host of other departments. This frustration gave rise to the apparently more responsive end-user computing approach. No one ever asked for a change control approval form when a user changed a spreadsheet.

Unfortunately, very few people ever questioned why all those procedures were there in the first place. The reasons for this apparently meaningless bureaucratic rigamarole have a direct bearing on the issues of software stewardship in an information center.

In the very early days of computing, none of these rules were in place. A programmer made changes as needed, usually at the verbal request of a manager, and usually without any regard for documentation. Those early days of data processing bore a strong resemblance to the wild and wooly era of the old West: the fastest draw was the biggest hero and the ability to live by one's wits was the most critical survival skill.

However, as data processing became an increasingly more important part of how an organization carried on its business, a new value system began creeping onto the scene. Dependability became more important than responsiveness. Unless a system performed the same today as it did yesterday, the business had no stable basis for its operations. Change was still important, but it was not to be allowed at the price of destabilizing ongoing operations.

The bureaucracy, then, was put into place to ensure the stability of the software components of the traditional systems. An organization designated a steward (usually a change control department) to patrol the border between test and production. This steward was to exercise the responsibility to protect existing assets by preventing uncontrolled change from destabilizing the software environment and to exercise the responsibility to the interests of the organization by allowing changes required to improve the quality and functionality of the software assets. This steward had to balance two conflicting forces, stability and change, and choose the best path for the overall organization (Figure 7-7).

The instigators of the end-user computing revolution are only beginning now to learn this lesson. As the spreadsheets and the ad-hoc reports become an ever-more-important part of the decision process of business, the same forces are at work. Change is an important component of successful end-user computing, but so is stability.

FIGURE 7-7   Software Stewardship

GOAL	POSSIBLE STEWARDSHIP ACTIVITIES
Enforce test/production border	Develop strict change control procedures.
	Monitor systems use for "test" systems used in "production" role.
	Ensure all applications are protected from inadvertent change or loss.
Provide stable tools	Implement change control procedures for all new releases of tools.
	Develop acceptance plan to test each new release of software tools.
	Ensure current system image is backed-up (not just original code plus "fixes" applied).

Chapter 6 highlighted the need for a clear border when developing prototype systems (see Figure 6-7). When dealing with end-user-developed systems, an information center must also carefully define the border between test and production. A production system might be defined as any spreadsheet, graph, ad-hoc report, or other system that is used by more than one individual or is used more than once is a production system. Although that definition might sound overly restrictive, it is important to look more closely at the needs. For example, once the system is removed from its creator, it also is removed from the best source of error detection. The creator understands what the software is supposed to do and the assumptions that are inherent in the spreadsheet, 4GL request, and so on. Any changes to the product by someone other than the creator may not fully integrate the assumptions or interactions among elements of the system. Once a piece of software leaves the hands of the creator, the potential for disaster multiplies. A "production" status may offer some protection against that disaster.

Similarly, the definition also calls for production status if the system is used more than one time. This is important because each iteration that uses the software implies an additional degree of confidence. If a spreadsheet has demonstrated correct results for two attempts, confidence tends to be high that the results of the third attempt will also be correct. This confidence may prove to be misplaced unless the software is protected from changes. Also, each iteration indicates that the software is fulfilling an ongoing business function and represents an asset to the organization. That asset needs to be protected for the business's own good. Thus, while the definition of a production system is indeed restrictive, it is also vital. (See Figure 7-8 for a summary of this discussion.)

Accordingly, every production system must be assigned a steward, who has the following responsibilities:

1. *Backout Recovery.* Whenever changes are to be made to a production end-user system (spreadsheet, ad-hoc report, etc.), the current ver-

---

FIGURE 7-8 "Production" System Definition

DEFINITION
A *production* system is any collection of software and data that is used by **more than one individual** or used **more than one time.**

More than one individual
Once removed from its creator, the software acquires a life all its own without the assumptions and instincts of the creator to control it.

More than one time
Once a task becomes repetitive, its results become less likely to be challenged. If an error is not discovered the first time, the probability of detection drops with each execution.

sion must be saved. Changes are made to a copy, never to the original. In this way, if the changes are not successful, the previously running version is always available. Ideally, at least the two most recent production versions should be kept.

2. *Change Protection.* Changes must not be made in the production version without the explicit approval of the steward. This may require encryption techniques, software-protection schemes, or physical security measures such as locks and keys.

3. *Backup Protection.* A copy of the current production version must always be maintained, and kept at a physically different location than the original. This procedure is markedly different from backout protection. Backout ensures that the immediately previous version is available if the new version is faulty. Backup protection ensures that the current version can be restored intact.

Once again, an information center's role with regard to software stewardship is that (1) it must clearly state the stewardship responsibilities of each user in a straightforward, written format; (2) it must constantly reinforce these principles in all of its training and consulting activities; and (3) it must take a critical look at itself to identify its own software stewardship responsibilities.

Tool-Kit Stability

As the previous section illustrates, a well-defined border is essential to separate test from production in end-user-developed applications. An information center clearly can help to patrol this border by providing a production library for fourth-generation procedures that is protected and regularly backed up. In addition, it can carry out spot audits of key user areas to ascertain that they are fulfilling their responsibility as stewards. However, an information center also has direct stewardship responsibilities in the software realm. While the previous section concentrated on developing a border for applications developed by the end user, the same concepts apply to the software stewardship responsibilities that are related to protecting the components of the underlying tool kit, such as the 4GL software itself.

Nothing in the information-processing arena stays the same very long. There always seems to be a new version of the software to install—a product that is faster, better, and cheaper than the existing system—and whole new categories of software seem to spring up overnight. An information center has the responsibility to step into this chaos, meanwhile trying to keep order within its own tool kit.

The vendor of the fourth-generation language software, for example, is constantly improving its capabilities and performance and new releases of the software seem to appear every six to twelve months. If an information center is to be faithful in its role as the steward of its tool kit, it must recognize the responsibilities that these new releases confer.

First, it is the responsibility of an information center to implement new releases as expeditously as possible. The new features and "fixes" in the new release may be required to solve critical business problems. The stewardship role always involves serving the best interests of an organization.

However, an information center also has a stewardship responsibility to protect the assets of the organization. In this case, protection means that the new release is to be thoroughly tested. Does it perform as promised? Are all of the new features available? More importantly, do all of the previous features still work, or will the changes in the software adversely affect existing systems? An information center cannot allow a new release to be implemented until it has concluded that the existing investment in the 4GL procedures is protected.

Third, the information center must ensure that the previous version of the 4GL software will be available if the new version fails to perform correctly. When installing version 7.0, an information center must make certain that version 6.5 can be restored as the "official" version if problems arise.

Finally, an information center must ensure that the current production version of the 4GL software is backed up in case of problems. It is not sufficient to keep the tapes supplied by the vendor as these "fixes" are often designed to correct problems in the software discovered after the general release. The backup copies of the 4GL software must always reflect its current state.

THE RESOURCE REALMS

One of the biggest myths of the end-user computing revolution was that many of the tools were "resource hogs," consuming far more computer cycles and disk space than their traditional counterparts. To debunk this myth, this section focuses on the fourth-generation languages and what really needs to be done from a stewardship perspective.

In one respect, there is really no argument: end-user computing tools such as 4GLs use more computing resources than their traditional counterparts for a given execution. The 4GL usually needs to interpret a request first, whereas the traditional request was preinterpreted through a compile process. This interpretation step puts a 4GL at a decided disadvantage when considering a single execution.

Focusing on the resources used in single execution, however, is unfair. Once the entire process from inception to production is considered, a different picture begins to emerge.

Size is one factor. A traditionally developed program is likely to be ten or twenty times the size of a 4GL procedure. An entire 4GL report request may require just thirty lines of code whereas the equivalent COBOL program may easily take 300–600 lines. Thus, the traditional program will need ten to twenty times more resources for entry and editing, as well as ten to twenty times the disk space to store it.

The process of debugging the code provides another point for comparison. The 4GL procedure has only thirty lines of code in which to make an error and is very forgiving about language syntax. The traditional program has many more places to make errors and the potential for many more errors because of the more rigorous syntax of the language and the nature of the compiler. As a result, the development process is likely to take ten to twenty times longer using traditional methods.

When viewed as a total resource, then, the implications are quite different. The 4GL may require thirty minutes of editing and three test attempts to be ready for production, whereas the traditional program could require days of editing, five compile attempts, and four tests! In reality, this means that the 4GL may actually use fewer total resources than the traditional program as development moves from initial concept to finished product. That is, although a 4GL procedure may use more of the computing resource for a single execution, it may actually use less overall. The 4GL exchanges the low, steady hum of the edit–compile–test cycles of traditional methods for the sharp spikes of a single execution. The 4GL doesn't necessarily use more resources; it uses those resources in a dramatically different manner.

In terms of stewardship, this means that organizations that try to limit the growth of their end-user computing tools because of resource constraints are approaching the problem from the wrong direction. The principles of stewardship do not prevent the use of assets, but only insist that they be used wisely. This is the key to resource stewardship in an information center: value must always be received from the resource used.

To provide that each value is received, an organization must designate a resource steward for each department (Figure 7-9). This person serves as an internal consultant to the department to advise the staff on the correct tool for a particular job. In trauma centers, such individuals are called "triage officers" (a concept discussed in Chapter 4). Their role is to separate the incoming injured into three categories: those who will die even with the best of treatment, those whose injuries are superficial and can wait for treatment, and those who require immediate treatment to save their lives. Similarly, the resource steward needs to look at each project to determine whether it fits into one of the following categories: those that are trivial and should not be automated at all, those that are best approached from a personal or departmental level, and those that are corporate in nature and require traditional development methodologies (Figure 7-10).

The resource steward, then, is the main point of contact with the traditional MIS department, and must set priorities and directions for the department's automation plan. The role of this steward is not to control

FIGURE 7-9   Resource Stewardship

GOAL	POSSIBLE STEWARDSHIP ACTIVITIES
Ensure correct tool is used.	Establish departmental triage officers.
	Produce guidelines for each tool to direct triage officers.
Ensure resource use has value.	Identify local resource stewards to monitor departmental and corporate activities.
	Monitor use of information center tools for anomalies.

technology, but to determine that the department and the entire organization receives value from the use of the computing resources.

An information center, in turn, has two key roles to play regarding a resource steward. First, if an organization does not have such a steward, it must take the political steps needed to get the position established. It need not be a full-time position, but can be added to the duties of an existing staff or line position. Then, once a resource steward has been clearly identified for each department, an information center must provide consulting support to help the stewards perform their function. A resource steward, with the help of an information center, can provide the best means for an organization to ensure that it is getting the best value from its computing resource.

FIGURE 7-10   The Triage Process for Resource Stewards

All incoming projects need to be divided into three categories:

- **Trivial**—Not really requiring any automation at all. No production (see Figure 7-9) applications will be needed.

- **Personal/Departmental**—Production systems (Figure 7-9) will be required, but can be developed at the personal or department level using spreadsheets, personal computers, fourth-generation languages, etc.

- **Corporate**—Because of significant transaction volume, complex processing, critical performance requirements, restrictive security requirements, or other reasons, the system is best developed at a corporate level using traditional methods.

SUMMARY

The fundamental tenet of this chapter is that an information resource belongs to an entire organization. However, an organization needs to appoint individual stewards to manage components of that resource in the best interests of the organization. These stewards are critical to the success of information centers. They make key decisions from a business, not technical, perspective. They assume responsibility for protecting the information assets of an organization. They lend a sense of stability to the environment. Finally, they afford an element of accountability that ensures that value is received whenever the computing resources are used. A successful information center uses stewardship to provide a controlled, yet responsive, end-user computing environment.

SUGGESTED PROJECT

Consider the following scenario:

The manager of the marketing department wants to use the employees in a very critical study of consumer behavior. She asks the information center to grant access to the employee information file. The information center forwards the request to the personnel manager (the designated steward of that file) for approval. The personnel manager denies permission, citing confidentiality as his reason. The marketing manager is informed of the denial and complains to the executive vice-president.

1. Analyze the scenario in terms of stewardship. Are the results consistent with the principle?
2. Predict the likely outcome. In your prediction, be sure to discuss how the results are (or are not) consistent with the principles of stewardship.

CHAPTER 8

Connectivity

One thing that can be said for the information-processing industry is that it has a marvellous ability to create new words to enrich the English language. One of these additions that arrived in the mid-1980s was *connectivity*. The appearance of this new word reflected a fundamental change in thinking about the online environment and the significant changes that were taking place in the data-processing world.

This chapter will examine the nature of the intermachine relationships and how those relationships affect an information center. However, it is not meant to be a complete description of the various networking protocols and architectures. The purpose is, rather, to provide a framework in which to consider the different ways to connect computers.

Thus, the chapter is divided into two parts. The first presents a model of connectivity technology that can be used to help understand the rapidly changing connectivity landscape. The second part focuses on the business issues that drive an information center to manage that connection.

CONNECTIVITY OVERVIEW

When looking at the issues of connectivity, the neophyte is quickly overwhelmed. There seems to be a bewildering array of "alphabet soup" terms (SNA, ISO, TCP/IP, among others) and an equally bewildering array of available options. Although there are a number of competing models and standards for connecting devices together, they all have one thing in common: the communication process is seen as a series of layers and a number of rules that define communication between those layers.

Communication between two devices should really be viewed as a series of transfers of a message down through the layers of one device, then across to the other device, where it is then transferred back up through the layers. For example, the OSI (Open Systems Interconnection) connectivity standard embraces a seven-layer approach, as seen in Figure 8-1. A different standard (such as IBM's SNA) may use completely different layers and rules to accomplish the same communication. However, rather than get into a highly technical discussion about competing standards, Figure 8-2 can be used as an idealized model to illustrate the concepts of a layered approach to connectivity. In this idealized approach, each of the layers in Figure 8-2 may correspond to a number of layers in the real standards (such as Figure 8-1) but the concepts will be equally applicable.

The Layered Approach

The layers in this simplified approach are fairly intuitive. The *physical* layer is responsible for managing the actual connection between the two machines. The *logical* layer is responsible for translating the electronic signals received at the physical layer into a logical message that can be

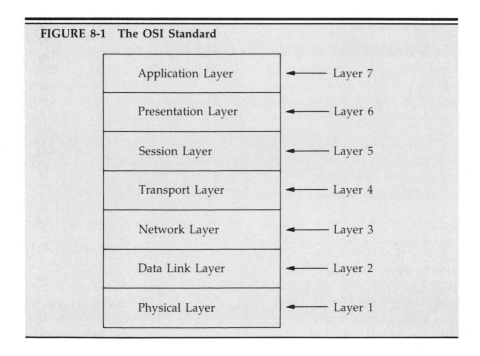

FIGURE 8-1   The OSI Standard

Application Layer	← Layer 7
Presentation Layer	← Layer 6
Session Layer	← Layer 5
Transport Layer	← Layer 4
Network Layer	← Layer 3
Data Link Layer	← Layer 2
Physical Layer	← Layer 1

acted upon, and the *local* layer is that portion of the system that performs the actual work.

The Local Layer. The activities of the local layer are directed toward the resources contained within the device. For example, the local layer in a simple terminal is that combination of hardware or software that manages the placement of the cursor, the display of characters or figures, and the

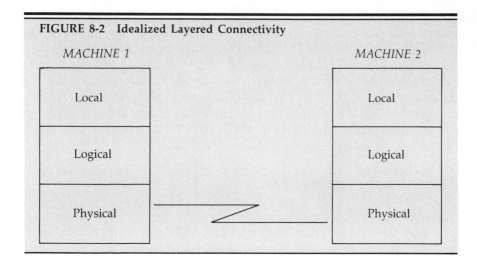

FIGURE 8-2   Idealized Layered Connectivity

MACHINE 1

| Local |
| Logical |
| Physical |

MACHINE 2

| Local |
| Logical |
| Physical |

collection of input from the keyboard or some other device. In a more intelligent device such as a personal computer, the local layer may also include software that can drive the printer or access local disk drives.

In this connectivity model, the role of the local layer is twofold: it may initiate a request to another connected device or it may respond to a request that has been received from a remote device. It fulfills both of these requests through interaction with the logical layer.

The Logical Layer. In the simplified connectivity model, the role of the logical layer is to translate between the needs of the physical layer and the needs of the local layer. For example, if one computer on a local area network (LAN) requests data from another computer, what actually happens is that the first computer's record request is passed to its respective logical layer. That layer rephrases the request into a proper message format according to the communications rules of that LAN and the message is then passed to the physical layer for actual transmission. When the transmission is received at the second computer's physical layer, the message is presented to the logical layer for action. The second computer's logical layer translates the request into a local request for action and passes it on to the local data-base server. When the record is retrieved, the desired record is translated into a message by the logical layer and returned by a similar mechanism.

For communication to succeed, however, the vocabularies of the logical layers of the two machines must match. The requests of the logical layer of the sending machine must be understandable by the logical layer of the receiving machine. This illustrates another important principle in connectivity—horizontal equivalence. If communication is to succeed, the functions at one level in one device must correspond with the functions at the same level in the second device.

The Physical Layer. The physical layer in this connectivity model is charged with managing the actual connection between the two devices. Its role is really very simple: to send and receive a series of electronic signals according to the rules of the network and the instructions of the logical layer. Once again, notice the need for horizontal equivalence. The transmission rules of the physical level of one device must match the reception rules of the physical level of the other. The physical levels have no need to be able to interpret the meaning of the message they are sending and receiving (that's the role of other layers), but they must treat that message according to a common set of rules.

Communication Among Levels

Among the benefits of considering connectivity from a layered approach is that each layer is concerned only with communication with the next layer. If machine 1 in Figure 8-2 is a mainframe, it can send a screen of data without being overly concerned about how it will be presented on the terminal (machine 2). The local application only needs to request its logical layer to send the data, trusting that when it gets to the terminal, the corresponding logical layer will know how to translate that data to the local layer for display. The mainframe is equally unconcerned about how the data is actually transmitted to the terminal. The connection between the two physical layers might be through a short (e.g., five-foot) cable, or it might be accomplished via a telephone modem over distances of thousands of miles. The management of that connection is carved out at the physical level and is of no concern to the application program.

Communication, then, is seen in two dimensions. The vertical communication passes a message from one layer to the next according to the identified rules. The idiosyncrasies of each layer are isolated from the transmission itself as the message moves up and down through the layers. The communication also has a horizontal component: the functions of a specific layer on one device must be equivalent to the functions of the corresponding layer in the remote device.

The principle of horizontal equivalence, however, does not require that the formats used in the logical layer of one device exactly match the formats used in the second. That would be contrary to the concept of layered communications. It only requires that they match functionally. It is perfectly acceptable for a message to say "ABC" when seen by one logical level and to say "0456" when seen by the other logical level. All that is required is that both logical levels understand the meaning of that request in the same way. The vocabulary must match in meaning, but not necessarily in format.

In reality, of course, there are many more than three layers. What is here called the logical layer may be composed of a number of different additional layers, each with its own role. The principle, however, remains the same: the process of communication between two or more computers is compartmentalized, with each layer providing a special service to the layer above and below it. The following examples, which are common to most information centers, illustrate how this approach works.

Example 1: Data Entry Screen on IBM Mainframes

Consider the FOCUS code fragment in Figure 8-3. The keyword CRTFORM tells the 4GL that a screen is to be sent and that a description of the screen follows. That description is expressed as a series of literals (e.g., "CUSTOMER NAME") and data fields (e.g., <CUST_NAME). This simple description represents the local layer in this transaction. When executed on the mainframe, FOCUS must translate this description into a string of data that includes not only the data values themselves, but also information about the position of each screen element, where data entry is to be allowed on the screen, and the identifier of terminal to which it is to be

---

FIGURE 8-3   A 4GL Data Screen

```
CRTFORM LINE 1
"                      ***** DATA ENTRY *****            "
" ⁄ "
"  CUSTOMER ID NUMBER: <CUST_ID   "
"   "
"  CUSTOMER NAME:       <CUST_NAME "
" " "
"  CUSTOMER ADDRESS:    <CUST_ADDR "
" " "
"  CITY  <CUST_CITY  STATE: <CUST_STATE  ZIP: <CUST_ZIP"
" " "


MATCH CUST_ID
ON MATCH......
```

---

sent. In this example, the process of translating the screen description into a stream of data represents the logical layer. This stream of data is then passed on to a portion of the operating system for actual transmission to the remote terminal (the physical layer).

Now consider a similar application using a more traditional approach, IBM's CICS online environment. In this version, the screen is defined using a series of commands (Figure 8-4). These commands are pre-processed and stored. When the program wishes to send the screen, it issues the command shown in Figure 8-5. Note how this local layer is dramatically different from the local layer in Figure 8-3. When the command is issued, CICS must use the preprocessed screen image to construct a data stream to send to the terminal. This data stream must also include positional and other control information. In fact, it will be identical to the data stream that was created by the logical layer in FOCUS. Thus, although the local levels in these two examples are radically different and the logical levels behave in completely different ways, the result that is passed to the physical layer is the same: a stream of data formatted with all of the information the screen needs.

Now consider the problem from the point of view of the terminal. A stream of data is received on a coaxial cable. This stream of data is passed to a circuit in the terminal that interprets the data stream into a series of positioning commands. Other processing circuits in the terminal then control the cursor as the operator enters data. This processing uses the control information in the data string to allow data to be entered in only certain locations on the screen.

FIGURE 8-4   CICS Screen Example

```
SAMPLE1   DFHMSD     TYPE=MAP,MODE=INOUT,CTRL=FREEKBD,        X
                     LANG=COBOL,TIOAPFX=YES
SAMPLE1M  DFHMDI     SIZE=(24,80)
          DFHMDF     POS=(1,20),LENGTH=22,ATTRB=ASKIP,        X
                     INITIAL='***** DATA ENTRY *****'
          DFHMDF     POS=(3,03),LENGTH=19,ATTRB=ASKIP         X
                     INITIAL='CUSTOMER ID NUMBER:'
CUSTID    DFHMDF     POS=(3,23),LENGTH=8,ATTRB=(NUM,BRT),     X
                     INITIAL='CUSTOMER ID NUMBER:'
```

The terminal behaves exactly the same for the FOCUS version of Figure 8-3 and the CICS version of Figures 8-4 and 8-5. As long as the data stream that it receives matches its expectations, it gathers and displays data regardless of which application sent the request. Notice how the principle of horizontal equivalence applies: The transmission on the mainframe side must be implemented according to the physical rules that the terminal expects. The message format that comes out of the logical layer of either application must correspond to the formats expected by the logical layer of the terminal. Finally, even the local layers are equivalent. The FOCUS and CICS commands both request the function "display screen." While the actual commands may take on a different format (CRTFORM vs. SEND MAP), they mean the same thing within their respective contexts. Furthermore, when received at the terminal, the screen is indeed displayed, just as the applications requested.

How can a personal computer be introduced into this process? First, the personal computer needs to be given the means to manage the physical connection to the coaxial cable. This can be done at a hardware level by designing an add-in board that has almost the same circuits as the terminal. Second, once the data stream is received by this board, the personal

---

FIGURE 8-5   Using CICS Screens

```
EXEC CICS
    SEND MAP    ('SAMPLE1M')
         MAPSET ('SAMPLE1')
         MAPONLY
         ERASE
END-EXEC.
```

computer must have some means to interpret the data stream into a series of commands to place characters in the appropriate positions on the screen and determine the characteristics of each. This logical level is easily handled by software. Finally, the personal computer must perform the actual entry of data, managing the cursor position and editing functions, just like the terminal. This local function is usually accomplished by terminal emulation software. As long as all levels performed according to the rules, the difference could never be detected. This type of communication is the basis for the popular IRMA card (DCA) and the IBM 3270 cards. The layers form the basis for communication through emulation.

Example 2: Upload/Download

One way to transmit data from one computer to another would be to add a new command to the local layers of each computer: "send file." If the first computer needs a file, it could transmit a "send file" request to the second computer. Recall from the previous example that the command may take a different format on each computer's local layer (much like "display screen" in the previous example). The logical layers on each machine must be capable of translating the local "send file" command to a common format and the physical layers must manage the actual transmission. As can be seen, the command "send file" performs very much like the command "display screen." It allows the two computers to communicate as peers as long as both devices recognize the command "send file" and both are capable of responding correctly.

However, there is yet another way that data can be sent without introducing a new "send file" command into the logical-level vocabulary of each device. If the terminal type device is sufficiently powerful, data can be transferred using the existing "display screen" command. In this approach, the personal computer user would request that the mainframe display the contents of the file on the screen. However, instead of using the received data stream to display the characters on the personal computer's monitor, the logical level now captures data from the data stream and creates a data record on the computer. By requesting additional displays, the personal computer eventually can capture the entire file from the transmitted screen images.

Notice how the layered approach is again at work. The only difference between the personal computer as an emulator and as a file-transfer device is the action of the local layer. Now perhaps the guiding principle of downloading from Chapter 7 becomes easier to understand: the ability to display data on a screen is equivalent to the ability to download data. All that changes is the function of the local level at the personal computer. Once seen from the perspective of this layered approach, the principle becomes obvious.

Example 3: Facsimile

The elegance of the layered approach becomes even more apparent from an examination of other connectivity issues. For example, although the electronic transmission of documents through a facsimile process is not part of the traditional realm of connectivity, by using the model, the same principles can apply.

In a facsimile system, there is a local layer, or that portion of the system that converts a document into a stream of data bits. There is also a logical level, that portion of the system that manages the format of that data stream and directs the response to the signals of other facsimile machines. Finally, there is a physical layer that actually transmits the data stream along with the control information from the logical layer.

By looking at this connection between two facsimile machines from this layered level, an interesting fact emerges: there is absolutely no requirement that the device on either end be an actual facsimile machine. For example, the sending device could be a personal computer that uses the layers to transmit a word processing document directly to a distant location without any paper being involved.

First, the personal computer would need a local layer that would translate the word processing document into a stream of data bits in the same format as created by a facsimile machine. A logical layer would also be needed to add the required control information to the data stream and to manage the physical connection. Finally, a physical layer would be needed actually to transmit the bit stream to the distant system. These layers could be implemented in a fairly straightforward fashion with an add-in board and supporting software.

The key point here is that the receiving facsimile machine will be unable to tell whether the document was sent by an actual facsimile machine or by a personal computer that had special hardware and software to perform the functions of the layers. This is the real secret of true connectivity: the actual device involved is not important as long as each of the layers performs its functions according to the rules.

The Benefits of Connectivity

The last example illustrates one of the principal benefits of the layered approach to connectivity. New developments in connectivity technology can be evaluated by asking four questions:

1. What are the functions of the physical layer?
2. What are the functions of the logical layer?
3. What are the functions of the local layer?
4. How do these new layers correspond to the existing rules in use in an organization?

The benefits of the layered approach now become obvious: as long as the physical layer of each device is able to respond according to the correct rules, and as long as each device's logical layer is able to translate the physical message correctly, then the issue of connectivity becomes straightforward.

If connectivity is this straightforward, then, why does it always seem to cause such problems in an information center?

THE PROBLEMS

Look again at the statement above that concludes, ". . . as long as the physical layer of each device is able to respond according to the correct rules, and as long as each device's logical layer is able to translate the physical message correctly . . .". These two "as long as" phrases are the real crux of connectivity problems.

As Long as the Physical Layer. . . .

The simple truth is that there is no clear standard for physical communication rules. Almost every vendor has a completely different set of rules that manage the physical characteristics of the transmission. (Sometimes even devices by the same vendor use radically different protocols!) Connecting devices from two different vendors is always a risky proposition.

An obvious solution is to develop a single and universally accepted communication standard for all devices. The key words here are "universally accepted." While the first steps toward this approach were take with the creation of the OSI standard (Figure 8-1), universal acceptance is far from certain. Until the standards are in fact standard, there will still be connectivity problems.

A second (and perhaps more realistic) solution to problems caused by different rules for the different layers, which was suggested previously, is that a third device is needed that can communicate with each of the two according to their own rules through emulation. Such a device is called a protocol converter and is illustrated in Figure 8-6. Notice that the protocol converter has a split physical and logical layer so that it can process messages from one device, and pass them up to its own local level and back down through different logical and physical layers to the other device. Any translations between the two sets of rules are made at the protocol converter's local level. This device enables communications between two otherwise incompatible protocols, such as a personal computer using a modem and an IBM mainframe. For example, such a protocol converter would translate the character-by-character transmission of the personal computer into the screen-by-screen requirements of the IBM mainframe. The bad news is that each different protocol requires a separate

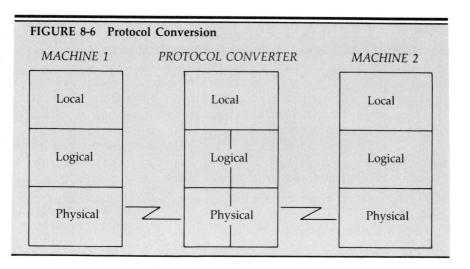

FIGURE 8-6 Protocol Conversion

conversion device. An organization that supports a number of different communication protocols may have a varied assortment of these converters, but that investment allows connectivity to be established while awaiting the issuance of universally accepted standards.

As Long as the Logical Layer. . . .

Reconsider the example of a personal computer communicating with a mainframe. From the mainframe's viewpoint, it is communicating with a terminal. It sends screen images of twenty-four lines of eighty columns each and receives similar screen images back. However, the device on the other end is a fully functioning computer with processor and disk resources of its own. Why must the format always be that 24 × 80 screen? Why can't the communications take advantage of these capabilities?

Remember the concept of horizontal equivalence? The problem is that the logical layer of the mainframe lacks the vocabulary to speak to that remote computer as an equal. Historically the mainframe was the master in the relationship and the logical layer was never designed to accommodate the transactions necessary to have the two machines communicate as peers. That logical layer only has the capability to send and receive screen images, not real interprocess communication requests. To use the language of the earlier example, the mainframe may lack a "send file" command in its local and logical levels, leaving data to be downloaded through the "display screen" approach.

This is the thrust behind recent technological developments such as IBM's LU 6.2 (or APPC, as it is sometimes called). With this major modification to the traditional IBM network architecture, the logical layers can be given the tools to communicate in new ways through new commands that allow the mainframe and personal computer to work as peers, not as a mainframe master and a slave terminal. When the proper changes have been made in the logical layers of the mainframe network and in the personal computers, the local application layers can start making requests to take advantage of the new vocabulary. The local personal computer can then request a single record or an entire file from the mainframe and have that request processed not as a screen image, but as a service request from a peer. This capability represents a significant change.

For a peer-to-peer approach to work, all of the device types in the network will have to change. Not only must the mainframe change to accommodate the new local and logical layers, but the logical and local layers of all of the other components of the network (e.g., terminal controllers and communications controllers) must also undergo changes to recognize that not all messages are sent in a pure master–slave relationship. Once again, the strengths of the layered approach become critical: the entire network need not change at once. As long as the old logical and local transactions are supported, the new versions can be installed piecemeal without interrupting the existing network. When enough of the network has been converted to new layers, the new functions can be used.

CONNECTIVITY MANAGEMENT ISSUES

The underlying concepts of connectivity provide for an interesting discussion, but what are its real implications for an information center? The answer to that question revolves around connectivity's costs.

Actual Costs

The fact is that connectivity costs money. Figure 8-7 illustrates some of the potential costs of connectivity based on the three layers of the idealized model. The following example utilizes these figures to compute the costs of a typical LAN to connect five personal computers together.

First, there is the cost of the computers. For this example, assume that they were already on hand and so represent no additional expense. Doing so permits the cost of connectivity itself to be isolated.

Another cost is that of the network cards—the devices that are placed in the personal computer to manage the physical connection. Such cards typically cost between $300 and $1,000 per computer. Next is the cost of the connecting cable between the computers, as well as of the labor to install it. Cable costs can range from $50 per machine in simple installations to $1,000 per machine in large buildings in major metropolitan areas. In addition, there is the cost of the network software. This software provides the logical layer that translates a request from the application into a network request, and can cost from $100 to $1,000 per computer, depending

---

FIGURE 8-7   Checklist: The Real Costs of Connectivity

PHYSICAL-LEVEL COSTS
- Cable costs
- Telephone charges
- Maintenance for cable or phone lines
- Special hardware
    Network cards for personal computers
    Protocol converters
    Modem costs
    Terminal controllers
    Communication controllers

LOGICAL-LEVEL COSTS
- Network management software
- Terminal emulation programs

LOCAL-LEVEL COSTS
- Special network versions of application systems
- New application development to use connection
- Format translation programs
- Changes to existing programs due to network

---

on the vendor, the number of computers in the network, and the type of network supported.

So far the connection among these four computers has cost between $450 and $3,000 per computer. Unfortunately, many information centers stop at this point in their computations without considering still other costs that can arise. First, a network version of a program costs significantly more than a single-user version. For example, a data-base program may cost $700 for a single-user version but $6,000 for the network version. If there are eight or more computers in a network, the per-station cost of the software is reduced. However, as there are only five computers in the example network, the cost per station is actually $200 *more* than for the single-user version.

Second, it is significantly more expensive to develop an application on a network than on a single-user system because the number of potential programming situations has increased. For example: what happens if two users want to update the same record simultaneously? While that problem could never arise on a single-user version, the network version must include additional code to handle this possibility.

Based on the checklist of Figure 8-7, actual out-of-pocket expenses for the example system would be somewhere between $650 and $3,200 per computer, not counting the cost of increased development time. Most likely, then, the initial investment would be approximately $1,500 per station. However, there are still more costs to come.

Human Costs

In addition to the obvious out-of-pocket expenses that must be met before a LAN can become operational, there are the costs of human resources to be considered—costs that can be easily overlooked. Figure 8-8 presents a list of some of the human costs of connectivity.

For the immediate future, no connectivity solution will ever be as simple as connecting cables and copying software onto the appropriate machines. No matter what the vendors claim, it is not as easy as plugging a telephone into a wall socket. Accordingly, a number of hours, or days, will be required to monitor the physical installation and troubleshoot the initial attempts at starting up the network. Additionally, a certain number of training hours will be needed to develop the expertise to monitor the installation. Depending on the complexity of the software and the physical system, an information center consultant may be asked to devote between forty and one hundred hours to initial training of personnel and installation support. With the basic skills in place, this investment in time will be substantially less for subsequent installations—perhaps twenty to forty hours.

However, no network stays static after it has been installed. New computers or other devices may be added to the network, new releases of the network software will require installation, and training will be needed to implement any new release. Additionally, as different people use the computers on the network, questions and problems inevitably will arise. It would be reasonable to assume that these maintenance activities will

---

FIGURE 8-8   Checklist: The People Costs of Connectivity

INSTALLATION COSTS
- Training costs
- Actual time spent in installation
- Time spent in problem resolution in initial time period

MAINTENANCE COSTS
- Time spent in controlling network configuration changes
- Installation of new network software releases
- Training time to learn new features with new releases
- Problem resolution—user support
- Performance tuning

ADMINISTRATIVE COSTS
- System backup
- Password administration
- Conflict resolution

require an average of two hours a week, or about one hundred hours for each year of operation.

Various routine administrative tasks also must be accommodated on the LAN. The shared data must be backed up, probably daily. If the LAN, like most, has a password scheme, some administrative time must be allotted to overseeing the security of the network. Finally, someone will have to play referee to determine priorities when two users need to use the same resource at the same time (e.g., a laser printer). Once again a conservative estimate of the time to be spent on administrative tasks might be approximately two hours per week, or one hundred hours per year, of operation.

As Figure 8-9 indicates, these costs have started to mount. Using the conservative values for each of the categories, that figure shows that the average cost for the example LAN over a three-year period would be $4,100, or $1,366 per year.

Of course, in actual situations, the costs may vary from this scenario. The important point, however, is that the cost of operating the LAN far outstrips the cost of its installation. Although human costs represent a significant management issue for any information center, there are yet other costs involved that, unfortunately, are even harder to measure.

Strategic Costs

The previous chapter proposed the following principle for stewardship:

> The information assets of a corporation are always to be considered corporate assets. However, the organization will appoint, either by explicit direction or by unspoken expectations, various distinct individuals (stewards) to protect those assets and to ensure they are used in the best interests of the entire organization.

This principle has a significant implication for the issue of connectivity: All data, whether stored in the corporate mainframe or in departmental LANs, must be considered a corporate asset. Any connectivity solution that makes that data a parochial, rather than corporate, asset is contrary to the principle and carries a significant strategic cost.

If a connectivity solution is to be in step with this vision, an information center must look beyond the immediate need to the long-term needs of the entire organization. For example, a marketing department wants to install a LAN to track the success of various marketing campaigns. If the information center blindly accepts the task and installs the network and appropriate software, it has missed an important point: the LAN solution requires that the marketing data be seen as the parochial property of the marketing department. If the same data is needed to support production planning or top management strategic planning, it is not available. Although the marketing department might have been willing to pay the dollar costs, no

FIGURE 8-9   LAN Cost Estimates

STARTUP COSTS
Per Machine

network card	$ 500	
cable cost	200	
for five computers		$3,500

Per Network

network software	$1,200	
network version of		
data-base software	3,000	
installation costs		
40 hours @ $20	800	
		$ 5,000

ONGOING COSTS PER YEAR

network maintenance		
100 hours @ $20	$2,000	
network administration		
100 hours @ $20	2,000	
		$ 4,000

Three-year cost estimate:

installation	$ 8,500
ongoing costs	12,000
total	$20,500
cost per machine	$ 4,100
or $1,366 per machine per year	

thought was given to the strategic costs created when the information was thereby made unavailable to the rest of the organization. The solution was shortsighted because it failed to recognize the value of the data from a corporate viewpoint.

The critical issue for an information center then, is to realize that the goal of connectivity-oriented tools must be to provide a corporate view of data, not a quick solution in isolation. An information center must pursue the ideal that all data, regardless of where it is stored, should be accessible to all authorized users.

Evaluating Connectivity Needs

In the previous sections, significant attention was paid to the cost of connectivity. How can an information center use these concepts to evaluate solutions to connectivity problems?

By this point in the book, the approach should come as no surprise: an understanding of the business problem must come first. As the examples have shown, implementing technology for its own sake may be expensive and counterproductive.

Consider the previous example of a marketing department staff that wanted to track the results of various advertising campaigns. Staff members described their problem to the information center as a need for a LAN. That is not a business problem; it is a technical solution. The real business problem might be stated as follows:

1. The department is unable to determine how a marketing campaign has created increased sales.
2. It already has invested in five personal computers and would like to capitalize on that investment.
3. The budget for this project is $8,500. The solution cannot cost more than that.
4. Staff members would be happy to devote time to solving the problem but not a lot of money.

Once the issue of technology has been removed from the problem, the consideration of alternatives can be discussed.

The results of a simple brainstorming session on possible alternatives to an LAN implementation are shown in Figure 8-10. Like the results of most brainstorming sessions, some of these alternatives will not afford a solution. For example, the "sneaker net" solution requires that files be shared by physically moving them from one computer to another. That is not very practical in this case. However, other alternatives may prove more practical. If the company has a protocol converter that allows a personal computer to emulate terminals using simple modems, developing a 4GL system on the mainframe might be much less expensive than the proposed network. Additionally, this approach would make the data available to other authorized areas of the corporation and resolve the problem of the strategic cost.

Once the problem is taken out of the realm of technology and restated as a business problem, the issue is reduced to a simple question: Which of the possible alternatives provides the best solution to the problem for the resources spent? Connectivity is now seen as a tool to solve the problem, not as a solution in its own right.

FIGURE 8-10   LAN Alternatives

- **Sneaker Net**—store data on one machine only. Carry diskette to other machine when sharing is required.

- **Switches and Cable**—connect peripherals with cables only. Use switching devices to connect right machine with right peripheral.

- **Zero-Slot LAN**—use serial (RS-232) port on each computer to connect devices. Purchase inexpensive software to redirect output request or file transfer requests to correct device.

- **Complete LAN**—implement a complete LAN including specialized cable, hardware cards, and networking software.

- **Tie into Departmental Computer**—use an emulation package to connect computers to departmental computer. Use departmental computer as hub of network.

- **Tie into Corporate Computer**—use an emulation package to connect computers to corporate computer. Use corporate computer as hub of network.

SUMMARY

The secret to understanding the technology that links two devices is not difficult to fathom. The fact is that the devices themselves are not really connected. The connection is better understood as links between layers in the devices. On a simple level, there are local, logical, and physical layers that communicate with each other vertically and horizontally to actually implement the link. To introduce a new type of device into the connection, that device merely needs to be able to support the functions required by each of the layers.

Just because two devices can be connected, however, does not mean that they ought to be. The real question, as always, comes back to the business problem and the connectivity technology must be seen as just another tool to solve that problem. To do otherwise reduces connectivity to a dazzling solution in search of a problem.

SUGGESTED PROJECT

Consider the following case:

The manager of customer service and the MIS director have asked the information center to assist in the evaluation of a new plan that will decentralize the customer data base. The country is to be divided into three support centers:

Seattle, Memphis, and Newark. The customer data base will be divided along these lines as well, and each customer will be assigned a service center. The software that will be developed will first look for the customer data at the local node in the network: if it is unable to find the data there, it will ask the other nodes in the network to supply the data. The assumption is that this will dramatically increase response time since the local data bases will be much smaller and more efficient, and since only a limited number of transactions will require a long-distance transmission. The information center has been asked to comment on this proposal.

Base your comments and analysis on the following questions:

1. What are the real business issues in this problem?
2. What alternative solutions might be considered?
3. Which of the alternatives is best?
4. For the solution recommended, identify the required functions at the local, logical, and physical layers at each location. What technology might be used to fulfill those functions?
5. Use the checklists in this chapter to identify potential costs, paying special attention to the human and strategic costs.

C H A P T E R 9

Training and Education

To those outside the classroom, teaching must look easy. All the instructor has to do is stand in front of a group of people and tell them what he or she knows. As the students hear and understand the explanation, they assimilate the knowledge and the learning process is complete. To the casual observer, it all seems quite straightforward.

That simplistic description does not reflect reality, however. The educational process actually is a highly complex interaction among a number of variables, including the clarity of the teacher's explanation, the readiness of the student to accept the new ideas, and the process by which the knowledge is incorporated into the student's understanding. Since information centers are charged with facilitating the transformation of data into information that managerial, professional, and support staff can use to solve business problems (see Chapter 1), understanding the nature of training and education is a very important part of managing an information center.

EDUCATION VS. TRAINING

Are education and training really two separate processes? If there is a difference between them, how can an information center use that difference to its best advantage?

Which course, for example—sex education or sex training—would be better attended on most college campuses? The answer seems obvious. As this slightly frivolous illustration shows, the term "training" conveys a sense of "hands on," whereas "education" implies a more conceptual approach.

Differentiating Training from Education

The following problem is posed to a class: compute the sum of integers from 1 to 100. To teach the students how to solve this problem, an instructor may choose from among three very different approaches. One method would be to use brute force, adding $1 + 2 + 3 \ldots$ until the answer is obtained. This method is not terribly elegant or error-free, but with enough drill and practice, it can accomplish the task. A second approach would be to use a formula from advanced algebra and solve it as shown in Figure 9-1. In this case, the solution depends on knowing the formula of the sum of the terms of an arithmetic sequence, recognizing that the formula is applicable to the problem, determining the proper substitutions, and performing the arithmetic. This method is far more elegant than the previous method and much less prone to error.

However, there is yet a third possible way to reach a solution to the problem, as illustrated in Figure 9-2. This solution is based on an understanding of the nature of integers (that there will be fifty pairs and that

---

FIGURE 9-1 Algebraic Solution

PROBLEM
Determine the sum of the integers from 1 to 100.

FORMULA
The sum of the terms of an arithmetic series is computed by:

$$\text{sum} = \frac{(f + l) * n}{2}$$

where: f = first term of series
l = last term of series
n = number of terms

SOLUTION

$$\text{sum} = \frac{(1 + 100) * 100}{2} = \frac{101 * 100}{2} = 5{,}050$$

---

all pairs will have the same sum) and of the nature of multiplication (adding a number of identical terms, by definition, is multiplication). This third solution is even more elegant than the second for several reasons.

First, the solution of Figure 9-2 is intuitively more plausible. The answer is far more believable because students can anchor the process in facts they already know. They do not have to accept on blind faith a formula that is somewhat obscure. Second, the solution in Figure 9-2 is portable. Instead

---

FIGURE 9-2 Intuitive Solution

PROBLEM: Determine the sum of the integers from 1 to 100.

SOLUTION: Group the integers as follows, noticing the pairs:

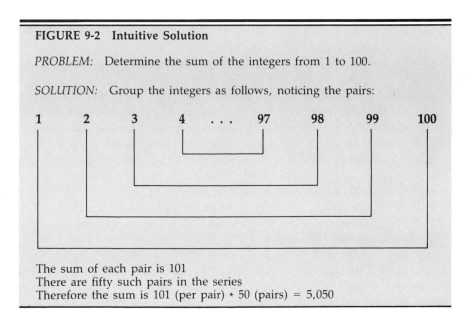

The sum of each pair is 101
There are fifty such pairs in the series
Therefore the sum is 101 (per pair) * 50 (pairs) = 5,050

---

of memorizing an apparently meaningless formula (only to forget it after the test), students can recreate the solution at will, as long as they retain a basic understanding of integers and multiplication and recall the enabling trick of pairing the numbers.

This, then, is the core of the differences between training and education. Training seeks to provide the procedures by which a solution can be obtained. It is based on formulas and algorithms, techniques that need to be memorized and applied. Education concentrates on the underlying concepts and provides a limited number of "enabling strategies" that allow a student to apply the concepts to solve a practical problem. The question is: Which is best for an information center?

Information Center: Trainer or Educator?

Is an information center to be a trainer or an educator? Predictably, the answer to this question is *"Both."* Instead of viewing training and education as a clear-cut dichotomy, an information center must see the process as a continuum with training at one extreme and education at the other. To concentrate on either extreme is counterproductive; instead, an information center manager must think in terms of selecting a strategy from somewhere in the middle of the continuum.

To illustrate, a person new to the use of a personal computer is faced with an almost overwhelming number of commands and concepts. In an effort to help overcome this confusion, many information centers offer a course such as "Introduction to Personal Computers," in which neophytes are taught such fundamental tasks as how to turn the machine on and how to perform such routine operations as formatting diskettes or making copies of files, as well as the basics of some common programs, such as spreadsheets and word processing. This is the training part of the course; information centers that understand the need for education will go a little farther.

In that case, as a part of the introductory class, the instructor might disassemble a computer and give a guided tour of its components. Seeing the central processing chip provides a certain level of concrete understanding of the debate about the respective merits of 80286, 80386, 80486, and 680X0 processors. Viewing the rows of RAM memory helps the student put the description "2 megabytes of memory" in perspective. Being shown the path through which data must flow as it moves from disk to memory helps the student appreciate the need for saving any work to disk periodically. The guided tour provides the basis for a better understanding of the training sections of the course.

There is a difference, however, between the way students interact with a computer in the classroom and what will happen when they return to their own computers. The classroom exercises are designed to assure that students do them successfully. If they get stuck, the instructor is always there, ready to offer a friendly word of advice. Training, by its nature, is success oriented, always trying to reinforce positively correct behaviors.

Reality is not so kind. Back in their offices, the former students can make horrendous mistakes, becoming hopelessly confused, and often walking away from the computer, vowing never to touch it again. The solution is to provide some level of reality education. The introductory class should include a built-in set of common disasters that the class will have to work through. For example, the monitor to one of the computers might be unplugged before the students arrive. The students then can discover the problem and solve it themselves. In showing how to format a diskette, the instructor might "accidentally" format the system hard disk, not mentioning the existence of backups until the students ask about them. Witnessing these disasters not only brings the class closer to reality, but also adds a practical aspect to the classes.

As these examples illustrate, training provides the means whereby students can move from incompetence to competence, whereas education allows knowledge to move from a student's consciousness into an unconscious, integrated understanding of the material. Without education, knowledge remains a skill that is characterized by syntax alone; that is, the student becomes capable of using technology, but only as a series of separate commands. Without training, the student cannot translate conceptual understanding into solutions to business problems (the original reason for setting up an information center).

Training alone is not sufficient—nor is education alone. Only when both are present will a course be successful. How, then, should an information center professional go about building the best program?

DESIGNING THE IDEAL CLASS

Designing an ideal class is much like designing an ideal program. The process starts with a top-down approach, decomposing the concepts into smaller, more manageable pieces. The actual materials and exercises are then developed at these lower, detailed levels. An example of the process might be the design of a course in basic reporting using a fourth-generation language (4GL).

Starting with the Business Problem

A recurring theme throughout this book has been the need to start with a business problem. Training is no different. Unless a training program solves a specific business problem, it is useless.

Determining the problem should begin with those who requested the program. What are their expectations? Why do they think the class is needed? What alternatives do they see? What would happen if the course were not offered?

The proposed participants represent another source of information. What do they think they need? How can the training help them do their job better? What do they perceive as possible pitfalls that training can help them avoid? What will they do if the course is not offered?

The results that come out of the answers to these questions should be a one-sentence description of the business problem expressed as a deviation from a norm (see Chapter 1). In the example of the 4GL course, the business problem might be phrased as, "Key support staff are not able to respond to information requests from management in a timely and accurate fashion." The statement includes a norm (information should be timely and accurate) and a deviation (unable to respond). With this business problem, as a basis, the course designer can move on to the next step—developing objectives.

After meeting with the requestor and the proposed participants, the course developer may learn that the two groups have radically different ideas about the business problem that the training is supposed to solve. In that case, the course would almost certainly fail to produce effective results owing to the conflicting expectations. By starting at the business problem, these conflicts can be identified early, thus avoiding wasted effort and poor performance.

Objectives: What Should the Students Learn?

An old cliche asks, "If you don't know where you are going, how will you know when you get there?" In designing an ideal class, the same principle applies. A designer who does not have a clear description of what the class results should be will be unable to determine whether the class was a success or a failure.

A complete discussion of the principles of designing instructional objectives is beyond the scope of this book. The basic concepts, however, are very important, and so this chapter will adopt an approach that uses a hierarchical decomposition of class objectives, similar to a top-down approach to program design.

First, what is the overriding objective of the course? A good starting point in determining an answer to this question is the business problem that was identified in the previous step. In the example of a course in 4GL basic reporting skills, that objective might be: "To be able to create 4GL procedures without information center assistance that will produce reports that answer a majority of current business questions."

How is this objective tied to the business problem? The objective is to remove the deviation (inability to respond rapidly and accurately) by providing skills that create 4GL reports (accurately) without the time-consuming intervention of an information center (rapidly). This objective, obviously, is limited in scope. The students are not expected to learn everything about reporting, but just about those facets of reporting that will allow them to meet most of their current business needs. The objective also is somewhat vague and not very well quantified. It did not say "that will meet 80 percent of their business needs" because introducing a quantitative approach at this stage is counterproductive as the arguments will then revolve around what constitutes 80 percent instead of what reporting techniques are needed. Quantitative measures come later, at a more detailed level. At this point, the overriding objective must be related to business needs, must be realistic in scope, and must not dwell too heavily on quantitative measures.

The second step in course dsign attempts to break down the overriding objective into a series of subobjectives. Ideally, no more than seven or eight of these second-level objectives should be identified, in order to keep the process manageable. Each of these second-level objectives, which should be much more detailed and much more measurable than the overall objective, may in turn be broken down into a series of third-level objectives, again in greater detail and more measurable than their predecessors. The process continues until the course designer feels an objective is sufficiently concrete to allow the development of objective-related course materials and sufficiently measurable to permit the construction of test questions that can unequivocally measure the student's level of competence on that objective. This process is summarized in Figure 9-3 and the results are illustrated in Figure 9-4.

The diagram of Figure 9-4 provides a designer with a convenient tool for organizing design ideas into related logical units in a top-down fashion. However, the design hierarchy is still incomplete. Since each box is limited in the amount of detail it can encompass, a designer should also develop an objective outline, as illustrated in Figure 9-5.

An objective outline is based on the hierarchy diagram, but expresses the objective of a box as a measurable student behavior. At the end of the course, success or failure is clearly defined by looking at the objective outline and determining whether the students have demonstrated that behavior. With regard to the phrase "demonstrated that behavior" two alternative objectives are possible: (1) "The student will understand the correct verb for a particular report." (2) "The student will select the correct verb for a particular report." Although both objectives state almost the same thing, the second is behavior related, whereas the first is almost impossible to measure. With no clear-cut measure for the first objective, how can the instructor determine whether the student "understands"? The second objective is clearly measurable: Did the student select the correct verb for the report?

This difference is not merely a pedantic exercise; it is the secret of quality courses. An information center may consider a course a success only if the students' behavior changes. Unless the objectives of the course are phrased in action-oriented terms, the course's value will always be a

FIGURE 9-3 The Top-Down Design Process

STEP 1.

Level 1 objective
Determine the single overriding objective for the course. This objective should:
- Meet real business needs
- Be limited in scope
- Be qualitative, not quantitative

STEP 2.

Level 2 objectives
Decompose the level 1 objective into no more than eight supporting objectives. These objectives should:
- Contain more detail that the level 1 objective
- Be more concrete in scope than level 1 objective
- Be more quantifiable than the level 1 objective

STEP n.

Level *n* objectives
Decompose *each* of the previous level's objectives into no more than eight supporting objectives. These objectives should:
- Contain more detail than the previous level's objective
- Be more concrete in scope than previous level's objective
- Be more quantifiable than the previous level's objective

FIGURE 9-4 Top-Down Objective Design

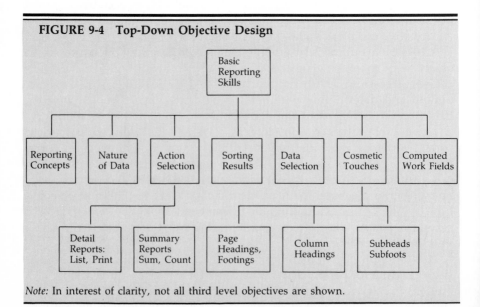

Note: In interest of clarity, not all third level objectives are shown.

FIGURE 9-5 Objective Outline Sample

BASIC REPORTING SKILLS

  I. Basic Reporting Concepts
      The student will . . .

  II. Nature of Data
      The student will . . .

  III. Action Selection
      The student will be able to select the correct verb for any report request.

     A. Detail Reports
        The student will use either the PRINT or LIST verb for detail reports.

     B. Summary Reports
        The student will use SUM for reports requiring totals, COUNT for reports requiring only number of occurrences.

  IV. Sorting Results
      The student will. . . .

---

subject of controversy. If everyone agrees on how the student's behavior ought to change, however, measurement of success is straightforward and unambiguous.

Methods: How Will the Objectives Be Met?

After identifying the objectives, the designer must determine the best method of accomplishing them. These methods essentially can be considered in one of three formats: teacher-oriented, student-oriented, or dialogue-oriented techniques.

Teacher-oriented methods center around a "telling" approach, including reading assignments and lectures. Communication is usually one directional, from the "source of knowledge" to the student. This approach is best for introducing material and for summarizing key points at the end of a presentation. It is not a good method for changing student behaviors, however, because by its very nature it requires almost no student interaction. Behavior changes only when a student has a chance to exercise a new skill.

Student-oriented methods center around a "drill and practice" approach that includes in-class exercises and homework assignments. This approach is directly related to the changes in behaviors that are specified in the objectives. It provides an opportunity for a student either to practice the new behaviors or to demonstrate mastery of the objective. As students

FIGURE 9-6   Methods of Instruction

METHOD	STRENGTHS	WEAKNESSES
Teacher Oriented	Good for initial presentation of material and review.	Not good for changing student behavior since students are "receivers" only.
Student Oriented	Good for giving student a chance to develop, demonstrate new behaviors.	Student may develop incorrect behavior in the absence of careful monitoring.
Dialogue Oriented	Allows students to "try out" new ideas, behaviors under controlled circumstances.	Very time consuming. Dialogue may shut out less vocal students, reducing them to listeners only.

work through these exercises, however, the exercises become highly prone to errors. Unless the methods are coupled with teacher-oriented methods to provide a direction and a basis for action, or unless the activities are closely monitored to prevent incorrect behaviors, they may be antithetic to the objectives.

Dialogue-oriented methods emphasize the interaction between the "source of knowledge" and the student. These methods, which include class discussions, interactive seminars, and guided exercises, allow the student to "try out" ideas under the watchful eye of the instructor. The student can clarify and strengthen concepts through interaction.

The methods are summarized in Figure 9-6. Since each method has both strengths and weaknesses, the ideal class must combine all three—a fact that an information center course designer must take into consideration and make sure to implement in planning class activities.

Materials: The "Stuff" Courses Are Made of

Once the objectives are identified and the methods are selected, choosing class materials is almost a trivial task. Teacher-oriented methods, for example, require materials that center around the "telling" process—such as textbooks and other reading matter, computer-based training materials, slides, overhead transparencies, and scribbling on blackboards. The main thrust of these materials is to inform the students of the skills or concepts needed to meet the objectives.

Student-oriented methods require materials that emphasize "doing"—for example, exercises, projects, and some computer-based training materials. The goal of these materials is to provide a framework for students that require them to perform activities that either build or demonstrate the new behaviors.

Dialogue-oriented methods require materials that will force interaction among students and teacher. Such materials might include discussion questions, team projects, and in-class experiments. Their goal is to stimulate discussion and to force participation by as many students as possible.

Materials, then, are designed to meet objectives and methods. They also should adhere to these basic design principles:

1. *Emphasize Clarity Over Cuteness.* While "cute" materials may capture student attention, clarity is the primary goal of any material. Pictures, jokes, and clever phrasing are all important, but not at the expense of clear explanations.

2. *Provide Anchor Points.* New material is best assimilated when it is related to previously mastered skills. Whenever possible, materials should be anchored in concepts and skills that are already part of the student's knowledge base.

3. *Provide Idea Frames.* New ideas should not be presented as a series of sequential topics, but should be organized in a framework. Materials should include outlines, previews and summaries of key ideas, and a conceptual framework into which the collection of new topics can be fitted.

Measuring Success

As described in the preceding sections, objectives need to be developed from a top-down perspective, they must be behaviorally oriented, they may be reached through various methods, and appropriate materials can be developed to help achieve those objectives. The final step in course design is to develop the means by which success or failure will be measured.

In the world of physics, one of the fundamental particles of matter is the electron, which may be considered as whirling around the nucleus of the atom. (This is a gross simplification of what is really happening, but it will do for the purposes of this discussion.) As physicists studied the electron, they discovered a fundamental principle: they could determine either the location of an electron at a given point in time or its speed, but never both, because the act of measuring one of the options always altered the other.

This principle (known as the Heisenberg uncertainty principle) can be extended to the nature of the education process by restating it slightly: "The act of measuring a behavior alters that which is being measured." One example of such an application might be the process used in most schools to measure achievement.

Once or twice a year, students are asked to take standardized achievement tests. These tests can create some interesting (and often unanticipated) behavior changes. First, they may induce anxiety in the students, thus reducing their ability to demonstrate their knowledge accurately. Second, if these tests are used to evaluate teacher performance, then even the best teachers will begin to alter the material taught to match the material on the tests. Instead of having the test measure instructional effectiveness, instruction becomes motivated by the measurement.

A second illustration of Heisenberg's principle outside the world of physics is the way in which most businesses evaluate their employees' job performance. In most cases, a job description is developed that lists the duties and responsibilities of that position. On an annual basis, an employee's performance is measured against this list in some quantitative fashion. Since financial incentives are usually based on this evaluation, an employee's behavior will usually change to conform to the evaluation used. The evaluation tool not only is the yardstick that measures success in the job, but it also becomes the model of behavior for people in that job. A job description that mentions "on-schedule" completion of assignments but not "error-free" work can result in sloppiness and poor quality. The measurement tool not only measures, it defines.

This is an important concept in developing training courses for an information center. Measurement of a course's success must always be tied to the objectives. Measurements that are not directly related to the objectives will create hidden objectives that become more important than the stated ones. If, for example, one of the objectives for a course states that students should be able to verify their results for accuracy using a test plan but the exercises merely move from one problem to the next, providing answers that show the correct report request for comparison, the objective becomes skewed. Instead of learning how to develop a test plan, students learn to depend on an outside source to validate the request. The objective said that the student should learn to develop test-plan validation, but the exercises emphasized code reviews by requiring the students to examine the code, not results. The objectives enforced by the materials and the evaluation will be the ones that alter student behavior, not those set forth in the course design. In good courses, the objectives, materials, and evaluations are synchronized.

COURSE DOCUMENTATION

In the world of traditional programming, the most ignored step is usually documentation. Course design, unfortunately, is no different. To be successful, the course designer should develop a documentation manual for each course. Since the original course designer may not teach a course after it has been presented a number of times, future instructors should have a source of information about the goals and objectives of the course. The course manual is this source of information.

The Course Manual

What should a course manual include? First, it should begin with the objective hierarchy that was developed initially (Figure 9-4). This diagram provides a single source that future instructors may use to understand the overall nature of the course. Second, the manual should include an objective outline that corresponds to the hierarchy (Figure 9-5). This also provides a sweeping overview of the basic structure and goals of the course.

Then for each of the boxes at the lowest level of the hierarchy, a detailed description should be provided. A sample of such an objective description is shown in Figure 9-7.

Note that the objective is clearly stated and includes a reference to the objective outline. Moreover, the methods and materials are clearly identified and cross-referenced where appropriate. In addition, the methods section includes all three types of methods—teacher-oriented,

---

FIGURE 9-7   Sample Objective Description

OBJECTIVE

III.B. Summary Reports
      The student will use SUM for reports requiring totals, COUNT for reports requiring only number of occurrences.

METHODS

1. Describe different verbs as part of basic reporting discussion.
2. In-class demonstration using sample file showing differences between SUM, COUNT, and PRINT. (See objective III.A.)
3. Student exercises for reinforcement.

RELATED MATERIALS

1. Student workbook pages 24, 27.
2. Overhead transparencies of workbook pages.
3. Example problem, teacher's notes page 10.
4. Student exercise set 3, problems 2, 5, and 9.

EVALUATION

1. Student will be able to develop the report requests for student exercise set 3, problems, 2, 5, and 9. Instructor assistance is permitted for these requests.
2. Report requests for remaining problem sets will use correct verb. Instructor assistance for those problem sets will be limited to new features, but student should be able to select correct verb for these remaining problems.

student-oriented, and dialogue-oriented methods—together with supporting materials. This chart provides a valuable validation tool. If all of the methods for a particular objective are teacher oriented, for example, then the course needs to be revised.

Finally, evaluation criteria are set for each objective that relates questions to the objectives and indicates the level of independence students are expected to demonstrate. By including the evaluation methods on the same page as the objectives, methods, and materials, the course designer can ensure that all components are objective based.

Updating the Course Manual

Courses, like computer programs, seem to take on a life of their own. They change to meet new needs or to incorporate better methods or materials. As every programmer knows, documentation is like radioactive material: in a certain period of time, half of it decays. If the course manual is to have any value, it must be accurate and as up-to-date as the course material.

Keeping the manual current may seem simple, but in the real world, it is almost impossible to accomplish. Unfortunately, there is no easy answer— except, perhaps, one dictated by discipline and pride. Course designers must take the responsibility *always* to update a course manual when materials or methods change. Putting off those changes never seems to work because the sense of urgency is gone and procrastination sets in. Finally, an information center manager needs to monitor the course manuals to ascertain that they are up-to-date. The short-term work caused by trying to keep the book updated is more than compensated for by the long-term improvement in clarity and continuity.

THE NITTY-GRITTY

In addition to the proper concepts and techniques, the success of an information center's educational program also depends on the facilities, staff, and procedures that will support the training—or what can be called the "nitty-gritty."

Facilities

The mind will continue to absorb only as long as the body is comfortable. Thus, if an education program is to be successful, the facilities must be comfortable from the viewpoint of both the participants and the instructors.

A lot has been written over the past few years about the ergonomics of office design. As a result, many training facilities have been redesigned

---

FIGURE 9-8   Facility Checklist

SIZE
- Is there enough space for each student to have a place for class materials and personal belongings?
- Will there be at least two feet between students?

LOGISTICS
- Can each student easily see the screen and blackboards?
- Are other facilities (restrooms, drinking fountains, etc., accessible)?

INSTRUCTOR SUPPORT
- Is all required audio-visual equipment easily accessible to the instructor?
- Can the instructor see each student and each student's work?

STUDENT EQUIPMENT
- Are there sufficient terminals to allow one device for every two students?
- Are the devices similar to those that will be used by the students in their own environment?

---

with the human factors in mind: the tables are at an optimum height, the screens on the terminals tilt and swivel, the screens are covered with a shield against glare, and students sit in $500 chairs that allow twelve different comfort adjustments. If an information center has the budget to invest in these wonders of modern design, that's fine—but a number of other things can be done that do not require a large investment of capital. Figure 9-8 illustrates some of these.

First, there is the question of the size of the training space itself. If ten students are crammed into a small conference room, their ability to learn will be markedly diminished. Students need space for their materials and personal belongings, as well as some personal space around them; they should sit at least two feet apart. If there is not enough space, an information center might borrow facilities from the training department or rent a meeting room at a local hotel.

Apart from adequate seating arrangements, students need to be able to see the screens and blackboards (or whiteboards) or they will quickly lose interest. Facilities to assure basic creature comforts are also important, including easily accessible restrooms, drinking fountains, and soft-drink vending machines.

From the instructor's viewpoint, teaching-related equipment must be easy to set up and use. An overhead projector, for example, must be at a comfortable level with its power cords safely out of the instructor's way. Additionally, the layout of the room should not make it difficult for the instructor to walk about and check on the students' work.

Finally, to assure maximum utility of the terminals, the classroom should include enough devices to allot one to every two students. This setup not only means lower costs for the training facility, but it also makes the training more effective. By working in a "buddy system," students can help each other while building skills. The insecurities and fears of confronting new material are greatly diminished when shared. Furthermore, the terminals should be similar to those used in the actual work environment. It is very frustrating for a student to learn a skill using one keyboard and to have to apply that skill using a different layout.

Staff

Figure 9-9 lists some of the key considerations in choosing a training staff. (Chapter 12 discusses the general staff of an information center in greater detail.) These are highly specialized skills; that not every information center staff member will possess, but at least some should meet the criteria.

The Figure 9-8 checklist is characterized by several basic themes. The first is preparation. It almost goes without saying that an instructor must be familiar not only with the subject of the course, but also with the materials that have been developed to present that subject. A "guru" who is not familiar with the course design and content has no place in the classroom.

The nature of the interaction between instructor and students is also important. An instructor must come across as a human being, not a teaching machine, creating an open atmosphere in which students feel comfortable about making mistakes and trying new skills. At the same time, an instructor must always be in control. The lesson must flow from

---

FIGURE 9-9   Staff Checklist

PREPARATION
- Does the instructor personally understand the material that will be presented?
- Has the instructor become familiar with the materials that will be used?
- Has the instructor worked the problem sets?

PERSONALITY
- Is the instructor nonjudgmental about students' ability?
- Does the instructor convey an openness to questions (not just in words but in actions)?

CLASS ACTIVITIES
- Is the instructor in control of the class without being controlling?
- Does the class move smoothly from one topic to another?
- Is the class interesting?

topic to topic, the topics must be clearly explained, and no one student should be allowed to monopolize the question sessions. Tact, honesty, openness, and a sense of direction are all hallmarks of a good instructor.

There is one other characteristic that a good instructor should possess—a sensitivity to the students' capabilities and goals. As every elementary school teacher knows, students learn exactly as much as the teacher expects them to learn. Study after study has shown that if a teacher believes that one group of students is incapable of learning a particular subject but that another group will excel at learning the same material, the second group will consistently outperform the first group on almost every evaluation. The instructor's expectations are translated into subtle subconscious messages that significantly affect a student's ability to learn. Thus, the instructor's attitude toward the class is a primary factor contributing to the success or failure of the class. Thus, to a good instructor's characteristic qualities of tact, honesty, openness, and a sense of direction must be added one more quality—faith in the students' ability to learn.

Administrivia

A final area of concern in setting up an educational program is that related to the problems of administration. These are the little nitty-gritty details that are so easy to ignore but nevertheless are so important. Figure 9-10 shows a checklist of items in two basic categories: registrar's functions and evaluation.

FIGURE 9-10   Administrivia

REGISTRAR FUNCTION

- Is there a good recordkeeping system to show who has signed up for a class, who is on wait list, etc.?
- Is there a clear policy for enrollment showing what management approvals are needed?
- Does each class have prerequisites? Are they enforced?
- Will there be a charge (however nominal) for the course? Who is expected to pay that fee?
- What is the policy regarding cancellation? What penalties will result from last-minute cancellations?

EVALUATION

- Will students be graded on a course (even PASS/FAIL)?
- Is there a class evaluation form that will be filled out by the students?
- How will the results of both the evaluations be communicated to management?

Once an information center gets into the business of education, it will have to face the same issues as any other educational institution. Students must be registered for courses, that registration must be subject to prerequisites and approvals, and there must be some type of control over "drops" and "adds." No university would think of supporting an unstructured approach to class enrollment, which is why the registrar's office exists. An information center must also establish a registrar's office, with a set of policies and procedures designed to keep the process under control.

It is also vitally important to the educational process to provide feedback, in a meaningful fashion, to both the students and the instructor. The students need to know how well they are meeting the course objectives. This evaluation can be formal (grades, tests, etc.) or informal (instructor comments during problem sets, postclass discussion, etc.), but it must take place. Without feedback, students cannot apprehend the value of the course and may have problems in applying the course material to the work setting.

Similarly, students should be given an opportunity to evaluate the course from their perspective in such areas as content, pace, instructor style, and instructor effectiveness. Submission of these student evaluations anonymously will encourage openness and honesty in the appraisals.

What will be done with all of these evaluations? Will the evaluations of the students be sent to their manager? The possibility that they will be passed on can have deleterious effects on class dynamics. Also, what will be done with the course evaluations completed by the students? Will they be transmitted to the information center's management? If so, how will they affect the willingness of the information center to try new, experimental topics and techniques?

There are no simple answers to these questions. The solutions will be different in each information center, but as the checklist in Figure 9-10 shows, a successful information center will have considered these questions and set a clear direction before the first class starts. The worst answers are always the defaults; explicitly selecting a policy from a number of alternatives is always better than doing nothing.

PREPACKAGED SOLUTIONS

This chapter has emphasized the need to start with the objectives, and then identify materials, methods, and evaluation criteria to meet those objectives. This approach clearly works when courses are to be developed "from scratch." However, what changes need to be made when an information center will be incorporating commercially developed solutions?

Types of Solutions Available

A number of different solutions are commercially available that an information center can use to meet training needs, including:

1. *Textbook/Workbooks.* Instead of developing written materials, an information center may choose to purchase them. Such materials usually feature high-quality graphics, charts, and multicolored text.

2. *Video Training.* Using the full power of the television medium, these materials present new ideas and skills through music, animation, attention-getting leaps from one topic to another, and actual demonstrations of skills and techniques. They often feature nationally known experts on a topic, providing access to this expertise in a cost-effective fashion.

3. *Computer-based Training.* Available on personal, departmental, and corporate computers, these courses utilize the computer's ability to display and receive data to inform the student, evaluate student understanding, and simulate software behavior in a training mode. In addition to prepackaged solutions, a number of packages are available that allow a course designer to develop an individualized computer-based training course.

A definitive discussion of each of these different types of media is beyond the scope of this book; however, Figures 9-11, 9-12, and 9-13 illustrate some of the differences among the solutions. In many cases, the benefits or drawbacks of each depend somewhat on the individual material. For example, a video-disk product is much more flexible than one that uses video tape.

FIGURE 9-11   Prepackaged Solutions: Textbooks/Workbooks

	FAVORABLE	*UNFAVORABLE*
"TAILOR-ABILITY"	Instructor explanation can easily enhance unclear material.	Additional material cannot be easily integrated. Must be included in an appendix.
FLEXIBILITY	Material can be presented in any order.	Format and content are predetermined.
INTEREST LEVEL	Attractive charts, tables can improve ability to hold student interest.	Passive medium: student still must be self-motivated and want to read material.

FIGURE 9-12   Prepackaged Solutions: Video Training

	FAVORABLE	UNFAVORABLE
"TAILOR-ABILITY"		Completely self-contained. Very little tailoring possible due to high production costs.
FLEXIBILITY	Video-disk-based media allow for random order presentation.	Videotaped-based media allow for only sequential presentation.
INTEREST LEVEL	In the "video generation," interest in visual images is virtually automatic.	Interest can become misdirected to the medium itself rather than the material.

FIGURE 9-13   Prepackaged Solutions: Computer-Based Training (CBT)

	FAVORABLE	UNFAVORABLE
"TAILOR-ABILITY"	Many systems provide access to the course through a separate authoring language.	Tailoring is often complicated and requires special training.
FLEXIBILITY	Some systems provide capability to vary presentation flow based on student responses.	If tailoring is not possible, course flow can be very rigid.
INTEREST LEVEL	Special features (animation, graphics) can enhance interest.	Interest can become misdirected to the technology itself rather than the material.

Evaluating Prepackaged Solutions

Having identified the major commercial solutions available on the market, the next question obviously must be: How does one evaluate different alternatives? The solution still starts with the objectives.

Using prepackaged solutions does not absolve an information center of the responsibility for identifying the objectives of a course. In fact, objectives become even more critical when considering commercial solutions. Unless the course objectives are developed in advance, there will be no honest way to compare commercial alternatives. Without those predefined objectives, an information center is tempted to select the option that is more pleasing aesthetically or can be most easily implemented. The only fair way to select a prepackaged solution is to clearly identify the evaluation criteria in advance by specifying objectives. According to the Heisenberg uncertainty principle discussed earlier, the evaluation criteria for materials will inevitably alter the selection process. Therefore, basing selection criteria on objectives will leverage the Heisenberg principle.

Purchasing commercial material also does not absolve an information center from the responsibility to ensure that the instructional methods are varied. For example, teaching basic 4GL reporting exclusively through computer-based training violates this basic tenent. It provides a teacher-oriented approach in the screens that show new material and a student-oriented approach in the screens that ask for a response, but it cannot provide dialogue-oriented methods owing to the nature of the medium. As this example shows, computer-based training should never be used as the sole instructional medium. It can be used as a preclass screening, as in-class exercises, or as postclass evaluation, but it must always be seen as part of a more comprehensive approach if all of the instructional methods are to be fully integrated.

This last example illustrates a key point—there is never one best way to meet a training need. The best solutions are dynamic in nature, frequently dictating changes in media and approaches to provide variety and to use the strengths of each approach to best advantage. There is never a "right way"; there are only more or less effective combinations of techniques and materials.

SUMMARY

The best classes are those that seem effortless. Students leave those classes with a solid understanding of the material, the teacher moves effortlessly from one topic to the next, and the exercises are positive experiences for the students. What this chapter has shown is that an effortless appearance is the product of planning. Course objectives must be specified from the top down, centering around objectives that are evidenced by a change in behavior. These objectives are met by developing methods and materials that reflect a number of alternatives. The success or failure criteria must be clearly expressed in evaluation methods that are directly tied to the objectives, and all of this should be documented in a course design manual. Additionally, an information center cannot forget that if it is to be in the training business, it must attend to the same details as all other training organizations. It must pay attention to facilities, staffing, and administration.

Finally, commercially available alternatives must always be evaluated in light of the objectives, not by aesthetics or ease of use. As is the case with any endeavor that seems effortless, it is only an appearance. "Effortless" usually means hard work and preparation.

SUGGESTED PROJECTS

1. Develop a course hierarchy for this or some other chapter. Be prepared to defend your choice of the first-level overriding objective. How can you justify your choice?

2. Using the course hierarchy of the previous exercise, develop course objectives like Figure 9-7 for selected bottom-level objectives.

3. For the course objectives of the previous exercise, develop course materials that might be needed to supplement this book. Be sure to include teacher-oriented, student-oriented, and discussion-oriented materials.

A Project-Oriented Information Center

Purgatory is said to be a place that lies somewhere between heaven and hell. It is the place where heaven-bound sinners are cleansed of the residue of their earthly existence. Those in purgatory are not sinful enough to go to hell, but are not quite pure enough yet to be accepted in heaven.

Information systems are similar in some ways. Some systems are clearly so complex and far reaching that they obviously need to be developed by the traditional MIS establishment using time-honored techniques. Others are so clearly idiosyncratic that they are best automated directly by the ultimate end user. However, there are other systems that seem to fall in between. These systems are not important enough to command the attention (and, therefore, the resources) of the entire organization but are sufficiently complex as to be beyond the scope of a single user.

These purgatory projects almost never show up on the list of project backlogs. Since they are not nearly as important as a new general ledger system or a rewrite of the order entry system, their sponsors never even mention them. These projects nevertheless represent the difference between a mediocre information center and a successful one.

DEVELOPMENT PROJECTS: WHY OR WHY NOT?

As pointed out earlier, an information center's role is that of facilitator. It is to help the managerial, professional, and support staff leverage technology into solutions for business problems. Historically, most information centers started out by training users to use the new technologies directly. The cardinal rule of early information centers was, "Thou shalt not write code."

Then a strange thing happened: outsiders found that they could perform some of the functions of those early information centers. A number of independent companies offered training in the basic tools using computer-based or video training. Other companies offered seminars on the tools of an information center. Retail computer stores discovered that training courses gave them a marketing advantage. In short, almost everybody felt they could do the job of an information center, and do it better and cheaper.

It wasn't only training-oriented information centers that found themselves on the way to oblivion. In fact, any information center that was founded to meet a single goal was in danger of becoming obsolete. In a November 1, 1987, *Datamation* article, Ronald Brezezinski told why, as vice-president of information systems at Quaker Oats, he ordered the information center to be dismantled. The purpose of the information center was "to act as an arm of the information services department, dedicated to providing technical support and services to Quaker's staff and management in acquiring and using personal computers."[1] Three years later, 2,000

---

[1] Ronald Brezinski "When It's Time To Tear Down The Information Center," *Datamation*, Nov. 1, 1987:73.

users had been trained, 1,200 personal computers had been installed, and 3,000 software packages had been purchased. However, when company managers began to look at new directions for the information center, they concluded that:

> Our talented information center staff was rapidly evolving into a maintenance mode, which didn't leverage their skills effectively. . . . In many ways the info center had evolved into a small business with its own set of technology inventory systems, chargeback processes, and service request procedures. The result was that the information center analysts, in their quest to be responsive to clients, were unknowingly propagating fragmented technology solutions. These "solutions" began hampering the IS department's applications and technology integration efforts."[2]

The issue of a project-oriented information center thus appears to be a double-edged sword. If an information center concentrates on training and consulting, it is duplicating services that can be provided by various outside firms better and cheaper. If an information center moves to take on some of the so-called purgatory projects, it risks being perceived as "propagating fragmented technology solutions." The truth lies somewhere in the middle. If an information center is to be truly successful, it must develop a project orientation by carefully selecting its projects, implementing them with an eye toward the corporate goals, and avoiding the appearance of becoming a second MIS department.

SELECTING THE CORRECT PROJECTS

The first step in selecting the correct projects for an information center starts with knowing the limitations of the tools and staff as well as the boundaries of the information center's charter. Certain projects clearly belong to the traditional MIS establishment whereas others ought to be implemented by the ultimate users themselves. A preliminary screening tool such as that shown in Figure 10-1 should be used to determine whether the proposed project is a likely candidate for the information center. The items in this questionnaire are not meant to be all-inclusive and each organization should develop a screening mechanism that meets its own needs. However, the purpose of this questionnaire is clear: to identify projects that are clearly outside the scope and expertise of the information center early in the process and to do so in an unambiguous manner that is clearly understood by all. To do otherwise reinforces an image of the information center as "propagating fragmented technology solutions."

Even if a screening tool is developed that is successful at weeding out projects that are best done by the users or by the traditional MIS establishment, many projects still remain that an information center might be able

---

[2]*Ibid.*, p. 76.

FIGURE 10-1   Initial Project Checklist

If the project involves reports only:
- *Is the data currently available?* (If not, a data definition project is indicated.)
- *How many files or data bases will be required?* (More than three files indicates a high level of skill will be required.)
- *Will data-base fields need to be recombined through computations or special handling?* (Complex calculations may require special expertise.)
- *Will this report be run on a regular (daily, weekly, monthly) basis?* (Regular reports will require documentation and special production handling.)

If the project involves more than reports:
- *Does the project require new data bases or enhancements to existing data bases?* (Good data-base design requires special expertise.)
- *How many people will be entering data at once?* (Concurrent data entry requires special techniques. Also, large number of simultaneous users indicates need for more traditional development methods.)
- *What other existing systems will be involved?* (The more interaction with traditional systems, the more likely it is that the project should be done by traditional methods.)
- *How many departments will be involved in entry and will receive reports?* (The more departments involved, the more likely it is that the system ought to be done by traditional methods.)
- *How critical are the backup and recovery demands?* (Systems that require up-to-the-minute automated recovery are best left to traditional development methods.)

---

to carry out. How can an information center select the correct projects from this list? Figure 10-2 suggests some criteria for project selection.

The Strategic Value Set

Chapter 3 discussed the concept of the strategic value set of the organization. An organization may be market driven, product driven, technology driven, or, rarely, truly bottom-line driven. If an information center has successfully identified the value set of the organization, selection of projects becomes much easier.

Suppose an information center manager must decide among three projects, each of which will require approximately one month of a consultant's time. The first project would analyze the accounts receivable system to find customers who took early-payment discounts to which they were not entitled. This project may generate as much as $350,000 in revenue once those discounts are collected. The second project will develop a prototype for an expert system to be used by the telephone sales staff to recommend the correct product based on a customer's responses to a series of questions. No direct operational savings are anticipated as a result of this

---

FIGURE 10-2   Selecting the Correct Projects

STRATEGIC VALUE
- Have the organizations strategic values been identified? (If not, see Chapter 3.)
- Can the benefits be phrased in terms of the strategic values?

BLITZKREIG EFFECT
- How long will the proposed project take?
- What is the ratio of information center people to user people required? (If two projects have equal strategic value, choose the one that better leverages the information center staff.)

TECHNOLOGY ISSUES
- What new technology will be involved in the project? (If two projects have equal strategic value and equal leverage, select the project with the newest technology.)
- What is the level of expertise in the required technology? (Are you biting off more than you can chew?)

---

project. The third project will analyze the sales file using a statistical sampling technique to determine if the recent increase in profits is attributable to last month's price increase or to an increase in sales volume.

The value set of the organization has a direct bearing on the project selection. If the organization is product driven, rapidly producing new products to meet old needs better or to meet newly identified needs, the second project is clearly the best choice. Even though the first project might generate a significant amount of bottom-line revenue, the strategic values of the organization would be best served by the expert system that can help place the new products in the hands of customers faster. On the other hand, if the organization has stable products but is constantly trying to improve its marketing strategy, the third project is far more valuable. Accurate knowledge of the effects of price changes can make a significant difference in the long-term success of an organization.

In both of these examples, the best decision was to avoid the straightforward reporting project that has an actual dollar value. In both cases, although a dollar return is important to the organization, the ability to deliver a service in a way that meets corporate values is far more important. When comparing projects of equal effort, the best choice is that which fulfils the corporate value set.

The Blitzkrieg Effect

World War II saw a complete revolution in the tactics of warfare. Hitler's army pioneered a technique that used tanks, airplanes, and troops in a lightning-quick strike that would burst through defenses keyed to a more traditional, slower-paced attack. This blitzkrieg offense almost overran Europe in a matter of months.

An information center's battles obviously are not as historic as those of that war, but the lesson remains the same. If it is to be successful, an information center must develop a lightninglike approach to problems. Given two problems of equal strategic importance, an information center should always choose the one that can be accomplished most quickly.

There are good reasons for taking a blitzkrieg approach to problem selection. First, the longer the time between the start of work and its completion, the greater will be the chance that the requirements will change. Second, the longer the project, the more likely it is to be too complex for the information center. Long projects are best handled by the department best equipped to manage them: the traditional MIS department. Finally, long projects seem philosophically antithetic to the general charter of an information center: to facilitate the work (not completely do the work) of managers, professionals, and staff. The best projects are those that allow an information center to stay "lean and mean."

The Technology Test

An information center must keep up with new technology. As new products and techniques come onto the scene, an information center must be at the forefront in evaluation and pilot projects, making sure that those technologies are in step with the overall corporate direction for technology. Accordingly, an information center has yet another criterion that can be used to evaluate projects. If two projects are equally important to the strategic values of the organization and will be finished in approximately the same amount of time, then the project that appropriately uses the newest technology should be chosen first. However, this criterion needs to be applied carefully—applying new technology for its own sake is always counterproductive. The technology must be a legitimate means to solve a business problem. For example, to try to force an expert system as a solution to a problem because "it hasn't been done yet" assures that the final results will meet nobody's needs. Technology is useless unless it solves business problems.

The technology test also must always be applied in terms of the "doability" of the project. It is foolish to attempt a major project using brand-new technology without a basic level of expertise in place. The level of expertise required should be directly proportional to the complexity of the project. A small expertise base is fine for small projects, but a large base of expertise is needed for larger ones.

Project Selection: Summary

Three criteria need to be applied as a part of the project-planning process. The most important is the relationship of the project to the strategic values of the organization. This criterion must be tempered by the blitzkrieg rule that states that short, quick projects are better than long, drawn-out ones. Finally, the tie-breaking principle is the technology test. If all other factors are equal, the choice should go to the project that uses the newest technology appropriately. It is important to note that this test is strictly a tie breaker: technology is *never* a primary decision criterion.

It is a sad but true observation that all of these guidelines may be overridden by contravening forces, such as politics or time constraints. These can quickly turn a rational project-selection process into a free-for-all. The next chapter examines these forces and determines some of the techniques that can be used to mitigate them.

PROJECT BACKLOG

Once the word is out that an information center will work on selected projects, it must be prepared for an avalanche of requests. Almost every area of the organization will come up with a "critical" problem. One of the side effects of project orientation is that there always seems to be a backlog.

As described in Chapter 2, one of the forces in the birth of the information center was the user reaction to the unresponsiveness of the traditional data-processing establishment. If today's information center is viewed as unresponsive, users might look for alternatives this time as well.

Causes of the Backlog

In economics, the classic definition of inflation is "too many dollars chasing too few goods." In similar fashion, project backlog can be defined as "too sparse a staff chasing too many projects." According to this definition, it would be very easy to assume that the obvious solution to the problem of project backlog would be to hire additional staff. It would also be very wrong.

Note that this problem statement has two components: sparse staff and too many projects. As the real cause of the backlog might lie in either of these elements, some of the techniques described in previous chapters must be used to deal with the problem correctly. For example, if the concept of cause-and-effect analysis introduced in Chapter 1 is applied, the resulting top causes may turn out to be like those shown in Figure 10-3.

FIGURE 10-3   Causes of the Project Backlog

TOO SPARSE A STAFF
- Not enough people
- Wrong skill mix
- Working hard, not smart
- Excessive overhead (e.g., meetings)
- Insufficient self-discipline
- Insufficient administrative support

TOO MANY PROJECTS
- Wrong type of projects
- Market forces
- Too successful—reputation creates additional demand
- Unclear mission statement
- Poor project intake procedures
- No project controls in place

Each organization will have its own list of causes, but the principle remains the same: to solve the problems of the backlog, first determine the causes.

Thus, the key point to be gleaned from this example is that just because the backlog is the result of too few staff members chasing too many projects, the correct action may not be to hire more staff. In fact, more staff may cause even more stress in dealing with the backlog since it will require additional communication facilities and more administrative overhead. Even worse, the problem might have nothing at all to do with staffing issues. Sometimes impersonal market forces (fueled by management action) are the cause.

In most organizations, the MIS department charges for its services. Users are charged for analysis, coding, testing, and maintenance of the system. By using the information center, a department might be able to accomplish many of the same projects without incurring these costs. In such cases, where the economics of the marketplace are driving the backlog, increasing the size of the staff will have very little effect. To deal with a backlog effectively, the first step is to analyze the causes.

Dealing with the Backlog

There are two ways in which an information center can work with a backlog: it can reduce it or it can manage its response to it.

As reiterated throughout this text, once the cause is identified, the solutions become much simpler. Since Figure 10-3 listed some potential causes of a backlog, simple brainstorming can generate a number of possi-

---

FIGURE 10-4   Possible Solutions for Backlog

CAUSE: Not enough people

POSSIBLE SOLUTIONS
- Offer internship programs with local colleges (for credit or for reduced salary)
- Create a "tour of duty" program to temporarily assign selected end users for intensive training program and project work
- Hire additional staff

CAUSE: Wrong skill mix

POSSIBLE SOLUTIONS
- Develop cross-training program
- Designate one staff member as senior consultant. Senior consultant does not actually get assigned to projects, but provides expertise to projects that get bogged down
- Provide additional product training
- Give priority to projects that require current skill mix while developing new skills

CAUSE: Wrong types of projects

POSSIBLE SOLUTIONS
- Back to basics: only accept strategically important, blitzkreig projects
- Develop new checklist for project acceptance
- Publish project acceptance guidelines for users

CAUSE: Market forces

POSSIBLE SOLUTIONS
- Increase (or start) charges for project work
- Offer incentives (delivery guarantees, reduced charges) for project work submitted well in advance of need
- Convince MIS to decrease charges project work to be competitive

---

bly useful solutions, as shown in Figure 10-4. This list will be different in each organization, but the idea is fairly clear: to reduce the backlog, use structured brainstorming techniques to identify the causes of that backlog. Then, for each cause, identify potential steps that can be taken to reduce the backlog. There is no magic way to deal with a backlog: each organization must apply the techniques of cause-and-effect analysis in a practical and honest fashion.

Even after taking these steps to lessen the backlog, there still may be too few staff members chasing too many projects. What can an information center do to manage the problem?

The Manic-Depressive Information Center

Psychologists often speak of a manic-depressive personality. Manic-depressives undergo tremendous mood swings: one moment they may be mired in deep depression and the next be cheerfully attacking a number of tasks simultaneously with surprising intensity. An information center with a large backlog often behaves like a manic depressive.

The management of a manic-depressive information center starts with reality therapy. To deal with the manic side, the manager needs to counsel the staff to use the "elephant approach": to eat an elephant, one must proceed one bite at a time. Managing the manic side requires a calmly articulated task plan that addresses needs in a priority order. Energy must be focused on the urgent first, then the important. Establishing task priorities becomes critical and the wise manager spends time keeping the staff isolated from the less critical tasks. Figure 10-5 illustrates some of these strategies.

Conversely, the depressive side of this condition comes from the feeling of being overwhelmed. When the burden of work remains oppressive for a long period of time, the manager must recognize the effects on the staff and refocus energy away from the amount of work involved. A manager might declare a certain time period as a "work-free zone" and encourage the staff to use this time in constructively "letting off steam." Recognition also goes a long way toward overcoming the depressive side. Once again, Figure 10-5 lists some alternative treatments that focus on the human factor. The important point here is simple, however. The backlog creates a level of stress in the staff that must be actively managed, not passively ignored.

FIGURE 10–5   Treating the Manic-Depressive Information Center Staff

MANIC TREATMENTS
- The elephant rule: one must eat an elephant one bite at a time
- Task plans focusing on the critical projects first
- Frequent review of the tasks in progress to ensure that top priority projects get first attention
- Increased emphasis on quality control

DEPRESSIVE TREATMENTS
- Designated "work-free time zones"
- Recognition of accomplishments
- Furlough programs—rotate staff members out to MIS areas or user areas for a period of time to get away from the demands and pressure
- Setting shorter milestones to increase the sense of accomplishment

"Do Unto Others": Taking a User View

The question now becomes one of how to manage the user needs and expectations generated by a backlog. The answer is learned in childhood: "Do unto others as you would have them do unto you."

The information center manager should step into the shoes of the user and ask how would he like it if a project were "lost" in somebody's backlog. Would he like frequent status updates or if there were alternatives to waiting? How would a user feel who only heard complaints about the backlog and how powerless the project manager was against it?

The answer is quite simple: one must manage the user view of the backlog with sympathy, empathy, and understanding, and with an abundance of positive communication. This compassionate management will have no real effect on the backlog itself (all the other strategies will work on that), but it does make the backlog a little easier to live with. More important, by managing a backlog according to the Golden Rule, an information center will build a reputation of cooperation with its users that can only improve its potential for forming strategic partnerships within the organization.

PROJECT SUCCESS FACTORS

Now that the project backlog has been managed, what will make the project, once started, a success? Traditionally, the MIS function has dealt with this question for many years. Information center managers have determined that the key success factors for projects include project plans, well-defined success criteria, intermediate deliverables, and user involvement.

The Project Plan

To reiterate: If you don't know where you are going, how will you know if you got there? With projects as well, if the expectations are not clearly identified in the initial stages and an accurate estimate of all required resources provided, the project is doomed to failure.

A plan for an information center's projects need not be complex, but should be limited to one page and emphasize clarity over form. In Figure 10-6, note that the scope of the project is clearly identified, that each of the objectives has been assigned to a specific area or individual, and that the time estimates are clearly stated. This simple plan can be used to judge the project's current status and estimated completion; it also includes a number of other concepts that will ensure success.

FIGURE 10-6   Sample Project Plan

PROJECT NAME: Quality Assurance Data Analysis
PROJECT SPONSOR: Manager, quality assurance
PROJECT SCOPE: This project will develop the system to capture
                       and analyze the number and types of errors at
                       each stage in the manufacturing process. Data will
                       be gathered for each operation and type of failure
                       at each step in every production run.

PROJECT OBJECTIVES

1. Who: Information center and QA staff
   When: Four days after project approval
   What: Develop the data-base design for the system. This includes all entit-
         ies, attributes, the final data-base description.
APPROVAL: Senior consultant and manager of QA

2. Who: Information center
   When: Five days after completion of objective 1
   What: Based on the data-base design from objective 1, develop programs to
         capture data gathered at each operation in each production run.
APPROVAL: Manager, quality assurance

3. Who: Information center
   When: Five days after completion of objective 1
   What: Develop programs to correct existing data through update or delete
         operations.
APPROVAL: Manager, quality assurance

4. Who: Information center
   When: Ten days after completion of objective 1
   What: Develop appropriate backup procedures for all captured data.
APPROVAL: Manager, information center

5. Who: Senior engineer, quality assurance
   When: Ten days after completion of objective 3
   What: Develop all required reporting programs.
APPROVAL: Manager, quality assurance

6. Who: Senior engineer, quality assurance
   When: Five days after completion of objective 5
   What: Develop all user documentation, including manuals, input forms,
         etc.
APPROVAL: Senior consultant, information center

ESTIMATED START DATE: 04/01   ESTIMATED COMPLETION: 04/25

Well-Defined Success Criteria

Every project that an information center undertakes should start with the
development of a written statement of the project scope. This scope statement must clearly delineate which business problems are to be included in

the project and which are not to be considered. Since this document is the first step in managing the expectations of the user, it must be written from a nontechnical perspective. Two examples are:

1. This project will develop the online programs required to maintain the following data-base segments: MRKT001, SUBM002, PRPN003, and PRDS001.

2. This project will develop programs to add, update, and delete data for market and submarket descriptions (including demographic data), product penetration at the submarket level, and product description information. A detailed description of the data to be captured (including validation rules) will be developed jointly in the first phase.

The first version is far more accurate than the second. It specifies the affected segments with no room for ambiguity. However, the user is given no idea of how the project is related to the user's business problems. The second alternative is much more closely related to the actual business problem since it expresses the activity in user terms. It may be wordier, but the meaning is far more understandable and more easily translated into agreed-upon success criteria.

In addition to a clearly defined scope statement, the plan needs clearly articulated objectives for the project. These objectives must show what is to be done, who is to accomplish the objective, and who will decide when the project is finished. Similar to the scope statement, these objectives must be stated in user-oriented terms that can be clearly measured. Objectives are always graded on a pass/fail basis: they have been accomplished or they have not been accomplished. The objectives must be so phrased as to make that grading unambiguous.

In many cases, the scope agreement and objectives may seem like unnecessary rigmarole. After all, as the project may only require a few weeks of effort to complete, why add one more step to a fairly straightforward process?

The answer lies in the following simple rule of thumb: "If a project moves from 0 per cent to 90 per cent complete in a time period N, the remaining 10 per cent of a project will require a time period of $N \times 2$." As this rule points out, the initial stages of a project seem to pass quickly. They are fueled by the fires of enthusiasm and naiveté. However, as the project nears completion, all of the little things that were overlooked in the initial stages start to appear. Without a well-defined plan to determine the appropriateness of these small additions or changes, the project will drag on well beyond the initial estimate. Even the simplest projects require agreement up front to determine what will be and will not be included. Short projects require short project plans (a memo, perhaps); larger projects require larger (but still simple) plans. Anything else only invites projects that seem to stretch on forever.

Project Management Software

What about the numerous software packages that are available to help manage projects through a number of reports and charts? Organizations that have relied on them heavily to manage larger systems development projects may be tempted to extend their use to information center projects, as well. Unfortunately, these project management packages are a mixed blessing for an information center.

Information center projects are small in scope and rapid in execution. Applying project management software to control simple, small, and quick projects is not a productive exercise. The value gained is simply not worth the work.

Parenthetically, in many organizations, the same can be said about the use of project management software in larger projects. Often it seems that the real role of the project management system is to be able to create four-color charts to dazzle management. The system itself is window dressing: the real day-to-day management of the project is accomplished by much simpler nonautomated alternatives.

This discussion will concentrate on the techniques that can be used to make sure the project is completed. Project management software is one tool that may be useful. A person who finds that this tool helps manage the project should use it, but if it adds no value to the management process, the tool should be ignored.

Intermediate Deliverables

Someone who is having a new house built will visit the site weekly to inspect the work that has been done. The person may not know anything about carpentry or plumbing, but seeing progress produces a feeling of satisfaction. If construction is delayed, the reaction is more likely to be one of understanding since the future owner has a sense of progress against which to compare the delay.

An information center project is no different. If the project has been selected according to the guidelines, it is going to fulfil a strategic need, will be delivered in an expeditious fashion, and will use some of the newest technology available. The wise information center manager will capitalize on this interest by setting up regular checkpoints where progress to date can be inspected. The sense of forward motion that such check-points create is essential to maintaining the user's interest in the project. As was the case with the new homeowner, the user is also less likely to be upset over unavoidable delays after gaining a sense of progress from the intermediate deliverables.

Another value of intermediate deliverables is that the quality of the finished product is greatly improved. Suppose, for example, that during an inspection tour the prospective owner discovers that the hot- and coldwater faucets have been reversed. The problem is much easier to correct if it is found before the plasterboard and tile are in place. Similarly, potential problems in the final product of an information center project are easiest solved when they are discovered early.

Note how each objective in Figure 10-6 has a distinct deliverable date. At each of these points, there will be a tangible deliverable, such as a database description, online programs, report programs, or a user manual. Progress in this project will be apparent at very short intervals.

User Involvement

The oracle of Delphi had an interesting approach to solving problems. When someone approached him with a question, the oracle would go off into the "divining cave" and return moments later with a highly ambiguous answer, for which he would collect a fee. A customer who wanted clarification, would have to ask another question and pay another fee to get a second ambiguous answer that was supposed to clarify the first.

Many data-processing projects have proceeded along a similar path. Users explained their needs at the beginning of a project, and when their answer came back, it might be perceived as incomplete, or simply wrong. To fix the first results, a user was told that it would require a second project with more questions, another period in the "divining cave," and another fee. Is it any wonder that the end-user computing revolution was so successful?

Experience shows that the most successful projects are those that have continuous high-level user support from the very beginning. There are two reasons why this involvement contributes to success. First, the level of understanding of the business problem increases dramatically when the user is directly involved in the design and implementation stages. The "oh, by the way . . ." statements that emerge with ongoing involvement make the final product a much more accurate reflection of the real business needs. Second, participation always generates a sense of ownership. The project is not just an information center activity, but is "our" project. By developing a sense of ownership, implementation and integration into existing work flows are greatly simplified.

How, then, is an information center to encourage user involvement from the beginning? The following suggestions are also summarized in Figure 10-7:

1. *Joint Design.* In the Chapter 5 discussion of techniques of data-base design, a cooperative, iterative approach was recommended to get the best results. There is very little in the data-base design process that is beyond the grasp of most users and the final product will reflect the actual business relationships much more accurately (objective 1 in Figure 10-6).

FIGURE 10-7   Involving the User

POTENTIAL USER ROLE	RATIONALE
Joint Design	User knows nature of business better than information center
Prototyping	Increased user ownership in project
	User can determine how system will fit into work flow
Test Plan	User knows real work flow and will be able to determine test cases better
Documentation	User will express concepts and procedures in more meaningful terms
Work Segmentation	User will develop reports and screens that reflect real business needs
	Reports are likely to change often. Putting development into the hands of the user improves ability to respond quickly

2. *Prototypes.* The degree of user involvement is inversely proportional to the length of time from design to tangible result. In the example in Figure 10-6, the lead times are short enough to hold everyone's attention, but long waits for the first screen or report mean markedly diminished interest. Chapter 6 discussed ways to use prototyping to shorten dramatically the time between concept and initial test version. The use of prototypes will keep user interest high.

3. *Test Plans.* Testing the system without a plan is not testing at all, it is merely fooling around. The user should be asked to develop a detailed test plan that shows the action to be taken and the expected results. Calculations must be done manually first to make sure that the results are correct. "Looks right" is not good enough; the user is best suited to determine what is actually correct.

4. *User Documentation.* Depending on the type of project, the user documentation may range from a simple paragraph to a complete book. Making the user documentation the responsibility of the users themselves has two benefits: it ensures that the users are actually exercising all of the system's options as they develop the documentation, while it dramatically increases user ownership of the system. However, this approach requires discipline. The project should not be considered complete until the documentation is finished. No matter how many tantrums the user throws, the in-

formation center needs to adhere to the following rule: the system does not go into production until the user manual is finished. Notice in Figure 10-6 that objective 5 regarding user documentation is to be accomplished by the user area but approved by the information center.

5. *Work Segmentation.* In certain projects, the work can be divided between the information center and the user department. For example, an information center may take responsibility for all data management, obtaining the required data extracts, developing the data-base load programs, and creating the online programs to add, update, or delete data. Using a 4GL the users will take responsibility for developing the reports required by the system, based on model procedures supplied by the information center. Division of the work makes the users active participants, not just advisors. Figure 10-6 illustrates this approach: the information center builds the data-maintenance programs and the users build the reporting programs.

THE MAINTENANCE BURDEN

Once the best projects for an information center have been selected and successfully completed, that success brings with it its own problems: the burden caused when changes are needed to the successful projects after they have been in operation for a while.

The Causes

Changes are required for a number of reasons, and if these reasons are understood, it may be possible to prevent wasting time making changes that are unnecessary.

Coding Errors. Even when using some of the elegantly simple tools such as fourth-generation languages, spreadsheets, and expert systems, it is easy to make errors in the formulas, algorithms, or validation criteria that make up a system. Careful testing according to a predetermined plan can go a long way toward reducing these errors, but it is almost inevitable that a small number of coding errors will be introduced into the production system. Careless coding errors are likely to occur more often than design errors or business changes even in a carefully executed project, but should be much easier to correct.

Design Errors. "But I meant . . ." Maintenance requests that start out like this mean that the system does not reflect the underlying structure and process of the business. Design errors are almost always the result of poorly articulated business rules, incorrect assumptions, poor communication, or aloof design techniques. Regardless of how sophisticated the system is, it will not solve business problems until a portion of it is structurally revised. Design errors are much harder to correct than coding errors as they can require a number of changes in a number of system components. Coding errors mean that things weren't done correctly whereas design errors mean that the correct things weren't done.

Business Changes. No business stays constant. The external economic environment changes, business tactics change, and occasionally even the strategic value set of an organization changes. As the business changes, so also must the system.

The simplest business-driven change is the need for new information. In such cases, there is no change to the underlying data structures. The only change is a new report or screen that presents the existing data in a new format. These new transformations of the data into information are usually fairly straightforward as long as the underlying data structures have been correctly determined and implemented.

However, sometimes even the underlying structure needs to be altered. In those cases, as long as the system has been properly designed, most of these structural business changes are accommodated in one of two ways: an attribute (field) is added to an existing entity, or an entirely new entity is added to the system. (See Chapter 5 for a description of these terms.) Under normal conditions, these changes can be isolated from the rest of the system, limiting the number of programs that need to be changed. Only those system components that are directly related to the new attribute or entity will require maintenance and the others can continue undisturbed.

However, in many cases, the fundamental business rules are altered and require a significant restructuring of the system. For example, a policy decision may be made that allows for matrix management within the organization. Accordingly, the previous one-to-many relationship between department and employee becomes many-to-many (see Chapter 5 for an explanation of why this is undesirable). In those cases where the business has undergone a significant change in its underlying data relationships, the maintenance efforts will be significant as well, perhaps requiring rewriting a major portion of the system.

Prevention and Cure

There are steps that a project-oriented information center can take to minimize the impact of maintenance requirements. These steps are summarized in Figure 10-8.

Coding Errors. The best prevention against coding errors is a comprehensive test plan that has been developed in conjunction with the

FIGURE 10-8   Causes and Cures Of Maintenance

SOURCE	POSSIBLE CAUSES	POSSIBLE CURES
Coding Errors	Carelessness	Imbed comments
	Unclear algorithms	Standards
	Uncontrolled ego	Naming conventions
		Test plans and walkthroughs
Design Errors	Poorly articulated business rules	User involvement
		Prototype
	Incorrect assumptions	Intermediate results
	Poor communication	Design notebooks
	Aloof techniques	Intense honesty
Business Changes	New information needs	Solid data-base design
	Simple structural change (new attribute, new entity)	User reporting
		Top-down development
	Complex structural change (change in current entity relationships)	

users. Each potential condition should be identified and executed to ensure that it is correctly handled by the system. As more efforts are put into testing on the front end, fewer errors will need to be corrected in a maintenance mode.

Even the best projects, however, may inadvertently overlook an error and so the next best defense is to plan for a certain number of errors. First, comments ought to be embedded within the code or spreadsheet, explaining complex algorithms or tricky logic. The developer must always assume that someone else will maintain the project and so leave behind enough hints to make the process a simple one.

Second, a simple set of standards must be created and enforced. An information center ought to have standards for the structure and format for spreadsheet macros and 4GL procedures. A standard structure makes it harder to make errors of omission and easier to identify the thought processes behind errors of commission.

Third, much as standards ought to be enforced for structure and format, naming conventions need to be developed for all files, procedures, and variables. The conventions should ensure that the names are meaningful and understandable. Who wants to try to determine what field "X1" means?

Finally, a development culture needs to be nurtured that encourages a "second set of eyes" for every activity. No information center staff member, no matter how senior, ought to be allowed to make changes without another person inspecting the change to make sure that the correct change has been made, that it has been done according to standards, and that it has been adequately tested. Uncontrolled ego is perhaps the most destructive trait in a project-oriented information center.

Design Errors. By and large, design errors are caused by incorrect assumptions and poor communication. Prevention, then, is merely adhering to the guidelines discussed throughout this chapter: involve the user from the start, use prototyping extensively, provide intermediate deliverables, and limit the scope of the project. Design should be the most time-consuming part of any project since design errors are the most costly to correct.

What if, after the best of efforts, a design error is discovered? One suggestion might be to keep notes at each step of the design process, documenting each decision that is made, each tough choice that is encountered, and each new revelation of information. These notes will prove to be a valuable resource if the system is to be redesigned. They also serve as a valuable learning tool. By documenting the design process, it is easier to determine how the design error crept into the project. Perhaps lessons can be learned that can keep it from happening again.

Even more important than note keeping is that, as soon as a design error is found, everyone involved in the project be told about that error as openly and as honestly as possible. Only when the problem has been identified and explored will the project have any chance of long-term success. Trying to patch something together secretly only delays the pain and needlessly complicates the rebuilding process that will inevitably be required.

This requirement for complete honesty regarding design errors is a difficult one for many information centers to meet. Most of them started out as successes in end-user computing and moving into projects may not have been an easy step. If the project is discovered to have design errors, the first impulse is to hide it so as to not blemish the record. In the long run, however, facing design problems with complete intellectual honesty is a far better strategy than allowing pride to find a stop-gap solution.

Business Changes. The basic premise of business changes and information center projects is as follows: The underlying structures of most businesses are remarkably stable. Changing business conditions most often result in a demand for new transformations of the existing data structures into new information. This premise means that if a system is implemented with a solid data-base design, the most likely type of change will be a new report or screen.

The implications of this premise are simple: train the users in the tools needed to create new reports or screens and the maintenance burden resulting from business changes will become almost insignificant. Much of an information center's maintenance burdens can be completely eliminated by a policy that says that the reporting components of any information center project will be the responsibility of the users themselves. After all, isn't that the underlying premise of end-user computing anyway?

Nevertheless, there will eventually be some business changes that will require changes to the underlying structure, especially a new attribute or a new entity. Thus, the effects of these changes should be minimized by developing projects in a modular fashion. This was the lesson learned from the structured programming revolution in the late 1960s. Each component of a project should be oriented toward a single function. The separate components are then connected to make up the system. A change in one component is isolated from the rest of the system. To minimize the effect of these types of changes, an information center's projects must always be developed in a top-down, modular fashion.

Finally, in the event of major structural changes in the business (recall the example of matrix management), an information center has very few choices with regard to maintenance. Major changes usually require a complete overhaul of the systems, perhaps even starting over from scratch. Although many of these changes can be prevented by using good design techniques, eventually the very nature of the underlying business relationships may change, requiring considerable maintenance effort.

SUMMARY

This chapter began with the premise that certain projects seem to be predestined for an information center. Not important enough for a traditional MIS group to undertake, yet too complicated for an end user to accomplish without assistance, such projects provide an information center the chance to escape the trap of training and consulting that seems to lead to oblivion.

However, if an information center is to succeed in project orientation, it must select its projects carefully, concentrating on the organization's value set, the blitzkrieg rule, and the useful application of new technology in the project. Then, once the project is undertaken, the information center must ensure its success through user involvement, intermediate deliverables, and well-defined criteria set forth in a written project scope.

Finally, the chapter discussed the maintenance implications of a project orientation, outlining the causes of system maintenance and identifying steps that can be taken to prevent the need for maintenance and to minimize its impact.

The first chapter discussed the prime directive of an information center: to facilitate the transformation of data into information that managerial, professional, and support staff members can use to solve business problems. As this chapter has shown, that mandate can also include a strong orientation toward development projects.

SUGGESTED PROJECTS

1. The information center at a major university serves the administration functions of the institution. It is faced with selecting one of the following projects:

   • Develop a "grade inflation" analysis system for the registrar's office. This system would track class grades over time and perform a number of different statistical analyses.

   • Develop an application-tracking system for the dean's office. This system would identify every open faculty position and gather information about every applicant.

   If you were the newly hired manager of the information center, how would you go about deciding between these two projects? What information would you need? What criteria would you use? Use your criteria to select one of the projects and justify your choice.

2. Using the project you selected in the previous exercise, develop a simple project plan. You may use the format in Figure 10-3 or develop your own format.

CHAPTER **11**

Quality and Ethics: The Realities of a Project Orientation

The mathematics of firing an artillery shell are fascinating. When the shell is fired, there are a number of different forces at work. First, there is the force created by the explosion at the breech of the gun that propels the shell at an angle toward the target. Second, there are the natural forces, such as the pull of gravity, that combine with the explosive force and describe a graceful parabolic arc between gun and target. The calculation of that path is essential to a successful artillery barrage.

What's interesting about this example is that to describe the path of the shell, a physicist must separate the forces into their vertical and horizontal components, called vectors (see Figure 11-1). Only when the problem has been described in terms of the underlying vectors can the physicist accurately predict the flight of the shell. (Even though the actual mathematics of Figure 11-1 are outside the scope of this book, the analysis is really quite elegant. The trigonometric functions should not be intimidating.)

A project-oriented information center can be likened to the flight of an artillery shell. It leaves the gun explosively, traveling in one direction, only to find that forces outside its control are pulling it into a completely different path. What are these forces that are working against an information center's success and how can an information center cope with them?

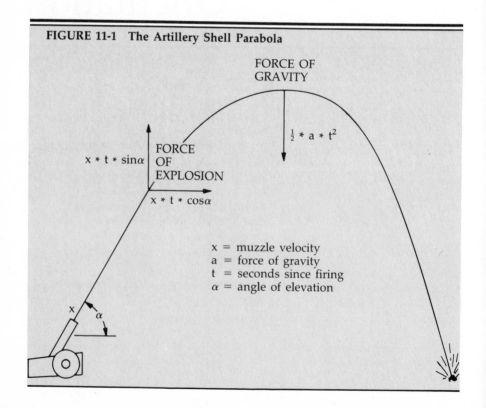

FIGURE 11-1   The Artillery Shell Parabola

FORCE OF
GRAVITY

$\frac{1}{2} * a * t^2$

$x * t * \sin\alpha$

FORCE
OF
EXPLOSION

$x * t * \cos\alpha$

x = muzzle velocity
a = force of gravity
t = seconds since firing
α = angle of elevation

VECTORS AGAINST SUCCESS

The artillery shell example was relatively simple: the forces at work were the horizontal and vertical components of the explosive force and the downward force of gravity. The vectors of success in an information center are more complex; they are shown in Figure 11-2. The upward and forward vectors are discussed elsewhere in this book, and so the following focuses on the downward forces that threaten the success of an information center.

Time Expectations

Deadlines are not new to an information center. Time expectations have always been an established fact of corporate life. However, not all deadlines are created equal, nor should all deadlines be treated equally. Among the different kinds of deadlines are:

1. *Legal Requirements.* All organizations are subject to the ever-changing legal environment. As laws change, the organization needs to be able to respond in a timely fashion to avoid penalties or liability. For example, when the laws about electronic banking transactions were changed to require a consumer advisory on each monthly statement, noncompliance by a given date carried significant legal penalties. The changes to the programs that printed statements had deadlines that were legally mandated.

2. *Critical Path Deadlines.* In complex projects that require coordination among a number of different areas of an organization, some tasks lie on the critical path. This means that any delay in those tasks will delay the entire project and will affect a number of other departments.

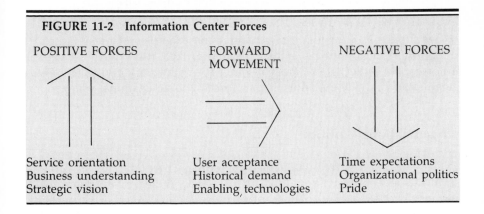

FIGURE 11-2 Information Center Forces

POSITIVE FORCES

Service orientation
Business understanding
Strategic vision

FORWARD
MOVEMENT

User acceptance
Historical demand
Enabling technologies

NEGATIVE FORCES

Time expectations
Organizational politics
Pride

FIGURE 11-3   Negative Forces: Time Expectations

LEGAL REQUIREMENTS
  • Regulation changes requiring customer notification.
  • Filing deadlines for forms, statements
CRITCAL PATH DEADLINES
  • PC installation and training required as part of larger project
  • Information needed as a condition of strategic planning
EGO-DRIVEN DEADLINES
  • Request originated at very high level of organization
  • Another organization failed in the task
EXTERNALLY IMPOSED
  • Management made promises before all specifications were known
  • Customers expect results by a predetermined date

---

3. *Ego-Driven Deadlines.* When the power of an information center's tool kit becomes known, it results in an overwhelming temptation to overpromise. However, once the project is started or evaluated in terms of other commitments, the promised date may prove unrealistic. In many cases, altering the deadline is not even possible because of the potential loss of credibility or the ensuing damage to the information center manager's ego.

4. *Externally Imposed Deadlines.* Related to ego-driven deadlines, these deadlines are the result of some other person's commitments. Often, these promises were made in the preliminary stages of a project and were never modified to reflect the changes in scope or deliverables. Other times, these deadlines have filtered through successive layers of the organization, picking up additional urgency and shorter time frames at each level. In these cases, it is the user's ego, not that of the information center, that drives the deadline.

See Figure 11-3 for a summary and some examples of these forces.

Although deadlines have the potential to ruin even the most capable information center, there are still other forces at work trying to militate against success. One of those other forces is organizational politics.

Organizational Politics

No organization is free of political pressures. There are always "up-and-comers," pet projects, key departments, and privileged programs. Additionally, for each real political force, there are any number of perceived political forces that information centers and their managers think ought to be appeased.

1. *Back-Scratch Power.* The ancient Romans had a term for it *quid pro quo* (loosely translated, "You scratch my back and I'll scratch yours"). In many organizations, almost nothing is done without marking an invisible score card. The obligations created by this approach become almost overpowering.

2. *People Power.* In every organization there seem to be people who command respect or fear. Alternatively, there are also those people who are tagged as "up-and-comers." Both types of people represent powerful political forces in the organization, and when an information center has a chance to carry out a project for these people, it is very tempting to agree to do so at the expense of other commitments and in spite of the manager's best judgment.

3. *Program Power.* Much as certain people seem to have inordinate amounts of power, so also do certain programs. These are the initiatives or projects that seem to have a life of their own and can siphon off substantial organizational resources, such as staff, funds, and equipment. For example, if the company president declares this to be the "Year of Quality," an inordinate amount of time and effort will go into such programs as a "Quality Improvement Council," "The Quality Index," or the "Quality Olympics."

4. *Strategy Power.* Finally, some projects and people demand priority treatment because they reflect the strategic vision of the organization. These projects are the tactical means that the organization will use to accomplish its strategic goals.

See Figure 11-4 for a summary and some examples of these forces.

FIGURE 11-4   Negative Forces: Organizational Politics

BACK-SCRATCH POWER
  • Key supporter of information center needs a special project
  • Projects for internal support areas (such as accounts payable, personnel) upon which the information center relies

PEOPLE POWER
  • Requests from the chairman
  • Internal projects for the information center manager's boss

PROGRAM POWER
  • Free support for the CEO's favorite charity
  • Requests from key support groups: quality assurance, finance, etc., in response to a crash program

STRATEGY POWER
  • Projects directly related to a strategic plan objective
  • Projects that relate to the nature of the organization (e.g., quality of care in a hospital)

Political forces are not in themselves wrong; in fact, no organization can succeed without politics. However, unless an information center looks closely at the political pressures, it may soon find it has lost control of its own destiny and will be buffeted about by the constantly changing political winds.

Pride

In traditional Greek tragedy, the hero's downfall was usually brought about through *hubris,* or overpowering pride. Because of such pride, the hero would overreach his abilities and challenge the gods in some inappropriately arrogant way. The lesson is an important one for most information centers. Since an information center is a new group with new tools and a new approach, there is a powerful temptation for it to think of itself as invincible. Some of the dictates of this "Superman" mentality are:

1. *Faster Than a Speeding Bullet.* The new tools that allow an information center to complete projects quickly have an interesting side effect: they build in a short-term reinforcement expectations. Information centers quickly become accustomed to producing results in hours instead of weeks. When a major project appears that seems to take longer than usual to complete, the length itself is perceived as a problem. In an effort to get rid of this long project that is interfering with fast turnaround, an information center is tempted to do dumb things.

2. *More Powerful Than a Locomotive.* Not only are the new tools fast, but they provide a sense of power. Soon the information center feels it can do no wrong. Doesn't it have the best tools and the best people in the organization? Soon any sense of limits disappears and the information center, feeling invincible, is tempted into projects well beyond its capabilities and scope.

3. *Able to Leap Tall Buildings in a Single Bound.* Did anyone ever ask Superman why it was important to be able to leap tall buildings? It was flashy, but it seemed to be a skill that lacked practical application. A similar force faces information centers: since the technology is so attractive and looks so good, there is a temptation to concentrate on the flashy at the expense of the useful. The result is isolated technology that looks good and attracts praise, but has only limited use from a corporate perspective.

See Figure 11-5 for a summary and some examples of these forces.

Forces against Success: An Analysis

In the artillery shell example of Figure 11-1, the forces seem fairly straightforward: there is the upward component of the explosion and the

---

FIGURE 11-5   Negative Forces: Pride

FASTER THAN A SPEEDING BULLET
- Underestimating project requirements
- Testing proportional to the development time (short development = short test cycle)

MORE POWERFUL THAN A LOCOMOTIVE
- Accepting projects too large in scope and requirements
- Using incorrect tool for project

ABLE TO LEAP TALL BUILDINGS
- Concentrating on the "razzle-dazzle" projects
- Grandstanding: projects that will gather praise but serve no useful purpose

---

downward force of gravity. The picture is incomplete, however, unless the nature of the forces is understood.

Once the shell is shot out of the cannon at a given muzzle velocity, its vertical upward component of velocity is constant. On the other hand, the downward velocity is not constant. As Newton first showed, gravity represents an acceleration and the downward component of gravity in Figure 11-1 will grow geometrically over time. The result is inevitable: the shell will not continue on the upward angle but will eventually crash to earth.

With an information center, the downward forces also increase geometrically over time. Shorter deadlines, more politics, and more ego problems will arise as time goes by. If an information center is to avoid crashing to the ground, it must counter the acceleration of the downward force by adding two other forces into the picture (see Figure 11-6). These new forces are *quality* (doing things right) and *ethics* (doing the right things).

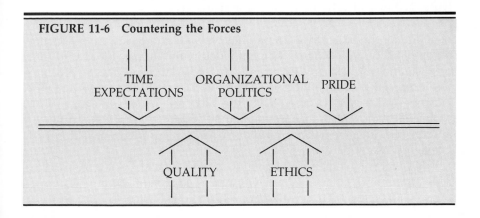

FIGURE 11-6   Countering the Forces

FIGURE 11-7 The Quality Rules

RULE 1: Do It Right Or Don't Do It at All
> People have a long memory for bad news, but a short memory for good news. They will remember a project was wrong and forget that it was on time.

RULE 2: The Individual Is Always Responsible for Quality
> In the final analysis, the quality is always the result of an individuals' choice to do the task right. Blame cannot be passed off to a committee or to amorphous forces such as "management" or "market."

RULE 3: The Walk Must Match the Talk
> An organization cannot bring quality into a product or process by using a jawbone. Every action and every decision must reflect the verbal commitment to do things right.

QUALITY: DOING THINGS RIGHT

In recent years, quality has become a buzzword in many corporations. In addition to the traditional quality-assurance function that always accompanied the manufacturing process, a number of organizations created high-level departments, such as "Quality Systems," "The Quality Institute," or "President's Q Team."

If an information center is to succeed over the long term, it, too, must pay very close attention to the quality of its products and projects. More than slogans and special task forces, however, quality in an information center revolves around attitudes and behavior, not platitudes. Three guiding principles, or *quality rules* (Figure 11-7), are proposed here that can apply to the forces working against success.

Rule 1: Do It Right or Don't Do It at All

To illustrate this rule, say a woman has won a flight to Hawaii. She departs on time, is seated in first class, is provided with fantastic meals and exotic drinks, and receives lavish attention. Upon landing, she is given the traditional lei greeting and is presented with the keys to a free rental car. However, she is also greeted by the airline's passenger agent with a chagrined look and the information that there has been a slight mistake and that her luggage has been sent to Acapulco, but that it should arrive in Hawaii in a few days.

What will the woman remember about the trip—that she departed and arrived on time, that she had wonderful food and drink, or that her luggage was lost? The truth about human behavior is that everyone remembers that something went wrong long after they have forgotten what went right.

In terms of an information center, this rule has a simple application: the best technology, the best people, and the best facilities mean nothing unless the results are correct. A "high tech" wrong answer is still wrong.

Rule 2: The Individual Is Always Responsible for Quality

No matter how piously an organization advocates quality, the quality of a product or a service is always the responsibility of an individual—not of management, the system, the procedures, or other people on the team.

For an information center's staff members, this quality rule ought to produce the attitude that everything they do should be of such quality that they are proud to be associated with the results. If circumstances and outside pressures are ruining the quality of a project, they cannot sit by and shrug off the results as somebody else's fault. The best approach to quality starts with individual responsibility.

Rule 3: The Walk Must Match the Talk

All of the management proclamations and team pep talks will become meaningless as soon as an organization pressures an information center to skimp on quality in order to meet a deadline or feed an ego. If the information center manager has been preaching quality to the staff and does not manage the department in a way that is consistent with that approach, the organizational schizophrenia is obvious to everyone. One organization proclaimed its policy to be, "Quality is the first among equals of quality, schedule, and cost." When that inherently contradictory statement met the test of real decisions, on-time and low cost triumphed every time. If an organization's executives continue to talk about quality but reward only on-time delivery, they can expect slipshod products that meet their schedules.

Quality Rules in Application

A case study will show how these quality rules might operate in a real situation.

The manager of the marketing department approaches the information center with the following problem: The chairman has asked her to present an analysis of the company's customer base at the executive summit meeting in three days. The data is located in five different application systems, and in each system the data has a different structure.

Additionally, a given customer may be on one or more of the application systems, but there is no common identifier positively to link the customer in one system with the same customer in another application. The marketing manager has been a stalwart defender of the information center at data-processing steering committee meetings and has been willing to dedicate budget money to support the concept. However, the manager of the information center knows that, owing to the complexity of the data structures, it will take a week of work to do the kind of analysis that is being requested. What should the manager do?

First, the manager should consider the forces that are at work in the problem. There are the political forces: the marketing manager has been a strong supporter and the project will provide exposure to the chairman. There are the time forces: the executive summit is to be held in three days. Because coordinating the calendars of executives would present a problem, it would be very difficult to change the meeting date. There are the pride forces: a "home run" here would be noticed by every top executive in the company. All of the potentially destructive forces are present in this one example.

It is time to apply the quality rules. Rule 1 says that it must be done right or not at all. A "crash program" might produce an analysis that could be presented, but there are risks: the analysis might be incorrect, misleading, or incomplete. If management decisions were to be based on the results of this data that has been "slapped together," significant resources might be wasted. The risks of failure far outweigh the potential benefits. Based on this rule, the information center manager needs to work with the marketing manager to determine a smaller-scale product that can be delivered with accuracy and confidence.

The second quality rule can also be applied to this case. None of the participants can be excused for a slipshod effort just because the request was initiated by the chairman. The quality is still the responsibility of the individuals involved. Poor quality analysis will be the responsibility of the people who produced the work and cannot be blamed on the time constraints or the outside forces that demanded the results. By applying this rule, the same conclusion is reached: only a smaller-scale project can yield a result that the participants will be proud to call their own.

When the first two quality rules are applied to the problem, the same result seems obvious: don't try to do the complete analysis as expected, but determine a smaller analysis that can be done well enough to make the participants proud. However, in most organizations, this alternative would not be pursued. Why? The answer is rule 3—the walk doesn't match the talk.

The issue of quality in an information center reduces to that of organizational schizophrenia. The information center manager and the marketing manager both recognize that the original request is far too ambitious for the time frame. They realize that the best solution is to produce a smaller-scale, but much more accurate, project. They also realize that they run the risk of incurring the chairman's wrath by doing the right thing. Doing the full analysis in a "crash program" seems to be the more attractive alternative, even though it's clearly not the best solution. In most cases, they will conclude that it is better to provide the appearance of meeting a need than to antagonize the chairman.

As this case study shows, the quality rules only identify the right way to do things. The other side of the coin is equally important: how to do the right thing.

ETHICS: DOING THE RIGHT THINGS

It is not enough to be able to know what ought to be done, as the best choice often is not available. There are some strategies that can be used when the ideal meets the real.

Deals with the Devil

In Steven Vincent Benet's short story "The Devil and Daniel Webster," a farmer faced a terrible dilemma. Years earlier, frustrated by trying to make a living on land of somewhat dubious quality, he had made a deal with the devil whereby he would be accorded success and fame for a period of years, in return for which he would forfeit his soul. In the story, as the promised period neared its end, the farmer became terrified at the prospect of paying the debt.

In many ways, the story is an image of the problems faced by many information centers when they confront the real world. The downward forces seem to be overwhelming and so a course of action is taken that meets the immediate need. Unfortunately, the results are the same as described in Benet's story: there will come a time when that debt will have to be paid. In the short story, Daniel Webster acted as attorney for the defense and negotiated the release of the farmer from his contract. Most information centers will not be so lucky.

The moral of the story is clear. The premise was well defined: the land was not fruitful enough to make the farm a success. The trouble began when the farmer jumped at an attractive solution without understanding the true cost of the bargain. The payback was far in the future, the payment was an intangible soul, and the pressures to do *something* were strong. The real problem was not the deal itself, but that the deal was made without fully understanding its implications.

Whenever the real meets the ideal, compromises will have to be made. These are the inevitable deals with the devil that are made in any business environment. The secret is always to know exactly what has been traded away.

In the example of the marketing manager, the reality of the situation is that a crash program will be launched to provide the complete analysis for the managers' meeting. When this decision is acknowledged as a deal with the devil, two further steps can be taken. First, the manager can look for alternative solutions to solve the problem, including:

1. Hiring outside consultants to do the job.
2. Shifting the burden to other departments, such as user areas, the MIS department, or internal staff support groups.
3. Setting up a crash information center program.

Once the crash program is seen as one of a number of alternatives, the chances of minimizing the long-term effect improve. The chances get even better when analyzed with regard to the potential costs in money, staff, resources, and reputation. For example, if the crash program is selected, the information center manager must understand that the solution will involve certain costs, such as:

1. User expectations. Once the word gets out about this crash project, how will the information center respond to other users with their own emergencies?
2. Staff morale. What will be the impact on staff morale if the job is perceived as one crash program after another?
3. Potential for error. If it all works, the information center is a hero; but if it fails, what are the potential effects on the information center's credibility and reputation.

Figure 11-8 provides a checklist to help analyze a deal for potential strengths and weaknesses. By using this checklist and looking at the problem in terms of a deal with the devil, an information center manager has a framework in which to make a decision, including alternatives to the deal and a fairly good estimate of the cost. If the decision is to go ahead with the crash project, at least the manager knows the implications of that decision. When the devil comes calling (usually in the form of a senior vice-president) to collect, at least it is not a surprise.

Disagreeing without Being Disagreeable

Another benefit emerges by looking at the problem as a deal with the devil: the information center manager has retained the right to say "No" and to suggest a counterproposition. After all, quality rule 2 says that the individual is responsible for quality and the marketing manager's emergency is not necessarily the information center manager's problem. The trick is to make disagreement palatable.

When dealing with two-year-old children, a simple "No" is best. No explanation is necessary. However, adults hate to hear No, regardless of

---

FIGURE 11-8   Checklist for "Deals with the Devil"

WHAT DOES THE DEAL GIVE AWAY?
What is the probability of failure?
What is the impact of failure?
- on the information center's reputation
- on the financial health of the organization
- on the organization's goals
- on the credibility of the people involved

What will really be required in terms of
- staff demands
- dollar cost
- other resources

WHAT DOES THE INFORMATION CENTER GET IN THE DEAL?
What are the direct benefits?
- billable charges
- improved techniques developed
- new technology acquired

What are the indirect benefits?
- prestige
- future considerations
- improved political leverage in the organization

WHAT ARE THE REAL IMPLICATIONS OF NOT DOING THE DEAL?
Organizational implications?
- strategic goals missed or attained
- real dollar cost

Legal implications?
- fines or penalties
- forced actions (e.g., closing the business)

Political implications?
- significant long-term changes (more than one year in future)
- will skipping the deal make information center look better (for integrity) or worse (unresponsive)

---

the explanation. The trick, then, is to find noncompromising ways to say Yes. This can be done with a response of "Yes, but . . ." The wise information center manager can then add conditions that put a price on the deal. When the marketing manager of the case study is forced to consider the cost of the crash program in meaningful terms, she may also become interested in considering alternatives to the proposed solution.

The biggest mistake in putting a price on a deal is to express that price in terms of money. Suppose the information center manager in the example responded to the marketing manager by saying, "Yes, we'll do the crash project, but it will cost you $10,000." Since the marketing manager is under great pressure, she may decide that $10,000 is a small price to pay for not being embarrassed at the meeting. It isn't her money and the worst that can happen is that she will be chastized at the end of the year for going over budget. In this case, the cost did not provide a sufficient incentive for the marketing manager to consider alternatives or to see the problem as a deal with the devil.

However, suppose the information center manager says, "Yes, we'll do the crash project for you, but we can do it only if your top staff person is assigned to us for the entire project to make sure the results are correct." The price now has been phrased in terms the marketing manager can understand. The project will affect every other task in her department and she has to determine if the crash project is worth the loss of an important staff member for a week. The manager's willingness to consider alternatives has increased dramatically.

Alternatively, the manager might respond: "Yes, we'll do the crash project, but only if you sign this memo that outlines some of the potential errors and poor quality that will result from the short time frame. This memo will be included in the appendix of the report." Once again, the cost of the crash project has been phrased in terms that the marketing manager can understand. She must go on record as having approved a project of dubious quality in order to meet a deadline. The information center manager is glad to carry out the project as long as the risks have been clearly identified and accepted publicly.

This is how the "yes, but . . ." approach works. An information center can still make its deals with the devil, but the cost of the deal is shared with others. If the cost of the deal is not shared, there will never be any interest in discussing alternatives or consequences.

SUMMARY

This chapter began with a discussion of the forces that are trying adversely to affect the course of a project-oriented information center. These forces are not unique to an information center, but are at work in every part of an organization. However, an information center is a relatively new part of most organizations and it has not been able to develop a natural resistance to these forces.

The tool to counteract such forces is simple: quality must be the organization's overriding value. This quality orientation cannot be expressed through signs, slogans, and empty platitudes, but must be an ingrained component of every decision and every action.

The real world, however, often forces an information center to compromise with what it knows is right. The way to manage the real world is to see each compromise as a deal with the devil. For each deal, there are always alternatives and costs that drive the decision. It's alright to make deals with the devil as long as the real price is understood.

There are ways to disagree without being disagreeable. When the deal with the devil is unacceptable, the best response is, "Yes, but. . . ." The price of the deal must be communicated clearly in understandable terms. Money is usually the worst way in which to express price; time, staff, or reputation often works best.

The forces that are trying to force an information center into a different path are not invincible and must be overcome. Remember what happens to an artillery shell at the end of its trajectory.

SUGGESTED PROJECTS

1. Defend or oppose the following assertion:

   Occasionally there are situations that demand that quality be sacrificed to meet another need.

   Be sure to include the following issues in your discussion: the cost of quality, political forces, and the short-term and long-term implications of choices.

2. In politics, it is considered highly honorable to resign when significant ethical or moral disagreements arise. Are there any situations in an information center that would cause you to resign rather than complete the project?

3. Consider the following situation:

   The MIS director has publicly stated that all personal computers will be purchased from a single source, the same vendor who provides mainframe software. However, the corporate director of strategic planning (who is widely acknowledged to be the next president) has completely ignored that directive and purchased twenty low-priced clones for his department. Unfortunately, he is now unable to connect them to the mainframe using the standard terminal emulation hardware. He has come to the information center for help.

   Analyze this problem in terms of the forces discussed in the chapter. As information center manager, what would you do? Be prepared to defend your answer in terms of the quality forces and ethical issues discussed in the chapter.

C H A P T E R   12

Staffing

In the English countryside on the Salisbury Plain near Wiltshire lie the remains of what may have been the first information center. On this site, known as Stonehenge, large stone slabs are carefully arranged in a pattern that the ancient Druids were believed to have used to predict the celestial events that directed their worship services. Today, however, the exact ways in which these stones were used to predict eclipses and solstices are for the most part unknown. All modern scientists can do is guess at some of the most obvious uses; the secrets of Stonehenge died with the Druids who erected the stones and used the site.

The modern information center can learn a number of lessons from Stonehenge, but perhaps the most important is the need for a highly qualified staff to make the technology work to solve business problems. Stonehenge without the ancient Druids is just a collection of stone; an information center without a competent staff is merely a collection of metal, glass, and silicon chips. It is important to examine the staffing issues of an information center from various perspectives, including the type of person needed and the techniques required to evaluate and train a highly qualified staff.

DIVERSITY AND UNITY

The people who staff today's information centers are marked by an incredible diversity of backgrounds. Some come up through the user ranks, others have been traditional application developers, and still others come into an information center directly from school. All of them, however, have a number of skills in common regardless of their backgrounds.

People Skills

The traditional systems development organization has always included people with strong interpersonal skills. Systems analysts had to be able to interview users to determine their needs and to express the required flow of information as a series of system and programming specifications. The managers of the traditional systems organization needed the same people skills as any other manager to survive in the organization and to accomplish their goals and objectives. The need to understand users and to express their needs clearly is not new; in fact, many of the people skills required for an information center are identical to those that a successful traditional systems development organization should have been using all along.

Listening. There is a marked difference between hearing and listening. There is no doubt that an overactive four-year-old hears the parent's voice, and understands the word "stop," but often there is no change in behavior

---

FIGURE 12-1   Listening Skills

Good listening requires more than hearing. It requires the listener to provide verbal clues and encouragement to the speaker in one of the following ways:
- Affirmation
   "Go on . . ."
   "Uh huh . . ."
   "I understand . . ."
- Reflection
   "I hear you saying . . ."
   "What I think you mean is . . ."
- Prospecting
   "Tell me about. . . ."
   "What were some of the things you did when . . .?"
- Probing
   "Wait. Tell me more about that."
   "What do you mean by that term?"
   "How so?"
- Colombo Approach
   "I'm confused . . ."
   "I don't understand . . ."
   "Can you help me with that idea?"

---

to indicate that the message was received. True listening is always reflected in a change in behavior.

What makes a good listener? First, the communication is active in nature. The active listener always seems to be interacting with the speaker. This interaction takes one of the following forms (summarized in Figure 12-1):

1. *Affirmation.* Good listeners encourage the speaker with simple phrases that indicate attention, such as "uh-huh," "go on," or "okay." These phrases in themselves have little meaning, but in the context of a conversation let the speaker know that the message is at least being heard.

2. *Reflection.* Affirmation isn't enough, because it only serves to reinforce the speaker to continue. Communication starts when a message is received, and so the good listener occasionally repeats to the speaker what the message seems to be. "What I think you have been saying is . . ." often is an excellent way to make sure that a message has been communicated.

3. *Prospecting.* Good listeners understand that communication is often like an iceberg, with the most important part remaining below the surface. They know that the best way to understand a message is to ask questions that do not have simple Yes/No answers. Instead of

asking, "Do you need to download that data?" the good listener will ask, "Tell me about the problem you've been having analyzing that data." The first message invites a "Yes" answer; the second asks the user to describe the problem in more general terms and can lead to a better understanding of the business problem.

4. *Probing.* Whereas prospecting is a useful technique to direct the discussion toward providing additional information, probing allows the good listener to get to the details. A simple "how so" or "tell me more about that" can often stop the discussion at the right spot and uncover important details.

5. *The Columbo Approach.* In the 1970s television series "Columbo," actor Peter Falk played a detective who perfected a technique for solving a mystery that became the character's hallmark—he played dumb. He acted as if he had no idea about a particular situation, even though he may actually have possessed all the details. By asking naive questions, he was able to disarm his subject and so gather further information about the crime. A good listener also must downplay any expertise on the topic at hand in order to entice the speaker to communicate the real problem. Often a simple "I don't understand" or "I'm confused" can lead to uncovering a previously unknown fact.

In all of these listening techniques, a single overriding fact begins to emerge—a good listener really wants to understand what the speaker is trying to say. Communication of the real problem is the most important facet of the interaction and a good listener knows that unless the speaker's ideas are clearly understood, communication has been a failure.

Speaking. Good listening is only half of the process of communication. The other half is the speaker's ability to express ideas clearly. A critical "people skill" for an information center professional is to be able to speak effectively using some of the following techniques (first discussed in Chapter 9):

1. *The 3-T Rule.* The best communication takes place when speakers tell their listeners what they are going to tell them, then tell them, and then remind them of what they told them. The preview provides a framework in which the listener can organize the presentation, the second "telling" actually fills in that framework, and the third "telling" makes sure that all of the main points were communicated.

2. *Anchor Points.* People communicate better when they can relate the communication to a previously known concept or idea. The good speaker makes sure that the listener can connect the point to ideas already clearly understood.

3. *Idea Frames.* The good speaker tries to provide the listener with a framework in which to fit the ideas. These idea frames may be verbal (as in the 3-T principle), written (outlines and agendas), or image oriented (metaphors).

Writing. The same concepts apply to the written word as to the spoken word. Clear written communication is marked by several characteristics:

1. *Clarity.* The best writing always communicates its message clearly and unambiguously. There should be no need for follow-up memos or further clarifications. If it doesn't clearly communicate its message, it ought to be rewritten.

2. *Brevity.* If clarity is the most important characteristic of good written communication, brevity is a close second. No one enjoys reading a long document—the length itself becomes a stumbling block that diminishes the ability to communicate. Memos should be no longer than one page, reports should always include a one-page summary, and any document that is over ten pages long should be immediately suspect.

3. *Bullet Format.* Good written communication ought to be pre-organized for the reader by presenting the primary points as short paragraphs called bullets. This approach provides readers with an idea frame in which to organize their understanding of the material.

Figures 12-2 and 12-3 illustrate these concepts. The structure of Figure 12-3 improves the clarity of communication, with a short, almost staccato, style that makes the same points as Figure 12-2, but in a much more forceful and commanding fashion. Even more important, the bullet format provides a structure that helps the reader understand the message. Admittedly, the second example is not as elegantly phrased as the first, but the greatly improved clarity makes an important difference.

In the discussion thus far of key skill areas, one theme emerges: the ideal information center consultant needs to understand that the ability to serve

---

FIGURE 12-2 Example of Bad Writing

Bad writing sounds like this:

After examining all of the parameters of the problem it can be concluded that the technical directions and the requirements of the user community can best be met through an aggressive proactive approach. This dynamic program will require the purchase of approximately twenty-three personal computers configured with appropriate peripherals (40 meg disk drive, 640K, 2400 baud modem, and a monochrome monitor) that will subsequently be installed in the user work area through a cooperative and combined effort of the information center staff and the technical support service team. Once installed, these devices will undergo extensive testing by field personnel using the standard installation testing checklist. When testing is completed, the information center staff will provide the required training in operating system requirements and special application oriented behaviors.

See Figure 12-3 for the improved version of this same paragraph.

FIGURE 12-3   Example of Good Writing

The improved version of Figure 12-2 sounds like this:

I therefore recommend the following actions:

PURCHASE

Twenty-three personal computers need to be purchased configured as follows:
- 640K RAM
- 40-Mb hard disk
- 2400-kb modem
- Monochrome monitor

INSTALL

This equipment will be installed in the user area as follows:
Technical Support Services:
- Phone line installation
- Communications system changes

Information Center
- Personal computer installation
- Operating system installation
- Hardware "burn-in"

FIELD TESTING

Information Center Staff
- Test the installation using standard field test checklist.

Technical Support Services
- Provide support as needed based on checklist results.

TRAINING

Training will be provided by the information center staff in these areas:
- Key operating system commands
- Application use

---

the users well is directly related to the quality of the communication. Listening skills help identify the real problem rather than the proposed solution. Clearly expressing ideas in verbal and written form completes the communication loop. Without that communication, an information center is useless. However, although these three people skills are necessary to a successful information center consultant, they are not sufficent. One other special people skill is required—empathy.

Empathy. *Sympathy* and *empathy*—both words have the same root, which comes from the Greek word *pathos*, or feeling, but the prefixes are markedly different. The prefix *sym-* implies same, so that sympathy connotes that one person can feel the same about a situation as another. Sympathy implies, "I know what you are feeling."

The prefix *em-* implies in, so that empathy connotes that the feelings of one person are taken into another. Whereas sympathy tells of understanding a feeling, empathy tells of sharing the feeling.

Although this etymology may seem out of place in a discussion of the people skills for an information center consultant, nothing could be further from the truth. A successful information center consultant is a person who can go beyond sympathy (knowing what the user feels) to empathy (sharing the feeling intimately).

Empathy brings with it a sense of passion, a passion for the problems and the needs of others. That is exactly what a successful consultant needs. With empathy also comes a sense of commitment, a drive for quality and an aversion to incomplete or short-term solutions. Empathy cannot be produced by training; it can only be nurtured and encouraged. The wise manager will seek out staff members with this characteristic and keep them out in the user community as much as possible.

Technical Skills

Good people skills are important to a successful information center consultant, but without a solid base of technical skills, all that can be offered is a sympathetic ear. The definition of an information center that was proposed in Chapter 1 spoke of the transformation of data into information. Without a good understanding of the technology, an information center is powerless to facilitate that transformation.

Gestalt Thinking. People develop technical knowledge in one of two ways: as syntax-based knowledge or as concept-based knowledge. Figure 12-4 illustrates some of the differences.

Syntax-based knowledge, as the name implies, concentrates on the predefined rules by which the components of computer systems operate. The syntax-based expert knows how to write the most efficient code possible, how to generate the parameters for an online network, and how to change the operating system to maximize the systems throughput. The syntax-based expert approaches a problem from the bottom up: do these things and the system changes as required.

Concept-based knowledge works on the principle: grasp the whole and the details will follow. To borrow a term from psychology, this "grasp the whole" approach can be characterized as gestalt thinking. The gestalt thinker starts by trying to determine the common underlying elements of all computer systems, understanding that all computer systems employ virtually the same techniques. The names and language syntax may differ, but the concepts remain constant. Gestalt thinkers always try to consider new knowledge in terms of the concepts that they previously determined.

FIGURE 12-4   Knowledge Styles

	SYNTAX BASED	*CONCEPT BASED*
BASIC APPROACH TO TECHNOLOGY	Bottom-up (master the technology first, then apply it).	Top-Down (see the technology in context first, then master it).
KEY LEARNING STRATEGIES	Concentrate on rules, "grammar," and formulas.	Concentrate on concepts and similarities with other technology.
USE PATTERN	Master details of technology first, then apply to problem.	Define problem first then use concepts to identify detailed knowledge needed to solve problem.

By its very nature, the technology of an information center is continually changing. New products are introduced at breathtaking speed and existing products are given new uses. To survive in this environment, information center consultants must approach technology from the perspective of gestalt knowledge. Every new data-base product is similar in some way to every other data-base product, every spreadsheet is similar to every other spreadsheet, every graphics package is similar to every other graphics package. The consultant with gestalt knowledge will be able to look past the syntax of the product and evaluate its use to solve business problems.

The Chapter 1 definition of an information center ends with the thought that the technology is to be used to solve business problems. The gestalt thinking consultant has the edge here, as well. By first seeing the conceptual framework underlying the business problem and by knowing the conceptual framework of the technology, the gestalt thinker has a good chance of matching the correct technology to the business problem. By starting from a solid understanding of the nature of the technology, the consultant is likely to discover new ways to use existing technology to solve the problems.

Gestalt thinking and detailed technical knowledge are not mutually exclusive, of course. It is the pattern of technical knowledge that is important for a successful information center consultant: the detailed knowledge proceeds from a solid understanding of the underlying concepts. Gestalt thinking does not absolve the consultant from knowing the details; it only provides the framework in which to understand the technology. Figure 12-5 summarizes some of the differences between these two approaches.

Multilevel Technology. The technical knowledge of an ideal information center consultant cannot be limited to the tool set discussed in Chapter 4,

FIGURE 12-5 Syntax Knowledge vs. Gestalt Knowledge		
	SYNTAX	*GESTALT*
LEARNING	Learns rules first	Learns concepts first
	Derives concepts from rules	Derives rules from concepts
PROBLEM SOLVING	Determine what programs are needed	Determine what technology best fits needs.
	Process oriented: What must be done to solve the problem?	Data oriented: What is the nature of the data that describes the problem?
NEW TECHNOLOGY	What are differences with current technology?	What are similarities to current technology?
	Looks for training in new language.	Sees new technology as extension of old.
		Training needed only in limited topics.

however. Gestalt thinking requires that knowledge of those tools be anchored in an understanding of the rest of the data-processing tool kit. For example:

1. *Traditional Development.* An information center has all of the fourth-generation languages at its disposal, but often the needed data is captured and massaged through third-generation applications. The successful information center consultant must understand the trade-offs and problems associated with these traditional application systems and be able to communicate any needs clearly to the development team.

2. *Technical Support.* Almost every large data-processing organization has a group that is charged with the care and feeding of the operating system and the online network. An information center consultant need not understand all of the details of the online network or the operating system, but the better the consultant is able to explain the technical details of the tools, the more support can be expected from the technical support group. A partnership with the technical support staff can only be built on respect and understanding.

An information center consultant need not be an application developer or a systems programmer, but an ideal consultant will be able to form strategic alliances with these two groups—alliances based on an understanding of the technology and respect for the needs of the other discipline. The ability to move among the technical ranks of the organization is indispensable.

Disciplined Technology. Although an information center consultant must be thoroughly grounded in the concepts of the technology and be able to learn the specific rules as required, technology without discipline is dangerous. An ideal information center consultant must be able to apply the technology using some of the following concepts:

1. *There Will Always Be Changes.* No matter how carefully implemented, any information center activity is always subject to change—even the simplest spreadsheet or most trivial data base. A disciplined information center consultant thus keeps careful notes and embeds comments into any project so that the next person to work on the project will know what has happened and why. A disciplined information center consultant knows that there will always be a "next person."

2. *Clarity Is More Important Than "Slickness".* While elegant and concise solutions make for efficient code, they do not always lend themselves to simple modifications. Since a disciplined consultant knows that there always will be changes, clarity becomes the most important attribute in technological solutions. Clear logic flows, meaningful data names, and a lot of helpful comments are always the mark of a disciplined professional.

3. *Focus on the Long Term.* A technological solution that is slapped together is a disaster waiting to happen. A disciplined professional knows the traps of simple looking shortcuts, time pressures, and a "close enough" mentality, and that each of these represents trading short-term for long-term success. A disciplined professional wants to do the job right the first time, realizing that an organization will remember the quality of the project long after it has forgotten that it was done quickly.

In the early days of information centers, there was almost a "Wild West" atmosphere. New technologies were emerging faster than the means to control them, and discipline often was sacrificed to the expedient. Now all that has changed. An information center is an established part of an organization and it is expected to deliver consistent, stable results. It is no longer a collection of toy computers and toy languages. It must be treated with the respect for discipline that any profession requires.

As this discussion has shown, information center consultants must live up to an exacting set of expectations! They must excel in the people skills of speaking, listening, sympathizing, and empathizing. They must understand the underlying concepts of the technology, be able to "hold their own" with the applications and technical support staffs, and be able to apply their technical knowledge with discipline. Finally, with all that there is yet one more thing required of these consultants: business knowledge.

Business Skills

The traditional applications programmer needed to know very little about the underlying nature of the business. All a programmer had to do was write programs that matched the specifications that had been developed by a systems analyst. The traditional systems analyst also needed to know little about the underlying business concepts: the analyst concentrated on the operational details of the business to determine how best to automate them. The assumption in many traditional development organizations was that it was a user's role to understand the business, an analyst's role to understand the operational needs of the business, and a programmer's role to translate the operational knowledge into software. These roles will not do for an information center.

Throughout this book, the strategic nature of an information center has been stressed. The ideal consultant cannot be content with seeing a business in terms of what it *does*, but must understand what the business *is*.

Traditionally, a user comes to an information center with a request, "Please provide an online screen that looks like this or a report that shows these items." An information center consultant with a strategic vision will not be content with this request, but will want to know why the request is being made. What is the business problem to be solved? How is this request related to existing programs? What are the implications for other areas of the organization? By combining the people and technological skills with a strategic drive, the consultant is able to see past the immediate request and perhaps create a solution that not only resolves the current problem, but may address future problems, as well.

An ideal information center consultant knows that users only appear to be bringing problems. Actually, they are bringing their own solutions, which they want automated. An ideal consultant who understands the nature of the business can cut through the apparent solutions and reach the real solution. Without a solid understanding of the underlying business problems, however, the real solution remains elusive.

Again, an information center consultant should demonstrate an understanding of the business as well as of the technology. An information center consultant in a bank, for example, must understand the nature (but not necessarily the details) of the banking business almost as well as the bankers. In a manufacturing environment, the consultant needs to understand the engineering concepts almost as well as the industrial engineers who developed the manufacturing processes. In a research organization, an information center consultant must understand the concepts of experiment design almost as well as the researchers. It is not enough to have people skills and to know the technology; an ideal information center consultant must be capable of functioning as an integral part of a business team.

The da Vinci Approach

What seems to be emerging from this discussion is that an ideal information center consultant needs to be equally adept at technology and business, and must also possess the interpersonal skills to tie them together. A consultant must have a wide, concept-based range of knowledge that is to be applied to solve problems.

The prototype for this type of person might best be epitomized by Leonardo da Vinci, the archtypical Renaissance man. Da Vinci was a painter, a physicist, an engineer, a philosopher, and a dreamer who was able to integrate concepts from all realms of knowledge. In the Renaissance, it wasn't so much that new ideas were being discovered at a rapid pace—almost all of the ideas that drove the explosive growth of the period had been known to the ancient Greeks or the early Moslems. What mattered most was that Europeans were finally able to assimilate those ideas into their own world view and to build on the conceptual framework they provided.

Da Vinci was a true genius, of course, which is not true of the average information center consultant. Nevertheless, the same forces that enabled da Vinci to excel are also the key to creating the best possible staff for an information center: broadly based, concept-oriented knowledge, with the details as needed, applied to business problems in a clear and unambiguous fashion.

To be sure, the ideal consultant does not exist, but there are steps that a manager can take to try to move the staff closer to that ideal.

HIRING THE IDEAL CONSULTANT

Which is the more important skill—hiring or supervision? An error in judgment when hiring can lead to years of frustration whereas an error in supervision is usually forgotten in a matter of months. This means that the best place to start the quest for an ideal information center consultant is at the resumé.

The Frankenstein Exercise

In this exercise, the reader is invited to step into the shoes of Mary Shelly's Baron von Frankenstein, the mad doctor who wanted to create life, and create an ideal information center consultant.

FIGURE 12-6   Resume Form for Frankenstein Exercise

Name: _____

Age: _____

EDUCATION HISTORY:

    Include undergraduate degree, major,

    as well as any graduate degrees

EXPERIENCE:

    Be sure to include any internal transfers as well

OTHER:

    Hobbies, avocations, interesting notes

The process is begun by filling in the sections on education, experience, and other interests in the resumé form of Figure 12-6. Spaces for name and age are also provided to make the resumé more personal. This will be the resumé of an ideal consultant, of course, and probably would not actually fit any specific individual.

The Frankenstein exercise is useful to determine the biases against and expectations for an information center manager. In trying to look beyond the details to determine the values that lie behind the resumé that has been created, some of the following questions might emerge:

1. *Education.* Was the ideal consultant given a varied background? As evidence of gestalt thinking, an exclusive emphasis on technical or business subjects seems contrary to the demand for gestalt thinking. A blend of academic interests is far more desirable. A person with a B.A. degree in music theory and an M.B.A. is a far better candidate than one with two degrees in MIS.

2. *Experience.* Does the resumé show that the ideal consultant has had a diversity of work experience? It is less important for a consultant to have worked at a number of different firms than at a number of different jobs. The ideal consultant should have made at least one major career change.

3. *Other.* Did the resumé provide the ideal consultant with interests outside of business? Real gestalt thinkers always find interesting ways in which to utilize their talents. They may be Sunday School teachers, bicycle racers, or experienced world travelers, but the diversity of experience is important.

A careful examination of the resumé that a manager builds in the Frankenstein exercise can determine the values that are important to the information center. The trick is making sure that they match the public pronouncements of strategy and tactics.

Interviewing the Candidate

The Frankenstein exercise is useful for clarifying the values that will be used to evaluate the candidates. These values, in turn, will prove useful in screening the resumés of potential candidates, but ultimately the final choice is going to be made on the basis of a combination of interview, resumé, and references. It is beyond the scope of this book to discuss interviewing techniques in detail, but relevant suggestions might include:

1. *Listen.* The ideal interview will consist of 90 percent "candidate talk" and 10 percent "interviewer talk." Rather than trying to impress a candidate with the interviewer's knowledge and experience, the interviewer should listen to the candidate. Too much interviewer talk gives a candidate an opportunity to determine what is important and to slant responses toward those points.

2. *Pose Open-Ended Questions.* The worst kinds of questions in an interview are those that can be answered with a single sentence. Asking about the candidate's level of technical expertise accomplishes only two things: it tells a candidate that technical expertise is important and it allows a candidate to get away with a simple answer, such as, "I am really good at the technical aspects of the job." Instead, "Tell me about that project you worked on," for example, will elicit evidence of technical competence.

3. *Look for Nondirective Responses.* When a candidate says something that needs clarification, nondirective phrases such as "How so?" or "Tell me more" will bring further information. The best responses will be obtained when the fewest hints have been provided to guide a candidate to the "right" answer.

4. *Keep Notes.* Rather than relying on memory to reconstruct an interview, by taking notes an interviewer can make a better evaluation. One technique might involve dividing the notepaper into quadrants labeled "technical," "business," "people," and "other." As the interview progresses, a lack of observations in a quadrant will indicate a need to find out more about the candidate's expertise in that area. For example, in Figure 12-7, the interviewer clearly needs more information about the candidate's ability to work with people, judging by the large amount of empty space in that section.

5. *Keep It Humane.* Interviews can be perceived as the Inquisition unless the interviewer acknowledges the human factors by offering amenities such as coffee and restroom breaks, keeping the interview

---

FIGURE 12-7   Interview Notes

Name _____ Date ____

Position _____ Interviewed by ____

Technical	Business
Bought Apple II in high school—early innovator *Only exposure to IBM mainframe was in school* *4GL experience seem to be concentrated on reporting skills*	*Degree in MIS concentrated on finance; possible use in upcoming CFO project?* *Actively trades corn futures for personal account* *• Conflict of interest?* *• Reflects good understanding of market forces*

People skills	Other
Tends to enjoy projects with high degree of autonomy	*Father plays golf with CFO* *Teaches tenth grade Sunday School—possible training role?*

---

to an hour or less, and never having more than one interviewer or more than one candidate present at a time. An interview must always be a one-to-one discussion.

There is no guaranteed painless way to select an information center staff, but by determining the desired values, evaluating the resumés according to these values, and taking simple steps to maximize the effectiveness of the interview, much of the pain will be removed from the process. Once staff members have been hired, the next task is to make sure that they grow professionally.

PROFESSIONAL GROWTH

Although it is obvious that no one individual could ever fulfil all of the qualifications of an ideal consultant, the development of such an ideal does help by defining goals for professional development. The only problem then facing an information center manager is to ascertain how to move the staff closer to that goal.

Using a Skills Matrix

The first step in staff development is to clearly define the skills that characterize an ideal information center consultant. Starting with the resumé of the Frankenstein exercise, for each of the points on that resumé, the manager needs to develop a list of discrete skills that would be required to demonstrate that capability.

The trick with this list is to express skills behaviorally. Instead of saying, "Consultant knows how to design data bases," the list should say, "Consultant designs data bases according to standards." The difference is that the first version requires a manager to evaluate what the consultant *knows*, whereas the second alternative requires an evaluation of what the consultant *does*. Again, instead of saying, "Consultant has good communication skills," the manager should say, "Consultant's written communications are clear and concise." The first version uses the somewhat ambiguous word "good," whereas the second version defines "good" as "clear and concise."

Once the skills have been identified, they should be divided into broad categories such as business, technical, and people skills. Adding a simple grid and the names of the staff results in a skill matrix that resembles Figure 12-8.

Individual Evaluation. In Chapter 9, the Heisenberg uncertainty principle was summarized by saying that the act of measuring always alters that which is being measured. In other words, the measurement tool itself starts to define behavior.

An information center manager thus must be very careful about the part the skills matrix will play. If it is to be an evaluation tool, the skills on that

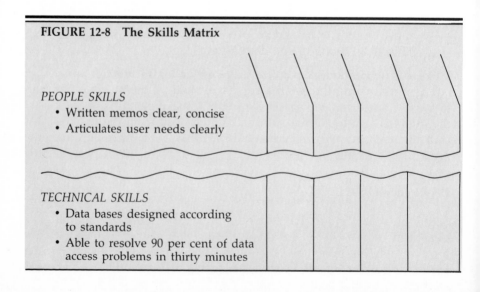

FIGURE 12-8   The Skills Matrix

PEOPLE SKILLS
- Written memos clear, concise
- Articulates user needs clearly

TECHNICAL SKILLS
- Data bases designed according to standards
- Able to resolve 90 per cent of data access problems in thirty minutes

matrix will become the de facto definition of a good consultant. If the manager makes sure that the matrix serves only as a guide for planning staff development, its power to change the characteristics of the job is markedly diminished. A manager must be very clear as to what the skills matrix is being employed.

The best role for the skills matrix is as a private tool with which a manager can assess the level of expertise of each member of the staff. It should not be used as a formal means to evaluate employee performance as that would greatly reduce its effectiveness as a development planning tool. This difference in roles is best explained by the level of accuracy required for performance evaluation as compared with development planning. The former determines promotions, raises, and perquisites, and so must be employed with a high degree of accuracy and diligence. When an employee's career is at stake, a "seat of the pants" evaluation is not acceptable.

When using the matrix as a tool for development planning, the implications of an incorrect evaluation are far less important. The worst case is that an individual might receive training in a skill that the person already possesses. Again, it must be emphasized that the skills matrix is to be used for planning employee development, not for evaluations. To use it otherwise is foolish and counterproductive.

Taking these caveats into consideration, an information center manager should then use the matrix to identify the skill level of each employee. The evaluation should not be complex: a consultant either has or does not have the skill. If in doubt, the conservative approach is best and the skill should be considered missing. Once the matrix has been completed, it can be used for two purposes: team evaluation and individual planning.

Team Evaluation. The pattern of the completed evaluation can prove enlightening to a manager. For example, the pattern in Figure 12-9 seems to show that employee 2 is clearly the expert in these skills and that employee 1 is the next best qualified, but employees 3 and 4 are not very skilled in this area. By contrast, in Figure 12-10 no one individual stands out as a specialist; the skills seem to be evenly distributed among all of the staff members.

The pattern can tell a manager a lot about the nature of the department. If the policy is to create generalists but the pattern of the skill matrix looks like Figure 12-10, the manager knows that remedial action is required. One value of the matrix is to identify where the policy doesn't match the reality.

There is another way that a matrix can prove useful. For every skill that is listed in the matrix, a prudent manager needs to have two consultants who have mastered that skill, in order to maintain the ongoing functioning of an information center in spite of vacations or staff turnover. The skills matrix exposes weak spots such as skills d–f in Figure 12-9. As the matrix shows, the loss of employee 2 would cripple the information center.

FIGURE 12-9   Specialist Pattern

	Employee 1	Employee 2	Employee 3	Employee 4
Skill a	x	x		
Skill b	x		x	
Skill c	x	x		
Skill d		x		
Skill e		x		
Skill f		x		

The matrix thus can be used to identify the differences between philosophy and reality and to highlight potential problems before they occur. The next step is to use the matrix to create a development plan.

The Development Plan. The previous steps identified skills that needed to be strengthened. The next step is almost embarrassingly simple: find a way to have the staff develop skills to fill in the gaps that were identified.

Probably the worst way to fill in such gaps is through formal training. A class can only provide the framework for a skill; unless the consultant can demonstrate that skill in a real-life situation, the training is worthless. Training for the staff should never be confused with mastering a skill.

Most of the skills of the matrix can only be learned "hands-on" and mastered by being exercised. This approach has a somewhat disconcerting side effect: a manager must allow employees an opportunity to fail.

Failure can be the best teacher for the skills in the matrix as long as a few important points are observed. First, not only must consultants be allowed to fail, but they must also be allowed to recover from the failure. The failure itself does not teach anything, but the recovery does. Second, there must always be a safety net. A manager must decide in advance just what level

---

FIGURE 12-10 Generalist Pattern

	Employee 1	Employee 2	Employee 3	Employee 4
Skill a	x	x		x
Skill b	x		x	
Skill c		x		x
Skill d			x	
Skill e		x	x	
Skill f	x			x

---

of failure will be acceptable and then develop a contingency plan to assist in recovery. No consultant should be allowed to feel responsible for the entire success or failure of a project. Finally, failure must not carry an excessive stigma. Failures mean that an information center is trying bold and innovative approaches. An information center that never fails is doing a mediocre job.

One other (and less painful) way to develop staff in a hands-on fashion is to go to the outside world. By actively participating in consortium groups (such as the local information center professional association) or by attending national conferences (such as the annual Information Center Conference and Exposition sponsored by the publishers of *Information Center* magazine), an information center consultant is exposed to new ideas, new techniques, and new colleagues. By taking advantage of these outside opportunities and integrating them into their own skill sets, staff members can gain valuable experience without the pain of possible failure.

The main point, then, is that a development plan is needed, not a training plan. The latter focuses on the formal education needed to improve skills whereas the former places stronger emphasis on the experiential. Understanding the difference between the two is critical.

SUMMARY

This chapter began by pointing out that the staff of an information center is its most important asset. However, that staff is markedly different from the rest of the traditional information systems team. An information center staff must possess a rare combination of people skills, technical ability, and business understanding—talents that are not intuitive but must be developed. The discussion included techniques to evaluate the current state of the staff and to put together a development plan. That development plan lies at the heart of an information center's success; without such a plan, it can soon turn into a modern-day Stonehenge.

SUGGESTED PROJECTS

1. Defend or oppose this statement:

    The ideal source of potential talent for an information center is the traditional MIS group.

    In your response, be sure to include such key concepts as gestalt thinking, people skills, and technical skills.

2. The text illustrates what it calls "the Frankenstein exercise" to develop the resumé of an ideal information center consultant. Complete the Frankenstein exercise and from that resumé develop a skills matrix like that in Figure 12-3.

3. Defend or oppose the following statement:

    It is better to staff an information center with a number of people, each of whom has a special skill set, than with generalists.

    In your response, be sure to include such key concepts as gestalt thinking, people skills, and technical skills.

C H A P T E R **13**

Audit

Parents often are able to exert some control over unruly young children excited by the prospect of Christmas by warning them that Santa Claus's elves are watching, making lists of boys and girls who are naughty and those who are nice. Not wishing to jeopardize their annual haul of toys, the children behave lest the elves snitch on them. Most data-processing professionals have a view of the organization's auditors that is not much different. The elves, who now wear business suits, are making lists of naughty and nice systems, but the concept is the same.

In reality, the audit function is a critical component of an organization's effectiveness and it behooves every information center professional to develop an audit mentality in managing end-user computing. The questions here are, what is required for an "audit mind set" and how can that approach help an information center?

RISK: THE ESSENCE OF AUDIT

After all of the layers of verbiage are removed from the official charters and job descriptions, the audit function is basically that of evaluating and managing risk. Some risks, such as a solar supernova, are trivial; others, such as employee theft, represent a real danger. The first steps in developing an audit mentality in an information center, then, is to determine what the term *risk* means and how to go about identifying and evaluating those risks.

A Definition

For the purposes of this chapter, risk is defined as follows:

> Risk *is an undesirable event that is evaluated in terms of its likelihood of happening and its potential impact on an organization.*

This definition entails three important concepts: undesirable event, probability (likelihood), and impact. All three concepts need to be considered in discussing risk.

With regard to the "undesirable event," the audit point of view is essentially pessimistic. Auditors tend to think that Murphy's law (anything that can go wrong will go wrong) is optimistic drivel. Good risk analysis starts by examining the current practices, policies, and procedures, and then tries to find all of those places where problems might arise. Risk analysis never spawns worries about success, unless that success creates new places for things to go wrong.

Risk always has a component of probability as well. If an undesirable event occurs repeatedly, a prudent organization will take steps to correct it.

Risk analysis, however, tries to foresee undesirable events before they happen and so must evaluate the likelihood that the event will actually take place. A supernova is an example of a trivial risk, not because it would have little impact, but because it is highly unlikely to happen. Other events may have different probabilities, depending on location. Earthquake, for example, is a very real risk in Los Angeles or Tokyo, but is a trivial risk in Miami or London. The degree of risk is always related to the probability that the undesirable event will occur.

The final concept of risk is impact. Although Murphy said that anything that can go wrong will go wrong, it is important to note that not all undesirable events are equally disastrous. For example, employee theft made possible by poor cash control is a serious problem, but improper parking in the company parking lot is relatively unimportant. The degree of risk is tightly coupled to the deleterious effects of the event.

Figure 13-1 shows a graphic way of looking at risk. Any undesirable event can be plotted on the graph based on its probability and impact, and its resulting position will dictate the level of concern and corresponding control that will be needed to manage that risk. The next task, then, is to determine how an audit-minded information center should set about identifying and evaluating these risks.

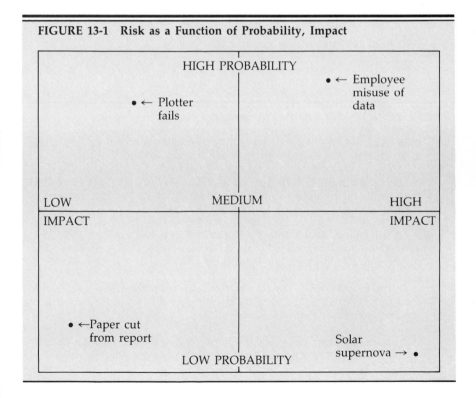

FIGURE 13-1   Risk as a Function of Probability, Impact

Identifying Possible Events

According to the definition of risk, it appears that a good starting point might be the identification of all possible undesirable occurrences. It is not enough to list all of the potentially bad things that could happen though, and so a bit of methodology (see Figure 13-2) might prove helpful.

First, isolate one area of the information center to undergo the risk analysis. Looking at the entire operation only scatters energy and seldom produces valuable results. One way to effect this division might be to use the realms of stewardship discussed in Chapter 7. Figure 13-3 illustrates some of the possible risk-analysis areas for each realm. The list is not meant to be comprehensive, but it does provide a good starting place for the analysis.

Second, risk analysis is best done as a group effort. As with the use of a structured group-oriented approach to solve other problems, such an approach is recommended for risk analysis as well, for several reasons:

1. No one individual can see all parts of the problem.
2. As each person contributes ideas, those ideas may inspire additional ideas from others.
3. Having the group analyze its own potential problems gives the group a sense of ownership of those problems.
4. The group approach emphasizes management commitment to quality and to trust in the group.

FIGURE 13-2   Risk Analysis Methodology

- **Select Isolated Area for Audit**—when energies are focused on a single functional area, the results are much more effective.

- **Use a Structured Group Approach**—the power of a group is more than the sum of the power of the individuals. The end results are always more effective with a structured group approach.

- **Identify First, Evaluate Second**—the most fragile moment in the life of an idea is the first minute after it has been articulated. Let the ideas flow freely and hold evaluation until the end.

- **Evaluate in Simple Terms**—a 1–10 scale is a terrible way to evaluate an idea. How can one tell the difference between a 7 and an 8? Use a simple scale like "low, medium, high."

- **Manage the Probability and the Impact Side of Risk**—Manage risks by either reducing the probability or reducing the impact.

FIGURE 13-3 Data Stewardship and Risk Analysis	
STEWARDSHIP REALM	*POSSIBLE AREAS FOR RISK ANALYSIS*
Data Stewardship	Data access
	Production vs. extract data
	Data migration procedures
	Disaster recovery
Software Stewardship	Test/production border
	Software installation procedures
	Disaster recovery
Resource Stewardship	Tool standardization
	Purchasing procedures
	Proper tool use by users

Third, the possible undesirable events should be listed without evaluation or comment. Comments tend to stifle the creative process and premature evaluation of an idea can bias the group concerning that idea and may inhibit another group member from adding a new item to the list for fear of being judged. In addition, the evaluation of risk needs to be removed from the realm of snap judgments and placed in a more rational process. Each of the potential problems must then be evaluated in a separate operation.

Rating Potential Risks

Figure 13-4 shows a sample list of potential undesirable events for the topic "data access." However, two other columns have also been included in the figure, labeled "Probability" and "Impact." As the definition states, a risk is an undesirable event that is evaluated for probability and impact. That evaluation is the next step.

The events in the sample list are difficult to evaluate accurately for probability. For instance, should the event "outsiders gain access to system" be assigned a probability of one out of 1,000 or one out of 10,000? Similarly, should the event "IC user transfers, should no longer have access to data" be assigned a probability of one out of one hundred or one out of twenty? To try to assign actual numbers to the various risks will soon mire the process in rather unimportant details. What really matters is that

FIGURE 13-4   Sample Risk Evaluation

SUBJECT: Data access

EVENT	*PROBABILITY*	*IMPACT*
Outsiders gain access to customer data.		
Unauthorized internal user circumvents data security rules.		
User data steward transfers, IC not told of new steward.		
IC user transfers, should no longer have access to data.		
Downloaded data after system rerun to correct problems.		
User uses incorrect field to answer query.		
Downloaded data is sold to competitor.		
User careless with password.		

the second risk has a significantly higher probability of occurring than the first. The probabilities should be grouped in broad categories rather than defined precisely.

The probability of an event should be evaluated in terms of low, medium, and high, as follows:

1. *Low:* The event is highly unlikely to happen within the next two or three years.
2. *Medium:* The event is likely to happen in the next two or three years, but will take place only once or twice.
3. *High:* The event almost certainly will happen in the next two or three years and may happen repeatedly.

Admittedly, no one person will be clairvoyant enough to be able to evaluate the probabilities completely accurately. Once again, an information center needs to adopt a group-oriented approach to the evaluation. The best way to implement such an approach is through consensus voting, in which each member of the group may vote that the risk is high, medium, or low. However, a simple majority vote is not sufficient. If a group of nine, say, splits five to four on a vote, the majority does *not* rule. Close votes usually indicate that the item is not clearly defined or that the group is not really certain about the probability. The item must be discussed and revoted until a significant majority can reach a conclusion on the probability. This is the major feature of consensus voting: the results need to be overwhelmingly in favor of one of the options. If they are not, the group has to reach a clearer consensus.

This first round of consensus voting concentrates only on the probability of an event's occurrence. At this point, the group should make no distinction between trivial and important events since impact evaluation occurs next.

After each of the events has been categorized as to high, medium, or low probability, the group should turn its attention to evaluating the potential impact of the event if it should happen. Once again, emphasis on an overly quantitative approach can complicate the process. As Figure 13-4 shows, no single quantitative measure can possibly assess each of the potential events fairly. Instead, broad categories of impact are utilized:

1. *Low:* Impact will be insignificant. Only direct participants will notice the effect.
2. *Medium:* Impact will be noticed but will not significantly affect the day-to-day operations of the organization.
3. *High:* Event will definitely cause a disruption in the organization's daily operations.

Once again, the group makes its decision by consensus voting, but this time the group ignores the probability of the event's happening. The vote should be based on the event's potential impact, if it should occur, without regard to the probability of that event's actually taking place.

Ranking Risks

Once the group has finished evaluating the possible events for probability and impact, the process of ranking the risks becomes fairly straightforward. The most important risks to manage are those that have both *high* probability and *high* impact. Clearly, these risks must be managed in any audit-minded information center. Conversely, those events that were rated as *low* probability and *low* impact are not worth any special efforts. A complete analysis of the combinations is shown in Figure 13-5. Of course, any evaluation must include an element of common sense. An event such as a solar supernova has a high impact and a low probability, but it would be foolish to assign it to the "important" category. As this example shows, the actual divisions are somewhat arbitrary, but reflect the following bias: any event with either high probability or high impact must be aggressively managed.

This grouping process is important for very practical reasons. An information center does not have the resources to manage all of the possible risks in its environment, and so must focus its attention on those few risks that pose the most potential for disaster. The process weeds out risks that can safely be ignored because of their low probability (supernova) or low

FIGURE 13-5 Risk Categories		
ACTION	*PROBABILITY*	*IMPACT*
Major risk	High	High
Must manage	High	Medium
	Medium	High
Important, but not critical	Medium	Medium
Manage if possible	Low	High
	High	Low
Trivial Risk	Low	Low
No management required	Low	Medium
	Medium	Low

impact (paper cuts from reports). Those that are left form a pool of risks that must be managed by an audit-minded information center.

Managing Risk: Reducing Probability and Impact

Again, risk is defined as an undesirable event that is evaluated in terms of the likelihood of its happening and of its potential impact on an organization. Once the process has identified and evaluated the risks faced by an information center, the next step must be to use that definition to manage the risk.

Looking again at Figure 13-5, if a risk that was graded high in probability and medium in impact were to have its probability reduced to medium, it would drop out of the category of "major risk" and be downgraded to "important, not critical." If a risk that was rated medium probability and impact were to have its impact reduced to low, it would drop to a "trivial" risk. This is the secret to managing risks: reduce probability and reduce impact.

After the group has identified and categorized all of the potential risks of an information center, its next step is to develop a plan to manage each of the major risks. Once again, through a process of structured brainstorming, the group needs to identify a series of activities for each risk that can be used to reduce the probability or impact of that risk. Figure 13-6 shows the result of such a brainstorming session. Note that attention is focused on only one risk at a time and that there are a number of ideas for both risk and impact, and also that some of the ideas clearly are not practical. During a brainstorming session, all ideas are written down without evaluation. Some of the apparently silliest ideas may trigger valuable suggestions.

With a list of alternatives developed for each of the risks to be managed, the group faces one last task––to examine the lists for those actions that the

---

FIGURE 13-6   Reducing Probability or Impact

RISK: User careless with password

PROBABILITY: High   *IMPACT:* Medium

ACTIONS TO REDUCE PROBABILITY
- Provide password protection training as a part of all information center classes
- Security software requires new password to be set every twenty days
- Spot inspections of all information center user work stations looking for passwords in plain sight
- Create corporate policy that declares disclosure of password a termination offense
- Ten-day suspension of information center access to any user who discloses password unless written exception granted by executive vice-president

ACTIONS TO REDUCE IMPACT
- Perform periodic review of all file access rights to make sure that no user has access to unauthorized data
- Require additional password for sensitive data
- Capture file-use statistics by user ID. Monitor for suspicious activity or use changes
- Encrypt sensitive data

---

group believes will be the most effective way to manage each risk. Once again, consensus voting is the technique that is best for this task. Unless there is clear agreement on the efficacy of an action, more discussion and clarification are needed. Once the group reaches consensus on an action, it may move on to the next activity.

The Cost of Control

One way to manage a security risk would be to assign a data security officer to stand at each terminal and make sure that passwords are used correctly. This action would certainly reduce the probability dramatically but is unlikely to be implemented. Obviously, the risk being monitored is not worth the cost of such a plan.

At what point does the cost become too great for the risk? Obviously, $1 million is too much to pay to manage this risk whereas $1 would be acceptable. In between is a gray area: What about $100,000, or $10,000, or $1,000?

Chapter 10 considered the problem of developing an effective cost/benefit measurement for an information center's projects. Whereas the costs were well known, the benefits were almost impossible to quantify in terms of dollars. The problem is the same with risk management: the impact of many risks can be measured in dollars, but others elude that measurement.

A very frightening equation occasionally emerges in product liability suits in which the defendants, as manufacturers, are accused of having intentionally ignored a potentially fatal design flaw in their products because it was not cost-effective to correct it. By estimating the possible loss in life and multiplying it by the estimated cost to settle each suit, they had concluded that the cost to repair the design flaw was not justified by the potential loss. From a purely cost/benefit perspective, they had made the correct decision, but from a moral and ethical viewpoint, such behavior was unforgiveable. Trying to evaluate alternative actions strictly on the basis of cost is dangerous and misleading.

In assigning an impact rating (low, medium, or high), cost is not a consideration. Rather, the focus is on the rating's effect on the business functions of an organization. The goal of risk management is to reduce the probability or impact and to eliminate those items designated as major risks in Figure 13-5. Once that goal is clear, the part that cost plays can be better understood: the prudent manager is looking for the most cost-effective way to move a risk from a higher risk category to a lower one. The action or combination of actions that accomplishes the goal at the lowest cost obviously is the best course to take.

Thus, although the cost of control is indeed important, it is seen only as a means to accomplishing a business goal. This approach does not try to mix measurements, but instead tries to advance the best program to accomplish the business objectives at the most effective price. This is the better way to determine the cost of control. The process is not driven by a dubious or inaccurate cost/benefit ratio, but by the need to accomplish the risk management objectives at the lowest cost.

At the end of the process, a comprehensive risk management document begins to emerge in which all of the major and important risks that an information center faces are articulated and evaluated. In addition, each risk is accompanied by a set of actions to be taken to manage that risk by reducing its probability or softening its impact. Furthermore, the alternatives have been analyzed to determine what actions or combination of actions accomplishes the goal of risk management in the most effective fashion. Using this document, an audit-minded information center can ensure that it has taken the first steps toward controlling its risks—the basis of all audit concerns.

CONTROL PROCEDURES

As described, the way to manage risks is to develop a list of actions that will reduce probability or impact. Such actions most often take the form of organizational policies or procedures. If these techniques are used to control the environment, they must be made clear and prove useful.

Policies: The Framework

The basis of the entire framework for the U.S. system of laws is a single, remarkable document—the Constitution of the United States. The key to understanding this legal framework, however, is to recognize that the Constitution is not itself a set of laws, but is the enabling document from which all laws emanate and by which the validity of all laws are judged. The Constitution serves as "metalaw": the law about law.

In a similar fashion, the first step in ensuring that an organization takes the correct actions in managing its risks is to develop a series of policies. In this regard, a policy can be defined as follows:

> A policy *is a written statement that describes in general terms a course of action for an organization.*

This definition has several important elements. First, a policy must be written. A policy has no value whatsoever unless it has been clearly articulated in a form that is available to all. If the purpose of a policy is to serve as a framework for action, it must be given some degree of permanence. The insistence on written policies provides that stability.

Second, a policy should be phrased in general terms. As was the case with the Constitution, a policy is not meant to be a checklist of actions, but to serve as a guide for developing more detailed action plans, called procedures (see Figure 13-7).

Third, a policy relates to a course of action. "Mom and apple pie" statements may sound good, but only those policies that can be used to direct a course of action are worth the effort to create them.

An example of a policy statement is presented in Figure 13-8. This statement does not go into operational details. It does not specify how the stewards are to be appointed or how they are to discharge their duties to protect, nurture, and use the data. Such details will be spelled out in later

---

FIGURE 13-7 Procedure vs. Policy

	POLICY	PROCEDURE
FORMAT	Written paragraphs	Written script
SCOPE	General	Very specific
PURPOSE	To enable action	To describe action

FIGURE 13-8   Sample Policy Statement

DATA OWNERSHIP POLICY

All data, whether stored on personal, departmental, or corporate computers, is to be considered an asset of the entire organization. Accordingly, each
collection of data will be assigned a steward on behalf of the corporation
whose role will be to protect, nurture, and use that data in the overall best
interests of the corporation.

---

procedures. The policy as stated here serves as a guide for action, clearly
establishing the ground rules for stewardship of data in such a way that
clear procedures can easily follow. The policy sets up the framework,
leaving the procedures to cover the actual details.

Procedures: The Gory Details

If the policies are to be the framework for action, the procedures are the
means by which this framework is implemented. Unfortunately, in most
cases, procedures wind up as exercises in futility.

Observation of any area of an organization will soon reveal a remarkable
fact: no one ever uses the written procedure manual. If an unusual situation arises, the person involved is most likely to turn first to a co-worker for
advice. If a co-worker is unavailable, the person is likely to turn next to a
"cheat sheet"—a handwritten set of notes that tell how to perform certain
tasks.

Why are the written procedures of a department so universally ignored?
Perhaps the reason is that they are so poorly written and presented. In
most cases, the procedures that govern a department are kept in a looseleaf
binder. Often they are written in difficult-to-understand "official-eese,"
but even in the better manuals, the procedures are likely to be described in
paragraph-oriented prose, such as shown in Figure 13-9.

Figure 13-9 is a good example of how not to write a procedure. To
understand the procedure, a person needs to read the entire document,
perhaps a number of times. The flow of paper and action is not clear from
the text: How many people are involved in the approval? What does the
data security coordinator do? How soon will the requestor know the
results? All of these questions are very difficult to answer without serious
study of the procedure. Is it any wonder that the procedure books in a
department gather dust?

In an audit-minded information center, procedures are the main means
of managing the risks. The information center manager thus must ascertain
that the group's actions are really reducing probability or impact, and that
all of the staff members will act the same way in important control situa-

---

FIGURE 13-9   Example of Poor Procedure Writing

PROCEDURE TO REQUEST FILE ACCESS

In order to obtain access to a file for reporting purposes, the requestor must complete a file access request, form AR-1776. The requestor must complete a different form for each file for which access is requested.

After completing form AR-1776, the requestor must obtain the signature of his respective division manager. When that signature is obtained, the form AR-1776 should be forwarded to the data security coordinator of the information center.

The data security coordinator logs the form into the security authorization system (see procedure DS-110), and forwards the form to the designated data steward for the file requested. The data steward reviews the request, indicating approval or disapproval, and returns it to the data security coordinator.

The data security coordinator then logs the response into the security authorization system (see procedure DS-110). If access was approved, the coordinator forwards the form to the manager of data security, who in turn modifies the requestor's security profile. Whether approved or disapproved, the final disposition portion of the form (section D) is returned to the requestor.

---

tions. How, then, should procedures be written to be useful enough actually to be used?

Script Procedures

Why is it easier to ask a co-worker for help than to refer to a procedure manual? The answer seems to lie in the response itself. A co-worker's reply is usually phrased in steps: "First you do this . . ., then you do this . . ., and finally you do these things." The response breaks the procedure down into a series of discrete steps, almost like the script of a play.

If written procedures are to be effective and usable, they also must express the action as a series of separate steps, as if each person were an actor. Each step in the procedure must clearly state *who* is to do the action, *what* action is to be performed, and *where* additional information is to be found. Figure 13-10 presents this approach, illustrating the same procedure as in Figure 13-9.

There is a difference, however. In Figure 13-10 each step is spelled out and the individual responsible is prominently identified. The flow of activity from one participant to another is clearly explained and everyone can see exactly what is required at each step of the process. Expressing the procedure as a script moves closer to the kind of help that is available from a co-worker.

FIGURE 13-10   Script Procedures

WHO	ACTION	RELATED DOCUMENTS
Requestor	Completes file access request, form AR-1776. Uses separate form for each file.	Form AR-1776
Requestor	Gives completed form AR-1776 to division manager for signature.	
Division Manager	Signs form AR-1776 and returns to requestor.	
Requestor	Sends form to information center data security coordinator.	
Coordinator	Logs request into Security Authorization System. Sends form to designated data steward.	Procedure DS-110
Steward	Reviews request, indicates approval or disapproval. Returns request to coordinator.	
Coordinator	Logs response into Security Authorization System. If request is approved, Then: Sends form to manager of data security for security profile change. Else: Returns form to requestor with reasons for denial.	Procedure DS-110 Procedure DS-112

Moreover, each step of the procedure starts with an action verb. Effective procedures must always be action oriented, emphasizing what must be done and the order in which to do it.

Finally, note that in the last set of actions for the coordinator, the IF logic is expressed in terms similar to that used in program coding. The main components of the decision IF and ELSE are capitalized, the actions are indented, and an explicit statement ENDIF is used to indicate the end of the decision. IF-THEN-ELSE logic needs to be used sparingly, however, and only when the decisions are clear-cut. A procedure should not be turned into a flowchart.

The purpose of a procedure is to describe how things ought to be done. Exception processing is to be described in a separate procedure, not as a collection of statements embedded in the main procedure. It is perfectly acceptable for a procedure to state, "If approvals are not obtained in three working days, use procedure AR-112 to guide follow-up activities." The procedure must be kept clear and flowing without a lot of logical pathways.

Obviously, clarity and action orientation are important in the creation of effective procedures. These characteristics can be implemented by incorporating standard audit principles into the procedures.

AUDIT PRINCIPLES

Auditors have developed a collection of principles that are important for the prudent operation of any business. How can these principles (which are summarized in Figure 13-11) be applied to an information center?

Separation of Duties

Parents of small children know how to avoid fights over the last piece of pie: one child is allowed to cut the pie and the other to choose the first piece. The almost surgical precision in cutting the pie that results from this approach illustrates an important audit principle: separation of duties. If tasks are carefully assigned, no one person can circumvent the procedures.

The same principle can be applied to the procedures of an information center. As long as any given task is the sole responsibility of only one individual, it is less likely to be done according to established procedures. In performing the task, the person will develop shortcuts and personal tricks that may seem to make the job easier, although they may actually

---

FIGURE 13-11   Basic Audit Principles

PRINCIPLE	WHY	EXAMPLE
Separation of Duties	To prevent any one individual from circumventing policy or procedures.	Data access approved by one person, implemented by another.
Redundancy	No single failure should cause complete and debilitating loss of function.	Cross-training staff in key skills.
Audit Trail	No change to a critical component should happen invisibly.	Date and time stamp placed on every change when moved to production.

circumvent the controls that were put in place to manage risks. It's fine for people to try to find new ways to do their jobs better; all this principle requires is that the written procedures be changed to show that better way and that a second person be involved to make sure that things are done correctly.

The principle can be put to work in a number of ways in an information center, as the following examples show:

1. *File Access.* The person who coordinates the file-access approval process should not be the same one who actually changes the security profile. Conversely, a list of all changes made to the security profile should be sent to the coordinator to check against existing records. This procedure ensures that no one individual can circumvent the stewardship approval procedure.

2. *Project Estimates.* The person who estimates the project should not be the same one who actually approves the work. This procedure can greatly reduce self-serving estimates and political favoritism.

3. *Work Schedules.* If the weekly schedule for help desk coverage is always completed by one of the persons on that schedule, there is always a temptation to assign the more favorable time slots in an unfair fashion. Either the scheduling duties should be rotated, giving each person a chance to make up the schedule, or scheduling should be the responsibility of an outsider, such as the manager.

4. *Data-Base Design.* No design should go to the coding stage until it has been reviewed by at least one other designer. (See Chapter 5, in which the design-review process was emphasized.) This review makes sure that the designer has not overlooked the obvious and that all business needs will be met.

Looked at pessimistically, the principle of separation of duties seems to be based on an inherent distrust of human beings. Actually, trust has very little to do with it. The principle merely recognizes that humans are creatures of habit and that good habits need to be reinforced and bad habits to be overcome. Separation of duties provides the means to build good habits in a positive environment.

Redundancy

It seems that every personal computer user needs to find out the hard way: critical data must be stored redundantly. Backup copies are essential to effective use of the computer since the original files are so prone to destruction or loss.

The procedures of an audit-minded information center should follow a similar path. Every critical resource, human and computer, needs to have a redundant backup. This backup either can be instantly available or "on standby," as the following examples show:

1. *Source of Key Hardware.* An information center may be a source of hardware for those who have none. For example, it may have a particular laser printer or plotter that can be used by departments that cannot justify the cost of the hardware for their own exclusive use. What happens if the printer or plotter fails just when a key user area has a critical project? An information center can protect itself from this eventuality in a number of ways. Critical hardware, for example, may be covered by a maintenance policy that promises free loaner equipment until repairs are complete. Alternatively, an information center may enter into mutual support agreements with other information centers in the city to provide emergency access to important equipment. However, the time to plan for these possible disasters is before the equipment fails.

2. *Source of all Knowledge.* Having only one individual who is knowledgeable about a particular tool is dangerous. The person becomes indispensable, and, even if not run over by the proverbial truck, a promotion to another job, or even a vacation, can create difficulties. A second source of knowledge must be made available through cross-training, better recruitment procedures, expert systems, and written documentation.

Aesop had it right: putting all of one's eggs into a single basket is risky. Critical functions must always have an alternative in case of failure.

Leaving a Trail

Spelunkers who are exploring a new cave for the first time ensure their safety by fastening a rope to the cave entrance and leaving a rope trail behind. In this way, if they get lost or become confused, they have a way to retrace their path and return to the surface. Exploring without such a rope trail is foolish, and may even be fatal.

Similarly, an audit-minded information center should concentrate on making sure that there is always a means to reconstruct a change history. No change should be made to a critical component of the environment without a clear path showing who made the change, as well as pertinent information about that change. For example:

1. *Production Code.* Chapter 7 discussed the need for an information center to establish a clear test/production border. Movement of code across that border ought to leave a trail, including a record of who made the change, who authorized the change, the date and time the change was made, and what happened to the previous version. This trail might be kept on paper or in computer format, but the important point is that it *is* kept.

2. *Project Logs.* Chapter 10 discussed the need for an information center to develop a project orientation. However, no project remains static,

and so it is important to maintain a trail of all changes to the scope and objectives of a project over time. Each change should be documented in a log (automated or paper) with the date of the change, who requested the change, who approved the change, and the nature of the change. Creating this trail makes sure that at the end of the project, no one asks, "Why are we doing this?"

3. *File Access.* The concepts of stewardship make an information center accountable to the data steward to ensure that the steward's wishes regarding file access are carried out. Accordingly, it is important to maintain a trail showing, for each user, the date the user was authorized to use the file, who authorized the use, and who changed the security profile. If the security system does not maintain this type of information, a separate automated or paper system must be created.

The process of leaving a trail has an interesting side effect: not only does it provide a level of comfort by affording a way to reconstruct how a particular event happened, but it also provides a means to identify the anomalies that may have crept into the system. Any component of the environment that does not have a corresponding change trail becomes suspect, since it may have entered the environment in an uncontrolled fashion.

Policy and Procedures: Summary

In summary, clear policies and procedures are the best way to implement the actions identified that would reduce the probability or impact of the risks for an information center. A policy is a framework that sets the direction for a course of action. The procedures are the means by which an organization specifies those actions, and it must do so using a step-by-step script-type approach. Furthermore, those procedures need to include the standard audit principles of separation of duties, redundancy, and change trails. Only one question remains—how to make sure that the policies and procedures are being carried out.

MONITORING THE RESULTS

Even if an audit-minded information center has carefully identified and evaluated risks and has developed clear policies and procedures to manage those risks, the results can still be a dismal failure. Developing a good audit mind set requires that the procedures actually be used. There are various ways in which an audit-minded information center can make sure that the business is being run according to the procedures.

Self-Audit

One of the standard management practices that is taught in basic business courses is that a manager monitors. Thus, in addition to the many other responsibilities of a manager of an audit-minded information center, the manager needs to spend some time on a self-audit.

A self-audit need not be elaborate or formal, but might take the form of periodic spot checks: Are the procedures being followed? Is the same task being performed by two people? Can the information center recover from hardware failure? Is every change documented by a change trail? The prudent manager will make time periodically to check those procedures that are managing the high-probability/high-impact risks.

The self-audit is not to be an inquisition. If a procedure is not being followed, there is always a reason. The manager needs to look beyond the simple issues of compliance or noncompliance and determine why there is a discrepancy. Often the answer leads to better policies and procedures or to different approaches to managing the work load. (Figure 13-12 illustrates this approach graphically.) If it is to be successful, a self-audit must be carried out in a nonthreatening, honest fashion.

This last point is important and bears additional emphasis. A self-audit is the best way for an information center manager to understand what is really happening. It cannot be done from behind a desk; the manager must observe the process at work. The fact that something is not being done according to procedure means one of two things: the procedures aren't understood or they need to be changed. However, if the self-audit is accomplished in a heavy-handed manner or it is punitive, any value is lost.

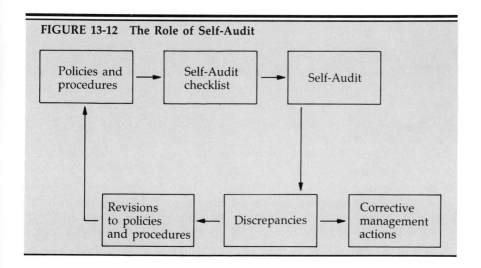

FIGURE 13-12   The Role of Self-Audit

The procedures will be followed to the letter while the staff is being observed, but will return to normal when observation ends. A self-audit is meant to evaluate the effectiveness of procedures, not the performance of the staff.

Voluntary Audit

Almost every reasonably sized organization has an audit group whose job it is to make sure that the assets of the organization are protected. Usually, the team's visit to a department is about as welcome as the plague.

This attitude is completely wrong. The audit process is not necessarily adversarial, but should be a welcome review of how well the department is protecting the organization's assets. Inviting the audit team to review the information center not only will throw the organization into shock, but may actually prove highly beneficial to the organization.

A voluntary audit has one overriding value. A second set of eyes looking at an information center from the outside can quickly identify areas of concern that are difficult to see at close range. What seems obvious and simple to the participants may seem complex and confusing to an outsider. The time to identify those discrepancies is before problems occur.

An information center manager should prepare for a voluntary audit by gathering all of the documentation that has been used in risk analysis and policy creation. The manager should then schedule a preaudit meeting to define the objectives of the audit and review the material, as well as a meeting with the information center staff to introduce the audit team and to make sure everyone understands the objectives. Once again, the audit is not an inquisition and the manager must emphasize that the goal is not to "check up" but to make sure that the department is behaving in a prudent fashion.

While the team is performing its audit, the information center manager should set up periodic meetings with the team to answer questions and share current findings. In this way, there will be no surprises when the audit is over. Once again, the spirit of the audit is as important as the actual findings. Open commitment to honesty and truth must be a prime force.

Once the audit has been completed, the manager of the information center needs to meet with the audit team to review the results. Since there will have been a number of interim meetings, the findings of the team should not be unexpected. After the results have been shared with the manager, a second meeting with the entire information center staff should be scheduled, at which the results of the audit will be reviewed, concentrating especially on areas where procedures are lacking or are not being followed. For each of those areas, the group needs to develop a plan of action to be used to remedy the shortcomings. Each member of the team should be given some responsibility for the plan.

In this nontraditional approach, instead of nervously waiting for the auditors to come in and hold an inquisition, the information center takes a proactive stance and invites an audit. Instead of being defensive, the information center makes the audit a team effort whereby it can discover ways in which to do its job better. The shock value of this approach might easily provide the information center with some welcome publicity in the organization.

The Secret of a Successful Audit

Whether the audit is to be self-directed or external, there is one principle that will make the process a success—that the devil knows is always better than the devil one doesn't know. It is painful to discover flaws in an organization, especially if there have been no catastrophes, but however painful such flaws may be when discovered during an audit, they are always more painful when they are not discovered and then cause a problem. A positive approach to the audit process provides the long-term results that are better for all concerned.

SUMMARY

This chapter began with a discussion of risk—the basis for developing an audit mind set. Risk was defined as an undesirable event that is evaluated in terms of probability and impact. Once the critical risks have been identified, a prudent information center manager will develop a risk management program of activities that can reduce either the probability or the potential impact of the event. Such actions usually take the form of policies and procedures. The policies ought to be general statements regarding the course of action to be taken, whereas the procedures are to be clear, explicit statements of each of the actions to be taken in a given event. Procedures are best written in a format similar to that of a script, listing each person and the person's actions. Finally, an audit-minded information center must continue to monitor its behavior to make sure that the procedures are being followed. To be effective, that monitoring must be done in an open and honest fashion.

This procedure may seem to involve a lot of effort—and it does. To act otherwise, however, abrogates an information center's responsibility to be a prudent steward of the corporation's resources.

SUGGESTED PROJECTS

1. The text states that it is impossible to fairly determine the cost/benefit analysis for any potential risk management option. Defend or oppose that position.

2. Develop a procedure to control the risks of final exams in an academic environment. Begin with the risk identification steps, include risk evaluation in terms of probability and impact, and recommend suggested risk management alternatives. Develop at least one procedure to control the risk using the script approach.

3. Consider the ways in which spreadsheets might be used in an accounting department at a major corporation. Use the audit principles of separation of duties, redundancy, and trails to suggest some potential risk management procedures.

Conclusion

Back in the preface, an effort was made to find a parallel between the information center revolution and Martin Luther's sixteenth century reformation. It's time to revisit that analogy.

It would be a serious mistake to see Luther as an innovative revolutionary. He did not view his movement as either bold or new, but considered his beliefs a return to fundamentals. He thought that the church establishment had lost sight of its original purpose, and that the theses he proposed would bring it closer to his vision of the traditional faith.

The information center movement needs to be seen in a similar light. Much like Luther's movement, an information center may appear to be part of a revolution, but in actuality it is a return to the fundamental principle that technology ought to exist to solve business problems.

Much like Luther's movement, as well, an information center often finds itself in a storm of controversy. It has alternately been the hero and goat in any number of organizations. Since Luther's movement left no clear victors in the ensuing four hundred years, it is unreasonable to assume that an information center will do much better.

Thus, there is little to offer, except a vision: that as a result of this discussion of managing an information center, each reader will leave with a new perspective on the old problems of data processing. With luck, that perspective will be centered around a new understanding of the role of technology in business and an increased understanding of some of the techniques that can be used to make that vision a reality. With that vision, nothing is impossible.

GLOSSARY

GLOSSARY

This glossary is not intended to be definitive or exhaustive. However, the following terms are either key concepts that appear in the text or are common industry terms that may not be generally known.

Anchor points — A communication technique that provides the listener or reader with a previously known concept that can be used as a foundation to understand new information.

APPC — **Advanced Program to Program Communication.** The facility in IBM's SNA (System Network Architecture) that allows two computers to communicate as peers, rather than in the more traditional master-slave relationship. Using this facility, a program running on a personal computer can request data directly from a mainframe system instead of having to rely on screen emulation techniques.

Artificial intelligence — Software that captures the inference patterns of experts or that mimics the thinking process of human beings to solve technical or business problems.

Attributes — The individual types of data that will be gathered for a particular **Entity**. For example, for an entity called *Student*, attributes might include *name, address, and telephone number.*

Backout — The process by which a software environment is restored to a previous state (usually after some alteration to that environment).

Backup — Creation of a second copy of the current version of software or data files to ensure that the current state of the environment can be restored.

Business problem — When used in this text, this term refers to a statement that presents a variation from expectation. For example, "We need a spreadsheet" is not a business problem since it neither states expectation nor variation. On the other hand, "We cannot analyze our data" states the expectation (data must be analyzed) and the variation (we are unable to analyze).

CAD — Computer-assisted drafting (also, computer-assisted design); high-resolution graphics software with special features that provide the capability to produce high-quality blueprints, plans, or detailed engineering or construction drawings.

CICS — A transaction-based online system used on IBM mainframe computers.

Connectivity — A term referring to the technology required to allow two devices to share such resources as peripherals, data, program logic, or processing capability.

Corporate computer — A computer used for enterprise-wide activities. Access to data is allowed (with proper security procedures) to all areas of the organization.

Data — Stored facts in context (see Chapter 1).

Data design — The process by which a logical structure for data is developed that corresponds to the underlying nature of the business. This structure is expressed in terms of **entities**, **relationships**, and **attributes**.

DBMS — Data-base management system. A software product that allows the programmer or user to concentrate on a logical representation of data rather than on the details of actual physical storage. This logical representation may be as **segments** (in a **network/hierarchical data base**) or as a series of **tables** (in a **relational data base**).

DB2 — IBM's relational data-base product.

Departmental computer — A computer used by a working group (department, division, team) for localized tasks. Access to this computer is usually limited to members of that group rather than to the whole corporation.

Entities — A representation of the people, places, things, and events about which a DBMS application will store data (see Chapter 5).

Entity-relationship modeling — The process by which the business relationships between two entities are captured and expressed. Some of these relationships might be *many-to-one, one-to-one,* or *many-to-many.*

Expert system — A type of **artificial intelligence** that captures the knowledge of a subject-matter expert as a series of rules. Conclusions are then inferred from these rules in a nonprocedural fashion.

Foreign key — The **attribute** of one **entity** that is also the **identifier** of another entity. For example, an employee entity might contain an attribute called "department number." That department number is a foreign key since it is the identifier of another entity, department.

4GL — **Fourth-generation language.** A **nonprocedural** software language that allows end users and professionals rapidly to develop software by focusing on the nature of the results rather than on the procedures needed to obtain those results. See Chapter 4 for a complete discussion of this term.

Gestalt thinking — A intellectual paradigm that seeks to "grasp the whole." Gestalt thinking proceeds in a top-down fashion, starting with understanding the concept and seeking to learn syntactical details in the context of the concept.

Hierarchial data base — *See* Network/Hierarchial data base.

Heisenberg uncertainty principle — A fundamental law of quantum mechanics that states one may either determine the location of an electron or the momentum, but never both. In this text, this principle is extended to the more general statement that the act of measurement alters that which is being measured.

Idea frames — A communication technique that provides the listener or reader with a structure in which to understand new material. Examples of idea frames include outlines, the 3-T principle, and topic headings.

Identifiers — That **attribute**, or set of attributes, that uniquely determines a specific occurrence of an **entity**.

Individual computer — A computer used by an individual for personal tasks. The resources of this device are completely local and are not shared with any other device.

Information — A meaningful interpretation of **data** that can be acted upon.

Information center — An organizational entity that facilitates the transformation of data into information that managerial, professional, and support staff can use to solve business problems.

Intersection entity — An **entity** whose purpose to to provide a cross-reference between specific occurrences of two other entities, eliminating the need for a *many-to-many* relationship (see Chapter 5).

IPO — Input/Process/Output. A traditional approach to system development that first identifies the desired **output**, determines the needed **input**, and then seeks to develop the **process** to transform the **input** to **output**. Contrast to the data-driven design techniques of Chapter 5.

LAN — Local area network. Hardware and software that connect a number of individual computers in order to share resources.

Mainframe — Customary term for a large **corporate computer**.

Microcomputer — Customary term for an **individual computer**.

Minicomputer — Customary term for a **departmental computer**.

MIPS — Millions of instructions per second. A measurement commonly used by computer manufacturer marketing departments to compare processing power. However, this measurement is often meaningless in real terms since the instructions used by one computer vendor may differ significantly from those of another vendor.

MIS — Management information systems. The department that manages the traditional data-processing activities of an organization.

Network/hierarchical data bases — A logical model of data that predefines some relationships among **entities** as *parent–child* while also allowing less restrictive logical relationships.

Nonprocedural — Any computer tool that allows the user to express the process in terms of the end results rather than the steps required to obtain those results.

Normalization — The process by which **attributes** are assigned to **entities** in a consistent and logical fashion. Based on some fairly arcane mathematical principles, the normalization process ensures that data is structurally consistent.

OSI — Open stystems interconnect. An internationally recognized standard for data communications. The standard calls for seven distinct layers that progressively translate the communications request from the user viewpoint to electronic signals and back again.

Paradigm — The model by which the nature of the world is understood.

PC — Personal computer; Another term for **microcomputer** or **individual computer**.

Process design — The steps taken to ensure that an application system behaves in a consistent and well-defined fashion by defining a set of standards for the structure and presentation characteristics of the software.

Protocol converter — A device that translates the communications messages of one device into the formats required by another, otherwise incompatible device.

Prototyping — An approach to application development that emphasizes rapid development through user interaction and multiple iterations.

Relational data bases — A logical organization of data into tabular rows and columns. These tables are independent of each other and are combined as needed to produce needed information.

RISC — Reduced instruction set computer. A computer that is able to process a limited number of operations very quickly. Theoretically, it is capable of exceptionally good processing performance; in reality, however, the high processing rate is somewhat offset by the number of RISC instructions required to perform an operation.

Risk — An undesirable event evaluated for probability and impact.

Segment — The component of a **network/hierarchical data base** that represents a type of **entity**.

SNA — Systems network architecture. IBM's network communications standard. Originally based on a master-slave principle, this architecture has broadened to include peer-to-peer communications and advanced facilities to support LAN access to mainframe resources.

Spreadsheet — A **nonprocedural** software tool that expresses the nature of data and the associated calculations as a series of cells arranged as rows and columns. A single cell of the spreadsheet may hold data, a literal expression, or a computation involving one or more other cells.

SQL — Structured query language. The most common data manipulation for relational data bases.

Stewardship — The concept that the information assets of a corporation are assigned to distinct individuals (stewards) to protect those assets and to ensure that they are used in the best interests of the entire organization.

Strategy — A process that defines the nature of an organization by stating what it is or what it needs to become.

SWOT — A technique for defining the strategic and tactical vision for an organization by concentrating on the *Strengths, Weaknesses, Opportunities,* and *Threats.*

Table — The component of a **relational** data base that represents a type of **entity**.

Tactic — An action that an organization plans to take to satisfy a **strategy**.

3-T Principle — A communications technique in which the speaker first *tells* the audience what he will tell them, then actually *tells* them, and finally *tells* them what he told them.

Triage — A process that divides a collection of items into three distinct groups to ensure resources are appropriately applied. For example, an information center's projects might be divided into those that are critical for the success of the organization, those that would be useful to the organization, and those that really have little effect on the operation of the business.

INDEX

INDEX